The Union Makes Us Strong

When the Union's inspiration through the workers'
blood shall run,
There can be no power greater anywhere beneath the
sun.
Yet what force on earth is weaker than the feeble
strength of one?
But the Union makes us strong.

Chorus: Solidarity for ever!
Solidarity for ever!
Solidarity for ever!
For the Union makes us strong.

The Union Makes
Us Strong

The British Working Class, Its Trade
Unionism and Politics

Tony Lane
Illustrated by Trevor Skempton

Arrow Books

Arrow Books Ltd
3 Fitzroy Square, London W1

London Melbourne Sydney Auckland
Wellington Johannesburg Cape Town
and agencies throughout the world

First published 1974
© Tony Lane 1974
Illustrations © Trevor Skempton 1974

Set in Intertype Times
Printed in Great Britain by
The Anchor Press Ltd., Tiptree, Essex

ISBN 0 09 908640 9

The first verse of Solidarity Forever, *beneath the frontispiece, is sung to the tune of* John Brown's Body. *Written in 1915 during a strike of West Virginia miners.*

Contents

Contents

Illustrations

By the same author

Strike at Pilkingtons
(with Kenneth Roberts)
Fontana

The people on the Rank and File Strike
Committee of the Pilkington strike in the spring
of 1970 said the strike had given them a bloody
good education. It did the same for me too.
Which is why this book is dedicated:

*To the Pilkington strikers and the working class
of St Helens.*

Preface

This is the place where writers reveal themselves as persons – by acknowledging their debts and allowing themselves a few expressions of sentiment.

My debts are numerous: and no one should assume that the order of their recognition is an order of degree of indebtedness.

Firstly to the historians whose works I have so liberally plundered. I don't agree with many of them, but I do admire their capacity for painstaking and careful research. Without them this book would have been immeasurably more difficult to write.

George Woodcock, Will Paynter, Lawrence Daly (who sings so beautifully and should record an album of labour songs), Alfred Allen, and Tom Jackson made me much more sensitive to the position of trade union leaders than I could possibly have been without their help. Some of them won't like this book very much, but that's the way it goes.

To my father, who was active in the labour movement at a time and place when it was not especially advisable if one was concerned with personal security, and who had the good sense to pass on his quiet and deep convictions to his sons. To my mother who shared and endorsed my father's beliefs.

To Huw who in many many ways will find a lot of himself in this book. To say the very least, he has a sharp eye for the apostrophe. To Peter and Martin and Ron and Gideon and Gerry who in their various ways have kept me down to earth.

To Diana who, though handicapped by three militant

children and a largely absent-minded husband, gave me more than I had any right to expect.

To Phil, Dorothy, Marg, Linda and Irene who typed most of the manuscript.

To the men and women of the labour movement whose story this is.

A Guide to Abbreviations

AEU Amalgamated Engineering Union.

ASCJ Amalgamated Society of Carpenters and Joiners – subsequently, in 1972, to be merged into an industrial union for building workers: UCATT, Union of Construction, Allied Trades and Technicians.

ASE Amalgamated Society of Engineers – the parents of the above.

ASLEF Associated Society of Locomotive Engineers and Firemen.

ASRS Amalgamated Society of Railway Servants – later to become the National Union of Railwaymen.

AUEW Amalgamated Union of Engineering Workers – grandchild of the ASE.

BISAKTA British Iron and Steel and Kindred Trades Association – i.e. the steelworkers' union.

CBI Confederation of British Industry – the capitalists' TUC.

CIO Congress of Industrial Organisations – half of the American TUC, and usually at war with the other half, the AFL – the American Federation of Labour.

CP Communist Party – its proper title is the Communist Party of Great Britain.

ETU Electricians Trade Union – now the EEPTU, Electricians, Electronics and Plumbers Trade Union.

GMWU General and Municipal Workers Union.

GNCTU Grand National Consolidated Trades Union – one of the earliest attempts at one big union.

ILP – Independent Labour Party – founded in 1893, forerunner of the Labour Party but always to the left of it. Still exists with a couple of hundred members and is a very rich outfit. Owns a bit of property and a big printing firm.

JIC Joint Industrial Council – set up in a number of industries towards the end of the First World War by behest of the government. The concept was peace and harmony in the factory.

MM Minority Movement – a Communist Party 'front' organisation of the twenties. Mobilised broad-front left opposition in the unions.

NAUL National Amalgamated Union of Labour – merged into the General and Municipal Workers in the twenties. Based originally on Tyneside and the north-east.

NAUPL National Amalgamated Union for the Protection of Labour – another of the early attempts at one union for all the workers.

NEDC National Economic Development Council – a Macmillan government creation of 1961. It was designed to bring peace and goodwill in industry. It is still around, though pretty insignificant.

NUGMW National Union of General and Municipal Workers – same thing as the GMWU, an aggressively right-wing union since the twenties.

NUR National Union of Railwaymen – it has a largely forgotten history of militancy.

OBU Operative Builders Union – an early and unsuccessful attempt at an industrial union for skilled building workers. These workers even now are amongst the worst organised.

SDF Social Democratic Federation – the first proclaimed Marxist party in Britain, it was disowned by Marx and Engels. Merged into the CP in 1920–1.

SLP Socialist Labour Party – the British off-shoot of the party of the same name in America.

T&GWU Transport and General Workers Union – the biggest union in Britain ever since the twenties.

TUC Trades Union Congress – the parliament of British labour.

A note on abbreviations used in notes

The term op. cit. is a latin term abbreviated from *opere citato* which means in the work cited. The term , therefore, is a handy device for saving constant repetition of a book's title which has already been given. The term ibid. is shortened from the latin *ibidem*—it is used to refer to a book which has been cited immediately above.

Introduction: The General Strike Tells the Story of the Book

THE
BRITISH WORKER
OFFICIAL STRIKE NEWS BULLETIN
Published by The General Council of the Trades Union Congress

No. 3.	FRIDAY EVENING, MAY 7, 1926.	PRICE ONE PENNY

TO OUR READERS

You will at once ask when you get this issue: Why is it only half the size it was before? The reason is that the Cabinet has stopped our supply of paper.

At the docks and in a mill there are supplies belonging to us. The Cabinet refuses to let us have them.

We are, therefore, compelled to cut down our size to-day. To-morrow, if Mr. Baldwin still declines to allow the Workers' cause to be defended by the General Council's newspaper, we may not be able to appear at all in our present form.

The Prime Minister, by attempting to stifle the voice of Labour, runs the very grave risk of undoing all the good that has been done by the General Council's daily appeal to

The General Council does not challenge the Constitution.

It is not seeking to substitute un-constitutional government.

Nor is it desirous of undermining our Parliamentary institutions.

The sole aim of the Council is to secure for the miners a decent standard of life.

The Council is engaged in an In-dustrial dispute.

There is no Constitutional crisis.

FAILURE OF THE O.M.S.

Truth About Situation at Newcastle-on-Tyne

The Organisation for Maintaining Supplies at Newcastle-on-Tyne has broken down completely, and the authorities have appealed for the aid of the unions," announced Mr. Connolly, one of the Tyneside Labour M.P.s, in the House of Commons on Thursday night. An hour later a Government representative told the House he had telephoned to Newcastle, and received a denial of the statement.

The BRITISH WORKER is able to publish the following account of the Tyneside situation, as given by the Worker's Chronicle, published by the Newcastle Trades Council.

The nine days' wonder was what Beatrice Webb called the General Strike. That was not the feeling of ordinary trade unionists at the time. On 12 May 1926 thousands of men and women were crammed into Birkenhead's Hamilton Square. An enormous wave of cheering was the response to the news that the Strike was over. Hardened shipyard, railway and dock workers soon realised their mistake: they had not won an historic victory, they had incurred an historic defeat. Not many minutes later men were seen to be crying as they left the Square in defeat and humilia-tion. There were Hamilton Squares throughout the country.[1]

By the 1970s the Strike had passed into the folklore of the labour movement. There were very few active trade unionists without some idea of 1926. They all knew – correctly – that something important for them had happened in that year. The story of that now-fabled and legendary strike carries within it most of the ingredients essential to an understanding of British labour. Of course it is not enough in itself: there would be no justification otherwise for the rest of this book. On the other hand this book *could* be read as a detailed account of the various tendencies shown in such sharp relief in 1926.

As an idea the big strike had a two-fold origin, although in terms of immediate issues it was bound up with the fortunes of the coal industry. The idea of a general strike was at least as old as Chartism. Chartists had talked of a 'national holiday', a 'sacred month' wherein all workers would strike simultaneously to force the government to concede universal suffrage. Much more recently, from the 1890s, Syndicalists* had urged the adoption of the general strike as the first step toward socialism. The trade unionists' conception of the big strike was more akin to that of the Chartists than of the syndicalists: they saw it as a means of coercing an obstinate government rather than as a means of dispensing with capitalism. For the trade unions the General Strike was a sympathy strike that had nothing in common with revolutionism. Not for nothing did the TUC's General Council insist on calling it the National Strike, insistently repeat *The General Council does not challenge the Constitution.*

*Syndicalists were socialists who argued that the socialist society could be achieved by the seizure of the means of production without recourse in the first instance to the seizure of the political machinery of the State. For them the socialist society would consist in a loose federal system of self-governing enterprises, the whole linked together by some kind of industrial parliament. All that was required as a first step was a simultaneous strike of all workers.

Red Friday was what they called 31 July 1925. On that day the Tory government, by granting a ten-month subsidy to the coal owners' profits, avoided a lock-out of the miners who had refused to accept a wages cut. The government also avoided a general strike: the TUC had agreed the day before to put an embargo on the movement of coal by all forms of transport, and had been empowered to call a strike on whatever scale seemed necessary. So the government had been defeated. But only temporarily. When Stanley Baldwin, the Prime Minister, was later asked why he had capitulated he replied: 'We were not ready.' By May 1926 they were.

In the ten-month interregnum the government set up a Royal Commission under Lord Samuel (a former Liberal Home Secretary) in the hope that it could find a solution to the coal owners' profitability problems that would not seriously antagonise the working class. At the same time it made arrangements on the assumption that the Samuel Commission would fail. The Royal Commission reported in March 1926. It offered the miners some reorganisation of the industry which left it in private ownership and would take years to accomplish. In return the miners were expected to take wage reductions.

The government, meanwhile, was concerning itself with more practical matters. Two days after Red Friday the Home Secretary sounded his warning: 'The thing is not finished. The danger is not over. Sooner or later this question has got to be fought out by the people of the land. Is England to be governed by Parliament and the Cabinet or by a handful of trade union leaders?'[2] No idle words these. In early October 1925 Baldwin promised the Tory Party Conference that he would consider prosecutions against the Communist Party – six days later there were the first arrests. Secret plans for a regional system of government, first drawn-up in 1923, were revised and updated. An apparently 'unofficial' body calling itself the 'Organisation for the Maintenance of Supplies' with a central council composed of generals and admirals and similar sorts of people, several of whom had close links with Fascist parties, quickly received quiet support from the government. Furthermore, although naturally no hard evidence is available, it would have been truly remarkable – given the more than century-long government policy of spying on the labour movement – if the network of petty informers, *agents provocateurs*, and spies was not greatly enlarged.

At the end of August 1925 the Communist Party's paper, *Workers' Weekly*, told its readers: 'Thirty-four weeks to go – thirty-four weeks to go to what? To the termination of the mining agreement and the opening of the greatest struggle in the history of the British working class. We must prepare for the struggle.' In the same month the *Daily Herald* ran a debate on 'Should the Workers Take Up Arms'. Yet despite the knowledge that there *was* a battle in the offing, despite the knowledge of government preparations, the TUC sat tight and did nothing. Even the ultra-cautious Citrine, acting TUC General Secretary and subsequently to be knighted in the 1930s, felt moved to urge some action.

Not until the last week of April 1926 did the TUC start thinking seriously about how it was to conduct the Strike – at the same time as its more prominent members were trying to negotiate a 'peaceful settlement'. Quite unknown to the miners' leaders (A. J. Cook and Herbert Smith) the TUC was ready to accept wage cuts on the miners' behalf provided the government was prepared to impose reorganisation on the coal owners. This was a stance which ran directly counter to its February declaration:

The attitude of the trade union movement was made perfectly clear last July, namely, that it would stand firmly and unitedly against any further attempt to degrade the standard of life in the coalfields. There was to be no reduction of wages, no increase in working hours, and no interference with the principle of National Agreements. This is the position of the trade union movement today.[3]

Still, this was a negotiating position, a public statement designed to show the government that it was in earnest.

The last few days of April and the first few days of May were those in which some members of the TUC's General Council began to forget what it was like to lie down between a pair of sheets: meetings in the House of Commons, at 10 Downing Street, at 11 Downing Street, at TUC headquarters. These men flogged themselves in their anxiety to avoid a general strike, grasped at every straw so liberally strewn before them by the devious Jimmy Thomas of the Railwaymen. Citrine's description of Thomas's style while the Strike was actually on stood equally well for his earlier activities:

Then we have Jimmy Thomas – always discovering new situations, with mysterious side glances and knowing looks – endowed with facile entry into the innermost circles of government. If we only knew what he knew! He had seen a Cabinet minister that day in the House of Commons, looking very worried. 'By God, our stock is up, but we must remember the serious consequences of any hesitancy.' Or perhaps a well-known capitalist, whose name he withheld for reasons which we would all understand, had winked at him, whereupon the said James required an urgent meeting of the Industrial Committee to debate the significance of the wink.[4]

But the 'well-connected' Jimmy had nothing to offer. Neither government nor coal owners were prepared to discuss reorganisation of the coal industry without a prior commitment from the miners to accept wage cuts. The TUC leaders were trying to bargain with a group of people who were unwilling to concede anything. No trade union leader, no matter what his politics, could accept that. And so the Strike was on.

A joint meeting of the executive committees of the unions affiliated to the TUC met on Saturday, 1 May. With the exception of the National Union of Seamen, the unions voted unanimously to strike in two waves. The first wave, consisting of workers in the transport, printing, iron and steel, metal and heavy chemicals industries, was to come out from midnight on Monday, 3 May. Engineering and shipyard workers were to be held in reserve to begin their strike one week later: with a group of well-organised workers such as these held in reserve there was thought to be a guarantee of the Strike becoming stronger as it went along.

The response to the strike call was overwhelming and far exceeded either the TUC's or the government's expectations. Julian Symons saw this middle-class scene on the morning of 4 May:

What people living in cities noticed first of all on that Tuesday morning was the peace and stillness of the streets. No trams or buses; none of the characteristic hurry and bustle of early morning. A breathless feeling of intense quietness, one observer noted, such as comes before a thunderstorm; another, in a manufacturing town, the strange clarity of air and sky.

The stillness did not last much beyond eight o'clock. The office worker, in London and other big cities, who had been told little but that he should get to work as and when he could, ate his breakfast and set off, on bicycle or by foot. The streets were crowded with bicycles, an army of people pedalling from the suburbs into the middle of cities.[5]

For the office-workers, commented Symons, it was all a bit of a lark. But the men who ran the State were not in joking mood, indeed were literally showing the iron fist. Christopher Farman described it:

All army and navy leave was cancelled and troop reinforcements were moved into London, Scotland, South Wales and Lancashire. The Cabinet had decided that troop movements were to occur 'as unobtrusively as possible', but in Liverpool two battalions of infantry landed from a troopship and marched through the city with steel helmets, rifles and full equipment while the battleships *Ramillies* and *Barham,* recalled from the Atlantic Fleet, anchored in the Mersey. Warships also anchored in the Tyne, Clyde, Humber, and at Cardiff, Bristol, Swansea, Barrow, Middlesbrough, and Harwich.[6]

The trade union movement was not accustomed, in practice or tradition, to unity. Every union was jealous of its own autonomy and used to going its own way regardless of other groups of workers. Yet an adventure like a national stoppage required – if it was to be successful – a sharp and radical change of direction away from sectionalism. The necessary unity never really emerged.

Right from the start the TUC had recognised its lack of unity: its strike call was phrased in the most general way and left it up to the individual unions to decide in what way to bring out its members, a decision which immediately gave rise to bickering as the various unions interpreted TUC instructions in different ways. These sectional rivalries were reproduced at the local level. The trades councils were, in a way, local TUCs and therefore quite as prone as the General Council to sectional dispute:

At Southampton there was friction between the transport workers and the trades council and at Middlesborough, Dunfermline, and Sheffield some individual strike committees were resentful of outside interference in what they regarded as their own affairs. At High Wycombe hostility between 'craft' and 'industrial' unions was intense, with the Furnishing Trades Association dominating the trades council and the NUR running a completely autonomous strike committee. In Leeds no less than four rival strike committees were set up and spent much of the time quarrelling over the use of a single telephone.[7]

Nevertheless local organisation and solidarity was,

in all the circumstances, extremely impressive. Where labour traditions or organisation and struggle ran strong, where the left-wing of the ILP and the Communist Party had a solid base, there also was strike organisation at its best. Where the tradition was absent, where left-wing politics was almost unheard of, there was organisation absent. The contrasts could be extraordinary. At Methil in the East Fife coalfield there was a Workers Defence Corps of 700 men who, under the command of ex-NCOs, were armed with pick-shafts and patrolled the area in disciplined columns. In Lowestoft in Suffolk the tramwaymen had returned to work within a matter of days, and the chairman of the strike committee had resigned and gone back to work.

Throughout the nine days there were constant rumours that the strike was crumbling. The *Kensington Strike Bulletin* hit on a novel way of coping with that in its issue of 7 May: 'The Strike is over. Only 400,000 NUR men are now on strike, plus 1 million miners and 2 million others. But three trains are running in Manchester and there is a five minute service every two hours on the tubes. A bag of coal has been brought from Newcastle today.' A bulletin issued in Monmouthshire carried a 'conversation' between a miner and his son: 'What is a *Blackleg*, Daddy? A *Blackleg* is a *Traitor*, my boy. He is a man who knows not Honour or Shame! Were there many *Blacklegs* in the valley, Daddy? No, my boy! Only the station master at Abersychan, and two clerks at Crane Street Station.'

The determination that was so evident in many localities was not matched by the TUC. Thinking there was more akin to Lowestoft than to Methil. ALL'S WELL! said the headline in the *British Worker* on the evening of Monday, 10 May: 'The General Council's message at the opening of the second week is "Stand firm. Be loyal to instructions

and Trust Your Leaders." ' But ALL was nothing of
the sort. The Strike was only three days old when
Lord Samuel entered the stage from the right. Setting
himself up as an arbitrator quite devoid of any government support, he contacted Jimmy Thomas (who else?)
with a view to obtaining a settlement. On the very
next day, 7 May, Bevin – who had become the
dominant figure in the day-to-day running of the
strike – was urging on the TUC the necessity for
reopening negotiations.

Samuel's mediation was one-sided: he had extensive
talks with TUC leaders, and none at all with the
Cabinet let alone the coal owners. The Cabinet knew
what was going on and gave quiet and indirect
encouragement – but nothing more. Effectively,
Samuel offered himself to the TUC as a face-saving
device.

By the evening of 11 May the miners' union executive had been informed of the General Council's
unanimous decision to call-off the Strike on the basis
of Samuel's memorandum – which in its main points
accepted wage cuts in return for reorganisation of the
industry. It was assumed, wrongly as it turned out, by
members of the General Council who were not on the
Negotiating Committee that had done the talking with
Samuel, that the Samuel memorandum had been
agreed to by the government. Bevin asked the Negotiating Committee: 'Does it mean, if we call the strike
off, that the Samuel document is to be made public,
that the Government is to accept it, and that lock-out
notices are to be withdrawn simultaneously with our
ordering resumption of work?'[8] *Yes* was the answer,
given prophetically three times.

As with Peter, the answer was false. The government had made no such agreement – and anyway the
miners found the proposals unacceptable. At noon on
Wednesday, 12 May, the TUC General Council went
to 10 Downing Street and surrendered unconditionally.

This was incredible because before going to Downing Street three points had been agreed: the Strike to be called off, discussion with a view to a 'no victimisation' agreement, and negotiations on the basis of Samuel's recommendation. In the event there was no discussion on the last two points: the surrender was abject and total. Even Lord Birkenhead, one of the Tory hardliners, 'Felt something akin to compassion for the TUC leaders as they trooped dejectedly out of the Cabinet room. Their surrender, he wrote later to Halifax, was "so humiliating that some instinctive breeding made one unwilling even to look at them." '[9]

The next day when the Strike was supposed to be over the total of strikers was up by 100,000, but leaderless the Strike inevitably crumbled. Alone, the miners stayed out for another six months until starved into submission. Although by the end of the week there had been a negotiated return to work in most industries, hundreds of employers seized the opportunity to rid themselves of militants and to otherwise harry trade unionism. Writing from Manchester, Fenner Brockway said it all:

A spirit of fatalism came over the workers. The TUC had ordered them back; there was no hope of concerted resistance – so back they went . . . Of course a General Strike must be revolutionary; it is of necessity a conflict between the workers and the capitalist state. The strike of 1926 was led by a General Council who did not realise this when they reluctantly authorised the struggle. And they drew back from it as soon as they understood its implications.[10]

The bitter irony of the Strike was that those who best understood were either in the Tory Cabinet or on the revolutionary left. The former could let the Strike take its course and be reasonably confident of victory. The latter could present its analysis, enter the struggle, and have few illusions about the outcome. As so often in this period, the Communist Party knew what it was all about – and was impotent to act effectively. Three days before the Strike began *Workers' Weekly* told its readers:

Our party does not hold the leading positions in the trade unions. It can only advise and place its press and its forces at the service of the workers – led by others. And let it be remembered that those who are leading have no revolutionary perspectives before them. Any revolutionary perspectives they may perceive will send the majority of them hot on the track of retreat. Those who do not look for a path along which to retreat are good trade union leaders, who have sufficient character to stand firm on the demands of the miners, but they are totally incapable of moving forward to face all the implications of a united working class challenge to the state. To entertain any exaggerated views as to the revolutionary possibilities of this crisis and visions of a new leadership 'arising spontaneously in the struggle', etc. is fantastic.

The major theme of this book is simply stated: trade unionism on its own carried within itself a politics of accommodation to a capitalist society. Trade unionism was not to be *equated* with socialism even though, as an organisational expression of the irreconcilability of labour and capital, trade unionism did point in that direction. But point was all it did. This comment is not levelled as an accusation with derogatory intent. It is not to suggest that trade unionism could have been other than it was. It is not to suggest that in some way or other the movement failed to live up to its promise. A cool, hard-headed look at the General Strike makes the point. In a compressed and exceedingly dramatic way there is a sense in which 1926 gives away the whole story. While it was true that some of the TUC's leaders were bunglers, liars, or both, such a moralising polemic hardly advances understanding. The plain and incredible fact was that the national leadership was so politically naïve as not to fully comprehend what a general strike entailed. They saw themselves as running a sympathy strike which quite

by chance happened to be of national proportions. The
TUC was not consciously and determinedly challeng-
ing the constitution, although their actions had precisely that implication – an implication that was
increasingly made clear to them as they engaged in
their frantic and last-ditch attemps to avert the Strike
in the last few weeks of April, and that confronted
them with a blinding clarity once the men and women
were out on the stones. Then, realising what they had
done, they were 'hot on the track of retreat' as the
Workers' Weekly had so accurately predicted.

Cowardly and treacherous panic was what rank and
file leaders tended to see on 12 May – and with some
justification. There really *was* a decadent and acrid
stink about the alacrity with which a number of union
leaders ditched the miners and large numbers of their
own members. However, 'treachery' and 'cowardice'
do not explain the greatest defeat in the history of the
British working class. While the exact nature and
terms of the defeat say a great deal about the personalities of the men who engineered it, it simply does
not explain the defeat itself. To uncover the meaning
of *that* we must look elsewhere.

Trade unionism in 1926, as in all the previous
decades (not to mention those that followed), was
about negotiating the terms between labour and capital
on an industrial and workplace basis. Trade unionism
brought workers together so that through their united
strength they could bargain with capitalists in a way
that they could not so long as workers were merely a
fragmented mass of individuals. Trade unionism
affirmed that the interests of labour were not in any
way similar or identical to the interests of capital.

Trade unionism encouraged and furthered the knowledge that the only way capitalism could be confronted
economically was at the point of production. Thus the
first and most basic form of class consciousness to
emerge in the working class was the 'us' versus 'them'

of the workplace, which meant in practice a consciousness of conflict that was mainly confined to *particular*
workplaces. Conceptions of unity, of 'us-ness' were
basically a feature of work in one place for one
capitalist. They could, of course, be broadened as they
were in the General Strike. Workers could, and did,
generalise from their own employer to all employers –
what might be called a 'boss consciousness'.

What trade unionism did *not* develop was a 'class
consciousness' in the full and proper sense of the term:
a consciousness which went beyond the workplace
antagonism of labour and capital; a consciousness
which, informed by a body of theory, could grasp the
total reality of capitalism and indicate strategies for
its eradication; in short a *socialist class consciousness*
which unerringly indicated *political* solutions to what
were superficially economic problems.

Since the practice of trade unionism could only seek
to adjust the balance of power between labour and
capital, and since the Labour Party was but a parliamentary expression of the trade union way of looking
at the world, it necessarily followed that the 1926
adventure was doomed to failure from the start. All
the epithets in the world could have been heaped on
the heads of the TUC worthies, and the caps would
mostly have fitted. But when it came down to it the
failure of 1926 was a failure of the politics of trade
unionism.

More generally about the book

Those who manage to get through to the final pages
might feel moved to complain that I have painted an
overly dismal picture; that the unpalatable has been
exaggerated at the expense of the palatable; that I
have allowed the 'good' to be submerged by the 'bad'.
I could sympathise with that sentiment while rejecting
the criticism implicit in it. I have not embarked on a

moral assessment, on a condemnation of this or that leader, this or that policy. I have sought rather to 'tell it as it was and is' and explain why – to understand and not to judge.

In particular I have set out to explode that hoary old myth, beloved of many socialists, that the failures of socialism can be attributed to a wearying succession of leaders who have 'betrayed' the movement. I have shown, I hope conclusively, that that story will not stand close examination.

Absolutely central to an understanding of the political condition of the working class is a clear and unembittered appreciation of that class's one durable monument: the trade unions. I have devoted a large amount of space to the union's history. In doing so I have not written a blow-by-blow account of every battle, great and small. Neither have I made any attempt to carry out any original research designed to reveal new facts. What I *have* attempted to do is to look at the past in terms of the present, to look to the past as a means of understanding current trends. The history as I have written it is not then of that sort popularly considered. Great men and heroic deeds do not feature in my story for I find little virtue in mythology and legend.

At every stage of development I have tried to identify the dominant trends at work and explain what they meant. I have been fully conscious that in every period the uneven development of capitalism ensured that there were always counter-trends and survivals from previous epochs. These I have mostly ignored, not because I consider them unimportant, but because I have not set myself the task of writing a conventional and definitive history. My concern with history, to repeat, is with its usefulness as an aid to analysing the present. For that purpose an outline of major currents is adequate.

What emerges is a repetitious theme – again and

again different men in different epochs appear to be doing and saying things that in principle do not differ too much. This appearance is no mere literary conjuring trick, no cunning device of my own creation to lull the unwary into an acceptance of my interpretation. I defy anyone at all knowledgeable of the contemporary scene to immerse himself in the history of labour and to subsequently surface without exclaiming to himself that he had been there before. The feeling is too overwhelming to be ignored – and so salutary an experience as to want others to share it. Thus emerges a subsidiary reason for writing an account of the historical process. An understanding of it mocks all endeavours to portray the present as unique in every respect – and better equips those who want to act in the future.

In the second half of the book I have tried to seize on the main themes I have identified in the first, and to colour them in with some descriptive and theoretical detail. There is an account of the mode of political consciousness of the rank and file; how it is produced by the practice of trade unionism, and with what consequences for the relationship between trade union organisations and their members. This is followed by a description of the relationships between shop stewards on the one hand, and the rank and file, employers, and union officials on the other.

The chapter on union leaders is the only one to draw on original material. In this chapter I have outlined the process through which leaders 'emerge', described the ways in which they become isolated from the rank and file and the character of their associations with employers. I have concluded with a statement of the means by which leaders maintain a dominant position within their unions.

A friend has told me that in the concluding chapter I have been 'rather naughty', and I am not sure what he meant. Anyway, what I have done is to bring together the various loose ends that I deliberately left lying around in previous chapters, and to develop a more detailed explanation of why trade unionism has taken its particular form. I have especially attempted to demonstrate that the tendency toward oligarchy amongst trade union leaders has never been more than a tendency, and that where it exists it is attributable to the nature of trade unionism in a capitalist environment, and not to the moral failings of union leaders or to bureaucratic forms of union organisation.

I have rounded the whole thing off with *A Personal Postscript* which could readily be interpreted as an attempt to block off certain obvious criticisms, and with some advice *On Borrowing or Buying Books*. This last item is included in the hope that readers will have had their interest sufficiently aroused to want to read more detail of the so many things that I have only lightly touched upon.

Trevor Skempton's illustrations are not wallpaper: just so much decoration to break the monotony of disciplined ranks of print. They are part of the argument and the story. The means of expression is different from words but the effect is the same. As Trevor himself says, illustrations are at the very least entitled to the same amount of attention as an equivalent area of print.

Part 1

The Inheritance

The tradition of all dead generations weighs like a nightmare on the brain of the living.

Karl Marx

1. Rick-burners, Machine-breakers, Humble Petitioners and the Emergence of the Sober Trade Unionist

this is to inform you what you have to undergo
Gentelmen if providing you dont pull down your
meshines and rise the poor mens wages the married
men give tow and sixpence a day the singel tow shillings
or we will burn down your barns and you in them this
is the last notis

from *Swing*[1]

You have no need to fear the power of Government,
the soldiers, bayonets, and cannon that are at the
disposal of your oppressors; you have a weapon that
is far mightier than all these, a weapon against which
bayonets and cannon are powerless, and a child of ten
years can wield it. You have only to take a couple of
matches and a bundle of straw dipped in pitch, and
I will see what the Government and its hundreds of
thousands of soldiers will do against this one weapon if
it is used boldly.

*Joseph Stephens addressing a meeting of Chartists in
Manchester, 1838* [2]

*To his Grace the Duke of Newcastle (Lord Lieutenant),
the Nobility, Gentry and Clergy of the County of
Nottingham*
   *The humble Address and Petition of the Two-needle
Framework-knitters*

We think we should be wanting in duty to ourselves
and families, were we not, with all due respect and
humility, to call your serious attention to those heart-
rending woes and severe privations under which
ourselves and families are now groaning, and to justify
ourselves in sending forth the present Address . . .[3]

The years between the passing of the Combination Acts in 1799 and 1800 and the last fling of the Chartists in 1848 were those in which various sections of the working-class-in-the-making tried to come to terms with the new order of industrial capitalism. Followers of the mythical General Ned Ludd, mostly craftsmen using centuries-old methods of textile manufacture, turned to destruction of new machinery which was turning them into semi-skilled factory hands. At their most active in the years around the end of the Napoleonic Wars, Ned Ludd's men amounted to '. . . a *quasi-revolutionary movement* which continually trembled on the brink of ulterior revolutionary objectives.'[4] Ludd's men were not primitive anarchists indulging in individual acts of sabotage through desperation. Desperate men they were – but they were also organised: they wrecked machinery in small, disciplined bands; they armed themselves, drilled, and attended closely guarded meetings on the moors at night. The State took them as seriously as they took themselves – in 1812 there were more troops stationed in Lancashire, the West Riding, and Nottinghamshire than Wellington had in the Peninsular War. Twelve thousand soldiers all told.

In the early 1830s it was the turn of the agricultural labourers, organised in the 'army' of Captain Swing. The farmworker had become proletarianised. Transformed from an in-servant to a casual worker hired and fired at will, precluded by enclosure of common land from supplementing his livelihood, he received a precarious cash wage which only at harvest time was likely to exceed subsistence level. His situation, intensified by the growing use of machinery and by an enlargement of his own ranks by population growth, touched off revolt.

Captain Swing was a mythical figure, a collective name adopted by farmworkers who burned ricks and barns, who destroyed threshing machines, who threatened farmers and parsons and justices of the peace with a roasting if they refused to redress grievances. Though organised, Swing's men lacked the discipline and secrecy that so effectively surrounded Ludd. Despite the efforts of the soldiery, government spies and paid informers, remarkably few of Ludd's men were caught and convicted. Swing's men were less fortunate: '. . . there was the solemn act of retributive justice, whereby nineteen men were hanged (all but three of them for arson), 644 were jailed, and 481 (including two women) were transported to Hobart and Sydney.'[5]

Insurrection, or 'collective bargaining by riot' as it has been so aptly called, was a traditional response of both urban and rural workers to pressing wrongs.[6] But it was by no means the only response; neither was it the most typical. Resort to fire and the sword and the musket was far removed from the minds of many of the craftsmen in the towns and rapidly growing cities. Organised in respectable – if not always sober – friendly societies based on particular trades, these were among the ancestors of modern trade unionism. If there was an element of guile and stealth in the respectfully worded petitions they 'humbly' addressed to their masters, there was a fair bit of meaning too. Although occasionally touched by some of the radical currents of the age, these were men who had something of a stake in the established order of things. When *they* wanted change they preferred it to come constitutionally. Even the great Chartist movements of the late 1830s and '40s which mainly agitated for universal suffrage failed to capture many of these men.

Trade unionism was not however confined to these men of modest and conservative temper. There were more militant sections of the working classes to be found in the various mining areas and the textile districts of Lancashire. Large and spectacular strikes often lasting for months at a stretch were a commonplace, especially in the years immediately following the repeal of the Combination Acts in the mid-1820s.* The men and women who struck their mills and pits practiced a form of trade unionism quite different from the urban craftsmen. Although millworkers and miners were more likely to be on strike as a means of either resisting wage cuts or restoring wages to levels prior to previous reductions, they were nevertheless engaged in straightforward confrontations with the owners. The craftsmen on the other hand were primarily grouped in combinations as a means of moving horizontally against other workers rather than vertically against their masters. Cabinetmakers and coachmakers, laceworkers and shoemakers and the dozens of other highly skilled trades sought to maintain their relatively privileged position in the economic pecking order by keeping out men who had not served an approved apprenticeship. These were men who tended to see other workers as their main enemy.

Chartists were clear about their enemy if divided as to how to attack him. The Chartists were against the landed aristocracy, the gentry and their bourgeois camp-followers who continued to dominate parliament and make laws in their own image. The Chartists tended to see society as divided into two classes: the productive classes consisting of workers and manufacturers who produced wealth, and the parasitical classes who lived off the rest through rent, taxation, and corruption. The aristocracy and their hangers-on were seen as leeches who controlled the State so as to carry on their bloodsucking ventures. The Charter was designed to sweep away such 'feudal' practices. The Charter – consisting of a monster petition calling for annual parliaments, universal suffrage, secret ballots,

*The Acts rendered liable to imprisonment any worker who combined with another to get an increase in wages or reduction in hours, who enjoined anyone to strike, or who objected to working with any other worker.

payment of MPs, no property qualification for MPs and equal electoral districts – was expected to have such persuasive effect that the stout parties in parliament would collapse under the weight of the people's voice. The 1839 parliament was deaf in one ear; the petition was rejected. A threat had accompanied the petition: if it were not accepted there would be a general strike of one month – the Sacred Month – and an organised run on the banks. The threat was idle. There may have been $1\frac{1}{4}$ million signatories but there were not $1\frac{1}{4}$ million organised and disciplined men. An abortive armed uprising in Newport, Monmouthshire ended in disaster and elsewhere virtually every Chartist leader was put behind bars. The agitation was renewed again in 1842 – coupled with widespread but not completely associated strikes in the North and Midlands. And yet again in 1848 – coupled with elaborate and unrealistic plans for an armed uprising. Both failed as completely as the first.

The first half of the nineteenth century was a period since unparalleled for the sheer variety of working-class organisation and political and economic practice. Movements rose and fell with astonishing rapidity; but only trade unionism in certain of its forms endured. There were good reasons (even if they were not understood at the time) for the extraordinary oscillations between limited insurrectionism and insurrectionism which nearly turned into revolutionism, timid trade unionism and militant trade unionism, radical parliamentary reformism and cautious reformism. And the reasons were basically to be found in the development of a capitalist economy. An economy which at once looked backward to the rural past of the eighteenth century and forward to the fully capitalist industrial society of the twentieth.

Precisely nothing of the years 1800–50 can be understood without the knowledge that it was more or less in this period that the basis of wealth changed from merchant and agricultural capitalism to industrial capitalism. True, the change had been in train since the early decades of the eighteenth century and was not to be effectively complete until the opening decades of the twentieth century; but by mid-century a new age had arrived and was being celebrated. Macaulay, one of the most flamboyant of Victorian chauvinists, was not speaking for himself alone when he said in 1846:

> . . . the greatest and most highly civilised people that ever the world saw, have spread their dominion over every quarter of the globe . . . have created a maritime power which would annihilate in a quarter of an hour the navies of Tyre, Athens, Carthage, Venice, and Genoa together, have carried the science of healing, the means of locomotion and correspondence, every mechanical art, every manufacture, everything that promotes the convenience of life, to a perfection that our ancestors would have thought magical.[7]

The accomplishments on which Macaulay laid such stress were those of industrial capitalism – yet as late as 1851 agriculture remained the largest provider of jobs. In that year some 25% of males over twenty were farmworkers. However, farming as a source of employment was in the process of protracted decline. At some time in the period 1821–51 a large proportion of villages and rural parishes passed their peak of population: a period roughly coincidental with a rapid growth of population in the nation as a whole. Britain's population doubled between 1801 and 1851, and it was in the same period that the new industrial towns marched so quickly over green fields. By 1851 one half of the total population of England and Wales was living in rural areas. The farm labourers were driven out of the countryside, along with rural craftsmen, by the same considerations that led to the Swing revolts. They became cotton-spinners, miners, foundry-workers, railwaymen, dockers, warehousemen, sea-men. Every expanding industry recruited its share of former farmworkers and their wives and children. Other families from the countryside joined that vast mass of unskilled labourers that lived in the teeming slums of the towns and cities, ekeing out a hand to mouth existence through an admixture of occasional seasonal employment, petty crime and begging.

New industries created new skills out of old. Old industries with new techniques displaced old skills altogether. Engineering, developed out of the application of steam power to cotton spinning and coal mining, got a new fillip from the building of the railways and then the steamship. Blacksmiths, millwrights, wheelwrights, watchmakers became fitters, turners, toolmakers, boilermakers. And they made and serviced the machines which ensured the death of the centuries-old skills of the textile industry. On the other hand many traditional handicrafts remained untouched until the later years of the century – shoemakers, silk-workers, lacemakers, printers. Yet others, such as the building trades, still remained largely untouched in the third quarter of the twentieth century.

The process of capitalist development was then extremely uneven. New industries existed side by side with others essentially unchanged for hundreds of years. Only with the gradual creation of large markets for goods that were once in short supply were old skills eliminated. Generally speaking development went in steps rather than in parallel: the growth of a new industry waited upon the development to a certain stage of one pre-existing. The generation and accumulation of capital in one industry would eventually spill over into others – which meant that the motive force of industrial expansion was not technical evolution, but the generation of a surplus of capital. Investment in new industries, or in expanding old ones, became progressively easier with the growth of specialist banking institutions. The country lawyer, who had played such an important part as a go-between with the landowner on the one hand providing the capital and the merchant and manufacturer on the other hand as consumer, was gradually displaced by country and national banks.

Overall the picture is one of an extraordinarily rapid sequence of events. In the space of fifty years or so all the essential features of a modern capitalist economy appear, become refined, and yet await consolidation. But it was not a *factory* capitalism. In 1851 there were more men employed in building than women and men in cotton, more blacksmiths than foundry-workers, more women sewing by hand as milliners, dressmakers and seamstresses than tended machines in cotton mills; one in nine of the occupied population were domestic servants. In the same year, of 677 English and Welsh engine and machine makers a mere fourteen employed more than 350 men and the bulk of the remainder employed less than twenty. As late as 1871 the average cotton factory employed only 180 people – and the cotton mill was the mother and father of the modern factory.

All this adds up to saying that the great majority of the emerging working class was not a factory proletariat. Only a small minority experienced the disciplines of the factory. Most people were either casual labourers, domestic workers pursuing traditional handicrafts in their own homes, or apprentices in small workshops working alongside their masters. Furthermore, in the large factories, mills and pits that did exist many of the workers were not directly employed by the owner but worked for sub-contractors who were themselves engaged by the owner. Labour-only sub-contracting was prevalent in mining and cotton where the typical sub-contractor was the individual worker who 'recruited' his wife and children. In both industries the skilled or semi-skilled workers could only hope to fulfil their contracts by exploiting their own families. In Lancashire, Cheshire, and Derbyshire in 1833–4 roughly one half of the mill-working children were employed by other operatives.

Factory capitalism as we know it today only emerged on a large scale in the last quarter of the nineteenth century. That simple fact goes far toward explaining why the working classes in the first half of the century were incapable of throwing up enduring organisations with a mass basis.

The accommodation between the aristocracy and the bourgeoisie

Capitalism could not proceed without political changes, for at the end of the eighteenth century there were still enough statutes on the books to severely impede the birth of the new order.

With some justification historians have characterised the first two decades of the nineteenth century as ones in which the old paternalist code was swept away. In the political system of previous decades the labouring classes got 'paternal protection in return for filial obedience';[8] in the new they were to have duties but precious few rights. Nothing made this quite so plain as the New Poor Law of 1834 which was designed to eradicate the system of poor relief, in which wages were subsidised from the rates, and force the poor into the workhouses. It was the declared intention of the Poor Law Commissioners '. . . to establish therein a discipline so severe and repulsive as to make them a terror to the poor and prevent them from entering.'[9] The New Poor Law, along with such other measures as the Act of 1814 which deprived magistrates of their previously held powers to enforce a minimum wage, was designed to help produce a malleable labour market – a market in which the buyers rather than sellers had the decisive advantage.

The Combination Acts of 1799 and 1800 served a dual purpose. Organisations of working men were looked upon as both nests of revolutionism, and as impeding the right of the employer to do as he pleased in the conduct of his business. In this last aspect, and as the Webbs put it:

From the very beginning of the century the employers had persistently asserted their right to make any kind of bargain with the individual workman . . . They had . . . adopted the principle, as against both the trade unionists and the Factory Act philanthropists, to perfect freedom of contract and complete competition between both workers and employers. In order to secure absolute freedom of competition of individuals it was necessary to penalise any attempt on the part of the workman to regulate, by combination, the conditions of the bargain.[10]

That there were similar restrictions on the rights of employers to combine seemed in no way inconsistent. As the Webbs also said: 'To the ordinary politician a combination of employers and a combination of workmen seemed in no way comparable. The former was, at most, an industrial misdemeanour: the latter was in all cases a political crime.'[11]

However, the fact that the Combination Acts were repealed in the 1820s – at a time, that is, when other restrictions on *entrepreneurial* freedom were being taken off the books – hints strongly at the *real* reasons for the notorious Acts: namely their politically repressive character. They were aimed not so much at incipient trade unionism (which largely continued despite the Acts) as against potentially radical organisations of workers. Nothing haunted the ruling classes in the thirty years from 1790 as much as the fear that the revolution in France would find its mate in Britain. For them: 'Pride and fear were bound closely together. As soon as disturbances broke out in the manufacturing districts the thoughts of politicians turned to two unforgotten outbreaks of violence, the Gordon riots in England (1780), and the Revolution in France.'[12] The spectre was not totally unreal, for the revolutionaries in France were not without their English admirers. After all, hadn't Tom Paine, that great hero of the politically conscious workman, taken himself off to Paris to throw in his hand with those 'abominable French upstarts'?

For much of the first half of the nineteenth century there were then two really significant types of legislation: that which freed businessmen from certain restrictions on their ability to accumulate capital, and that which was designed to keep the increasingly volatile working classes in their place. That such wide-ranging and far-reaching changes were in the air meant that the structure and composition of the ruling classes was changing. By the turn of the eighteenth century Britain was a capitalist country as much in the outlook of its rulers as in its mode of production. If Britain retained its landed aristocracy and gentry, among whom there were many yet to be converted to a total belief in the full rigours of *laissez-faire* doctrines, it was an aristocracy and gentry that had been leavened, permeated, and often rescued from financial oblivion by parvenu merchant capital and its sons and daughters. It was an aristocracy that knew about capital investment and practised capitalist agriculture. It was, said E. J. Hobsbawm, 'by continental standards, almost a form of bourgeoisie'.[13] When Napoleon spoke with contempt of the English as being a nation of small shopkeepers he had in mind the English ruling classes, and the aristocracy in particular. British aristocrats did not disdain to let commerce and finance trickle through their fingers, nor even to admit the newly rich to its ranks. This did not mean, however, that the mercantile and rising industrial bourgeoisie were rapidly and willingly assimilated into the ranks of the aristocracy. Control of the apparatus of the State was too firmly in the grip of the corrupt landed aristocrats for there to be an absence of political resentments. Nevertheless, throughout the opening decades of the nineteenth century there was a progressive diminution of the conflict between the landed aristocracy and the bourgeoisie. And it was not merely the result of economic alliances: fear of the subordinate classes – who were growing insubordinate – provided a potent glue.

Where the aristocracy and gentry were afraid of the dissolution of their agrarian society, for their part the merchants, bankers, and newly rich manufacturers, while not greatly enamoured of government by a corrupt aristocracy, were considerably less enlivened by thoughts of a revolt from below. They accordingly fell in behind the Whig patricians and the Tory monarchists in defence of the established order. It is too much to say that the bourgeoisie demanded their price for co-operation. They did not and neither did they need to. If they had little love for the aristocracy, that very grouping was nevertheless busily creating an environment economically conducive to bourgeois interests. It was entirely credible that this should have been the case. Ater all, many of the great landowners were busily exploiting the mineral wealth lying beneath the ground on their estates, and others, in the 'railway' age of the 1830s and '40s, were buying their way into the railway companies.

Still, the traditional Tory paternalist never quite disappeared. The ethic of *noblesse oblige* was not a completely spent force even if it was often reduced to a genteel form of agitation. It left its mark on the first phase of *laissez-faire* liberalism in the form of the Factory Acts. But that it was reduced to the marginal role of attempting to ameliorate the worst excesses of the factory system was nowhere better illustrated than by the complete failure of the romantic Young England movement to revive the traditional (and idealised) conception of the paternal aristocrat as a dominant political force.

Not until the closing decades of the century did the new bourgeoisie come to dominate parliament. The 1832 Reform Act enfranchised but a small proportion of this new class and provided a few sops to it by eliminating most of the grosser corruptions of the rotten boroughs. That the new bourgeoisie took so long to rise to political pre-eminence was not however especially significant. The important thing from its point of view was that the legislature should not do anything disastrously inimical to its interests. That the Houses of Parliament did not do so is conclusive proof of an aristocracy and gentry predominantly possessed of a bourgeois view of the world. With enemies like these the manufacturers needed few additional friends.

The working class response: old remedies and new departures

Labour's response was not in chorus, nor was it continuous: conditions made either impossible. Not all workers suffered equally from the new climate of *laissez-faire*, and very few workers were in situations favourable to combination or political organisation. Exclusion from the political processes of parliament meant that labour was dependent either upon sympathetic voices within it or upon extra-parliamentary agitation. It is not surprising then that this period was one in which the various segments of the working class were, so to speak, in search of an economic and political theory suitable for the new order. And given the extremely uneven nature of capitalist development, in which archaic work and employment practices existed alongside the more modern, it is not surprising either that the various sections should come up with different answers and tactics.

Broadly, the working-class-in-the-making came up with four distinct answers. Craftsmen, such as hand-loom weavers and agricultural workers, turned sporadic-ally to insurrection with the former also prominent in the Chartist movement. Urban artisans in relatively sheltered trades, as yet largely untouched by capitalist development, tended to lock themselves up in their exclusive trade societies, making only occasional ventures into fringe parliamentary politics. Other urban artisans in less protected trades sought collec-tive defence through trade societies, alliances with bourgeois radicals inside and outside parliament, and were prominent in Chartism. Workers in the newer industries such as engineering, cotton textiles and coal mining turned to trade unionism and Chartism.

This classification is not meant to suggest that the various sections always acted in ways that the cate-gories indicate. The men of Ludd were influenced by the populist Jacobins of the French Revolution as were some of the urban artisans and workers in the newer industries – and all sections practised some form or other of trade unionism. The truth of the matter is that there was a considerable commingling of move-ments and ideas:

As movements faded into one another, a continuity was provided by the personnel. Many of the leaders, at both national and local level, were in all . . . movements. A working man of radical inclinations did not limit himself to one particular cause, but rather supported all types of political agitation in the belief that they were all part of a general movement for change. (J. F. C. Harrison)[14]

No phenomenon of the first half of the nineteenth century captures the political condition of the working classes quite like Chartism. Chartism was unique because it represented the only major attempt at a working-class political organisation of national proportions. That it fell apart ten years after its first appearance in 1838 demonstrated that at that time there was no possibility of bringing together into a united front such a fragmented and sectionalised class. Chartism was essentially a catch-all movement, a movement providing a single response to a multitude of discontents. It brought together parliamentary reformers, displaced or threatened domestic workers, struggling trade unionists. It also brought together all the leading spokesmen of those groups that contended with each other in explaining the nature of the new order and offering programmes of action for the working classes.

The uneven nature of capitalist development – such that some industries in the nature of their practice looked back to the eighteenth century or even earlier, while others already foreshadowed the tightly integrated capitalism of the future – meant that the available 'manifestos' of political and economic analysis *roughly* reflected that stage of development. Robert Owen, mistakenly hallowed in legend as the first English socialist, sought to effect a marriage between factory capitalism and the Tory pastoral ideal of serfs happy in the knowledge of a benevolent squire. For Owen, as V. A. C. Gatrell put it:

What the village portended was clear: that the relationships, close, deferential, and interdependent, which were thought peculiar to pastoral Britain, were capable of reconstitution within industrial society. They could, in short, be reconciled with the machine and not least with the growing numbers of the poor. In this, every conservative instinct of the age could find hope for the survival of its values.[15]

Still, if Owen was as 'firmly paternalist and as essentially authoritarian as a Tory reformer',[16] he nevertheless captured the imagination of large numbers of working-class people – especially artisans working in traditional trades.

Owen started his political career as a benevolent entrepreneur at the New Lanark mills in Scotland. He built substantial cottages for his workers, provided schools for their children, closely regulated working hours and conditions in the factory. In all respects he was a model paternalist employer – and ever afterward based his politics on what he had accomplished. His was not a politics that sought to mobilise the working classes:

. . . the notion of working class advance, by its own self-activity towards its own goals, was alien to Owen, even though he was drawn between 1829 and 1834, into exactly this kind of movement. This can be seen in the tone of all his writings. He wished (he said in 1817) to 'remoralise the Lower orders'. Next to 'benevolent' the words most commonly encountered in early Owenite writings are 'provided for them'.[17]

With New Lanark as a model, what Owen sought to achieve was a society in which the profit motive disappeared and in which production was based on small communities co-operatively organised. This was a conception of society almost tailor-made for the artisans who were '. . . inheritors of long traditions of mutuality – the benefit society, the trades club, and chapel, the reading or social club . . . Owen taught that the profit motive was wrong and unnecessary: this keyed in with the craftsmen's sense of custom and the fair price' (E. P. Thompson).[18] Inspired by this vision thousands of artisans at various times organised themselves in producers' co-operatives, and some of the more adventurous attempted to establish independent communities. Failure attended all these attempts to re-create the mythical Merrie Englande: of those producers' co-operatives that did survive, they did so by becoming straightforwardly capitalist organisations.

Owen merely gave his followers a moralising rhetoric with which to attack capitalism, a rhetoric

From a rural workforce to the beginnings of a factory
proletariat . . .

which in wit and bite was vastly inferior to that of Thomas Carlyle, an arch-Tory. However, few of Owen's followers were true disciples. What most Owenites found was less of a doctrine and rather more of an expedient; an expedient which could offer a way out of intolerable hardships, and offered a vision of a society closely related to that cherished in folklore. If Owen 'simply had a vacant place in his mind where most men have political responses'[19] the same was not true of supporters who had been more lightly touched by his brush. The logic of Owenism was an opting out of established society – a utopian formula altogether too fantastical for the worker 'two-blocks-up' against a brutish reality. The importance of Owen rested not in his critique of capitalism (he didn't have one); it lay rather in the fact that his ideas, merely by being critical, raised the level of consciousness of large numbers of workers and made them readier to join in movements like Chartism.

The main thrust of Chartist polemic was of an egalitarian strain which reached back at least as far as those British artisan admirers of the French Revolution in the last decade of the eighteenth century. As P. Hollis put it: 'For twenty years (i.e. 1810–30) . . . working class theorists had recognised that there was a gap between what the labourer produced and what his wage would buy, and in turn taxation, upper-class parasites, the theft of land and competition were held to account for it.'[20] What these theorists noticed was *political oppression* rather than *economic exploitation*. And that was not surprising. A theory of exploitation would have called for a close look at the role of the emerging class of manufacturers; but since these critics were themselves small masters or close enough to them to aspire to their ranks, there was a natural propensity to lump manufacturers and labourers together as constituting the productive classes. For them, enfranchisement was the burning question, and universal suffrage the answer to all ills – an illusion the depths of which still remained to be plumbed in the 1970s.

The Chartist programme of universal suffrage and the like, while patently the work of Tom Paine's descendants, nonetheless provided a rallying-point for almost all sections of the organisable working class. The Charter was a sort of 'lowest common denominator'. It indicated a direction of change which could be understood as generally favourable to the working classes. This catch-all character of Chartism was at once the source of its superficial strength and its underlying weakness.

On the face of it Chartism was a mass movement of dimensions previously unknown in British history. Indeed it was the *first* mass movement of modern times. The 1839 Chartist petition had $1\frac{1}{4}$ million signatures, that of 1842 well in excess of $3\frac{1}{4}$ million, and that of 1848 somewhat short of 2 million. But signatures on petitions are like crosses on ballot papers: they point only to the momentary acts of isolated individuals. It is arithmetic that makes the crosses and signatures collectivities, and arithmetical collectivities should not be confused with the more viable kind to be found in a mobilised and organised mass. When the testing time came for Chartism its numerical strength was found to be infinitely weaker than its internal divisions.

From the beginning in 1838 there had been a fundamental split in the movement. There were the 'moral force' Chartists who believed in a strict adherence to parliamentary and constitutional practices, and there were the 'physical force' groups who argued for a resort to arms in the event of the failure of peaceable methods. This division between reformers and revolutionaries accurately pinpointed one of the major cleavages within the working class which has already been referred to: namely, the reformers tended to be the artisans in the more sheltered trades who could see themselves as having some stake in society as constituted; the revolutionaries, by contrast, were largely composed of distressed domestic workers, such as handloom weavers, and the less 'privileged' of the urban craftsmen. Straddling this polarity, tending this way or that depending on local circumstances, were such workers as those in the pits and cotton mills struggling to develop a viable trade unionism. Another, much larger, section of the working class – the great mass of casually employed, semi- and unskilled labourers in the large towns and cities – might occasionally have swelled the ranks of the demonstration but were not, properly speaking, part of the movement at all. Henry Mayhew, the most astute observer of the time, had this to say:

The unskilled labourers are a different class of people. As yet they are as unpolitical as footmen, and instead of entertaining democratic opinions, they appear to have no political opinions whatever ; or, if they do possess any, they rather lead towards the maintenance of 'things as they are', than towards the ascendency of the working people. I have lately been investigating the state of the coal-whippers, and these reflections are forced upon me by the marked difference in the character and sentiments of these people from those of the operative tailors. Among the latter class there appeared to be a general bias towards the six points of the Charter ; but the former were extremely proud of their having turned out to a man on the 10th of April, 1848, and become special constables for the maintenance of law and order on the day of the great Chartist demonstration . . . The artisans of the metropolis are intelligent, and dissatisfied with their political position : the labourers of London appear to be the reverse ; and passing from one class to the other, the change is so curious and striking, that the phenomenon deserves at least to be recorded . . .[21]

Although the various Chartist movements were riddled with government spies, *agents provocateurs* and petty informers peddling trivial titbits to pop-eyed magistrates and parsons; although the soldiery was widely deployed and in constant communication with the Home Office,[22] F. C. Mather's assessment of the Government's role in 1838–9 stands equally for the later movements of the 1840s: '. . . the government showed a scrupulous anxiety to keep within the law in dealing with Chartism, and its policy was in no sense systematically repressive.'[23] While the localised insurrections of Chartists in 1839 and 1848 inevitably brought down a heavy-handed State, the failure of the movements lay in the internal contradictions – precisely the same sort of contradictions that from thenceforward always bedevilled the trade union movement.

The most durable product of the years to 1850 was the trade union. Pedestrian when compared with the excitements of Chartism, Ludd and Swing, it was nevertheless a very considerable achievement. While the unions may have had more limited aims, they were often thought of by the ruling classes on the ground (as distinct from that section of the ruling classes that held the levers of State) in the same lurid terms as rickburners and machine-breakers.[24]

It was not merely that they were regarded as a threat to the established order of things or even that today's trade unionist was yesterday's follower of Ludd; rather there was a deep-rooted feeling of outrage that the 'lower orders' should have the audacity to organise. The way the officers of the British navy regarded the mutinous seamen in the 1790s was the way magistrate, parson, landowner and millowner thought of their workers some fifty years later:

The Georgian plutocrats had invented a character for the British sailor – mentally inferior, simple, jolly and loyal. He was by nature lazy, so the bosun's mate used a knout to send him up the shrouds. He was improvident; therefore pay only indulged his weakness. He was a drunkard; so he must not be allowed ashore. He was a child who looked to the captain and the admiral as his father . . . The mutiny – with its skilful planning, determination and discipline – wrecked the jolly jack tar mystique. It was hard for most officers to believe in the new man who had come so unexpectedly on deck. It was hard for some of the men too. (J. Dugan)[25]

The 'new man who had come on deck' had not wrought a total revolution within himself: he could be quite as perplexed as some of his masters with the new order. Some of the urban artisans – still relatively privileged, clinging to vestiges of independence and aspiring to be masters themselves – though on balance conservative, were showing signs of movement:

Though notoriously divided into many small societies (the London carpenters) had since 1823 held annual united dinners of all societies. In the 'twenties the toasts had been to the king, the House of Hanover, the army and the navy, Mechanics' institutions, and the *Trades Newspaper*. But by the 'forties they had changed to toasting the People's Charter and having Chartrist guests . . . (I. J. Prothero)[26]

Among the new factory workers without either a foot on the ladder or a tradition of craft:

. . . new attitudes, new community-patterns were emerging which were, consciously or unconsciously, designed to resist the intrusion of the magistrate, the employer, the parson, or the spy. The new solidarity was not only a solidarity *with ;* it was also a solidarity against . . . Magistrates rode through thronged neighbourhoods a few hundred yards from their seats, and found themselves received like hostile aliens. They were more powerless to uncover trade union lodges than Pizzaro's freebooters were to uncover golden chalices in the villages of Peru. (E. P. Thompson)[27]

The Combination Acts did not kill trade unions. They either went underground as secret societies operating to regulate work customs and practices, or disguised themselves in ill-fitting clothes as friendly societies for the provision of sickness and burial benefits, etc. Artisans persisted with their traditional combinations which in a number of cases could trace descent to the early decades of the eighteenth century, and the habit spread to workers in the newer trades of cotton textiles, engineering and mining where they often operated quite openly. The large wave of strike activity which followed the repeal of the Acts showed that many more had been leading a furtive existence. The repeal, incidentally, by no means entailed a complete change of heart on the part of the ruling classes: unions continued to be regarded as conspiracies in restraint of trade and had no legal protection for their funds.

Virtually every historian of the labour movement worth a mention has noticed the astonishing speed with which trade unions rose and fell in this early period. This pattern of rapid entry and equally rapid exit was due to the fact that the trade in the locality was the normal focus of organisation. Sidney Pollard's description of the Sheffield situation makes the point very well:

The traditional industries of Sheffield produced a large variety of articles, and in the course of time a high degree of specialisation had created minute sub-divisions among the local trades, each with its own trade society, its own piece-rate list and its own traditions. Each narrow trade, in turn produced goods of innumerable patterns and qualities, few of which had a mass market.[28]

A comparable point was made by Prothero (mentioned above) with respect to the London carpenters. In normal times then, any town or city of reasonable size would have a number of different societies catering for the same trade; and in those times the societies were at once both social clubs and mutual benefit societies running a variety of insurance schemes. When times were not so normal – when the masters either singly or in unison attempted to effect reductions in their lists of prices for various categories of labour –

then did unions make an appearance. Early unions, that is to say, were typically loose federations of trade societies temporarily united to fight issues that extended to whole trades. Thus, as the Webbs put it, there were 'practically two constitutions, one for peace and one for war.'[29] Once the war was over, the unions tended to dissolve because the primary basis of allegiance was the trade.

Naturally defeats in battle hastened the end of many a *union*, but much more rarely did it mean the permanent end of associations in trade societies – 'a trade "out of union" was easily re-formed into a society, with much the same membership and the same officials, and the sense of belonging to one's trade was strong' (S. Pollard).[30] Thus, with the survival of the small societies there continued to remain the basis for a survival of unionism. However, trade unions were as likely to dissolve after victories as after defeats. A fact which doubly underlines the primacy of the trade over the union. Still, this narrow sectional self-interest, itself a reflection of the stage of economic development, was not the only factor inhibiting the development of permanent unions.

A common cause of complaint amongst employers in the first half of the nineteenth century was the indiscipline of their workers. The 'indiscipline' took the form of a refusal to work beyond hours that enabled workers to secure sufficient money to ensure the customary standard of living. Needs were simple then; there was no hint of the grotesqueries of the acquisitive culture of capitalist societies in the late twentieth century. Weekends would last from Saturday through to Tuesday, and wages would be made up by working late into the evenings of Thursday and Friday. These practices made it hard for employers to maintain continuity of production and fully utilise their plant. But, and much more importantly, they also created problems for trade unions. Effective trade unionism depends, amongst other things, on the standardisation of wages and hours. Indiscipline with respect to these things could accordingly weaken, or even make ineffective, trade union organisation. Certainly this seems to have been the case with the pottery workers: 'Because of their inability to deal successfully with hours, potters' unions found themselves seriously handicapped in their efforts to standardise and raise wages.'[31]

While 'indiscipline' certainly contributed to the organisational problems of the early unions, the fundamental issue was the proliferation of the small trade society. The fragmentation of trades into thousands of small workshops each catering for a local or specialised market, and the unreliability of transport and communication made this pattern almost inevitable. Not until the advent of the railways, national markets, and large-scale factory production did the unions emerge as national organisations. It was significant that it was in coal mining and cotton textiles – both tending to operate on a national scale and bringing together large numbers of workers in one workplace – that the first attempts to create national unions appeared.

Toward the end of 1829 Lancashire cotton spinners founded the Grand General Alliance of All the Operative Spinners of the United Kingdom with branches in Scotland and Ireland. But before that – in 1810 and 1818 – there had been other attempts at a general union based on the region. In 1810 in South Lancashire there had been a four-month-long strike of spinners centrally organised from Manchester and described at the time as 'the most extensive and persevering strike that has ever taken place'.[32] Both strike and union were defeated. Manchester was the scene of another attempted federation in 1818. Known as the Philanthropic Society, it was based on the cotton industry, though also affiliated were societies of hatters, bricklayers, sawyers, machine-makers, colliers and shoemakers. Formed to provide mutual assistance in strikes, it foundered on yet another abortive strike.

The 1829 venture of the Grand General Alliance followed lengthy and unsuccessful spinners' strikes in Stockport and Manchester. Within six months the union became the National Association of United Trades for the Protection of Labour with the ambitious aim of uniting all workers regardless of trade into one union. In 1830 its affiliations were from 150 societies spread over twenty trades. While the main strength came from Lancashire cotton workers, others included miners from most of the northern and midland districts, potters, millwrights, mechanics, and blacksmiths. By 1831 it claimed a membership of 100,000. By 1832 it had disintegrated into its various parts.

There had been problems of leadership, but they were secondary and largely derivative of the *real* problem, which was the incoherent market structure of the industries in which the affiliated trade societies were operative. Each of the various societies had, understandably, joined with the larger body in the belief that it would get support from other workers for its struggles. When the National Association found that a large proportion of its constituents all needed to fight at the same time it found its task impossible. Not only did the various sections not understand the complexity of the environment in which they collectively worked, but market circumstances ensured that operatives, far from making their own initiatives, were forced to respond to those of their employers. Such was the diversity of trades, and the diversity within trades as between localities, that sectionalism and indiscipline rather than strategically planned action became the dominant mode of activity. The formal unity of a National Association could not in any way cope with the actually existing disunity.

Events overtook other similar attempts at National

Unions in the 1830s, though the ostensible reasons for collapse varied.[33] The London-based Metropolitan Trades Union of 1831 federated a number of trade societies. It amounted to very little because its activists were much more interested in the National Union of the Working Classes which was mainly concerned with agitation for the constitutional reform of parliament. The Operative Builders Union formed in the same year had a rudimentary national organisation and a number of local victories to its credit in 1832 and 1833. In the latter year the OBU came under Owenite control, the Owenites seeking to take over the industry by forming a Grand National Guild with associated workers' co-operatives: simultaneously the union was being beaten to its knees by an employers' lockout. A succession of other defeats, coupled with internal dissent, led to the dissolution of the union into its separate elements in 1834.

The Operative Builders Union's misfortunes were closely bound up with those of the most ambitious attempt of all – the Owenite Grand National Consolidated Trade Union (GNCTU). The GNCTU, like the Chartist movement which it in some ways foreshadowed, was an excellent example of how in this period working-class movements could with great rapidity oscillate between narrowly economic and broadly political action. Certainly, as A. E. Musson said: 'There was a strong sentiment that trade unionism was one thing, politics another, and that trade societies should confine themselves to trade affairs, unless politics obviously impinged upon them . . .'[34] But politics often did impinge, for there was nothing quite like a trade depression for providing an indirect revelation of how little the established political machinery spoke to working-class needs. Thus when circumstances provided that revelation, the moment was opportune for such organisations as the GNCTU.

The GNCTU belied its title for: 'Its immediate

object was nothing less than the entire supercession of capitalism and of the system of competition by a co-operative system of workers' control. It aimed, not only at controlling industry, but at superseding parliament and the local governing bodies, and at becoming the actual government of the country' (G. D. H. Cole).[35] The GNCTU's 'immediate object' also belied its objective basis: trade societies affiliated with it for much the same reasons that had led them to previous affiliations with the other nationals – namely, the need for an organisation that could supply them with a strike fund of a magnitude beyond their own resources. The GNCTU could not meet that need any more efficiently than had the NAUPL and the OBU. It exhausted its funds after supporting locked-out workers in Derby for four months, and duly collapsed as the various trade societies withdrew. William Lewis, a tailors' leader from London, commented: 'Some trades are withdrawing themselves from the Consolidated; this is wise; let each trade act on a reciprocity of interest, but let each trade be governed by its own executive.'[36] Sectionalism got its just deserts once again.

The idea of One Big Union endured right into the early decades of the twentieth century, though by then it was too late to be applicable since it cut across the aims and policies of well-established unions even though the nature of the economic terrain was by then more favourable. In this earlier period the nature of the terrain was favourable only to the highly specific, locally-based union of tradesmen and other workers who for one reason or another could regulate entry into the labour market. It was such unions, limited in their aims though often ready to join in the grander schemes, that survived in modified forms to become the ancestors of the unions of the late twentieth century.

In the years until mid-nineteenth century the world

of the labour movement reflected all the conflicting tendencies within the working class. Ambitious, forward-looking projects such as the national unions rose and fell. Others less forward-looking, such as the utopian Owenite movements, rose and fell too. Yet others showed all the marks of desperation – Ludd and Swing for example. Ideological, theoretical, tactical and economic differences ensured that the working classes never offered a united front. And not surprisingly.

With the very fabric and texture of society changing so rapidly, few people were clear as to the exact nature of the relationships between the classes; generalised ideas certainly, yet none tangible and coherent enough to stun people into an aggressive unity. Doctrines were abundant to explain the nature of the world and each gathered its groups of devotees. But none of the doctrines had any quality of blinding clarity, and many obscured more than they revealed. The stark fact was that a pervasive industrial capitalism was too recent a phenomenon to be fully comprehended, and the unevenness of its development sufficient to ensure intellectual confusion. Trade unions and other working-class movements were then, almost inevitably, caught up in the pursuit of Owenite red herrings, doomed insurrections, and Chartist blind alleys.

The gut basis of the narrowly conceived trade lay at the root of all enduring organisations, for: 'Although the arguments for uniting appeared irrefutable, and the weakness of the isolated societies was only too obvious, most of the members showed no great enthusiasm to join up in regional organisations. Parochial isolationism, national rivalry and jealous zeal for local autonomy all contributed towards the delay.'[37] John Child was talking there of compositors, notoriously amongst the most conservative of workers, yet in their insistence on local autonomy they were thoroughly typical. Even so, local loyalties did slowly start to break down at the same time as a very diffuse and general consciousness of class started to break the surface. Sectionalism, while dominant, did not tell the whole story. In the three years 1810–12 'the small society of London Goldbeaters lent or gave substantial sums, amounting in all to £200, to fourteen other trades', and in 1823 the Home Secretary was informed that a Bolton society of cotton-spinners 'had received donations, not only from 28 cotton spinners' committees in as many Lancashire towns, but also from 14 other trades, from coal-miners to butchers.'[38] Ideas of solidarity, going beyond those of the locality, began to take root. But primitive understanding of class solidarity is not the same as a fully awakened class consciousness. The latter is dependent on an over-arching political theory.

The years to 1850 left no such theory to succeeding generations. Ideas of wage-slavery and exploitation anticipating Marx and Engels made an appearance, but not in the context of a worked-out and integrated theory. Solid practical lessons in the matter of organisation and tactics, in the true anti-intellectual tradition of British 'common sense', were the main components of the legacy. What was found to work on a limited scale – at least as far as skilled workers were concerned – was control of entry to local labour markets, and the provision of welfare benefits. Other workers, such as miners and cotton-spinners, learned that strikes, provided they were launched when markets were buoyant, could be an effective weapon. The lessons learned related more with how to cope with capitalism, and less with how to overthrow it. They were to dominate the thinking of the labour movement late into the twentieth century.

2. Respected and Respectful Men: The Years of the Top-hatted Trade Unionist, 1850-1890

There are thousands of well-to-do workmen who own houses, have shares in building societies, and money in banks; men also who, by reason of their 'push' and energy which have, as a rule, enabled them to accumulate money or property, are among the most influential of their class, and these men are keenly opposed to anything that tends to trench upon the 'sacredness' of individual property, or about which there is any savour of the levelling doctrine.

The Journeyman Engineer in 1871[1]

The managers of the Great Exhibition, held in 1851 but three years after the last Chartist movement, '. . . had continued to fear that the working classes would make of its opening an occasion to exploit class ends and to embarrass and humiliate their superiors . . . Many responsible persons thought that the opening ceremony should be private, lest Chartists or foreigners should make trouble' (G. Best).[2] Their fears were ill-founded. 1851 was a year of working-class passivity and bourgeois self-congratulation. Thousands of working-class families had trooped around the Exhibition in an orderly and dutiful manner.

Their masters had cause to be complacent, for Britain was unquestionably the world's dominant economic and political power. The labour aristocracy of artisans and skilled workers had reason to share that complacency for they too were getting their cut. Even the great mass of the population, the casually employed urban poor, took a marginal bite out of the growing prosperity between 1850 and 1875. In that period the rich were getting incomparably richer. Simultaneously the distribution of inequalities within classes, as well as between them, was changing its shape. In the ruling classes the dominance of aristocratic landowners was being progressively diminished with the growth of vast bourgeois fortunes made in industry and commerce. In the working classes the labour aristocracy became further differentiated from the semi- and unskilled labourers.

The various engineering industries were becoming the backbone of British capitalism, employing in 1891 twice as many workers as they had forty years earlier. Only agriculture – on a continual decline – employed more. Not a few of the rural workers, driven from the land by unemployment, found jobs in pits and on quaysides, although most of them found their way into the transportation industry which showed a two-and-a-half-fold increase of employment from 1851–91. Many of the daughters became domestic servants (country girls being considered more pliable than their town counterparts) – one in six of the occupied population were 'in service' from 1871–91.

The rural workers' often traumatic experience of being uprooted from traditional communities, never to be subsequently paralleled, was not simultaneously even yet equivalent to the creation of a factory proletariat. Domestic outwork continued on a considerable scale, though now mainly located in the slums of the large cities and towns; sub-contracting of the labour-only sort predominated in the Midlands ironworks, shipbuilding, quarrying, and in the large and growing building and construction industry; the engineering trades still largely consisted of small workshops. Nevertheless, the wage-earning factory worker in the direct employ of the entrepreneur was growing in importance, especially in the capital-intensive industries and in others where the activities of large numbers of workers needed to be co-ordinated. Overall, one thing is clear when we survey the employment situation of the working class as a whole: the vast majority, as in the earlier part of the century, worked in situations where the money-bond between worker and capitalist was obscured. That is to say that where in fact the only tie between them was one of cash, that fact could be obscured by a close working relationship with the master of a small workshop who worked at the bench alongside his men, or by indirect employment through a sub-contractor or the middle-man in the domestic system.

The bourgeois take-over

'(In 1873) about 80% of the kingdom was owned by about 7,000 families. At the apex of the social pyramid was a group of men with property larger than several sovereign states and rent rolls greater than national treasuries . . .'[3] In other words, the landowners were still pretty important people. Yet the fact that the landed aristocracy and the gentry dominated parliament until 1885, the Cabinet until 1905, and effectively controlled entry into the Civil Service until the 1870s and into the ranks of the Army officers until 1871, was of no great consequence: '. . . the laws which were passed and executed by landed parliaments and governments were those demanded by the businessmen and . . . their intellectual masters.'[4]

The leavening process which had been going on for 200 years or so, in which new wealth bought its way into the aristocracy and gentry, quickened in the second half of the nineteenth century. Industrial wealth followed merchant wealth and acquired land and country mansions. If it could not buy estates and mansions it built them up from scratch, often on the rural fringes of the large cities. It did not do so under the same political pressure as previously for successive reform acts had broken, or were in the process of breaking, the connection between landed property and parliamentary representation. The impetus now came from a desire to ape established wealth and claim acceptance. Land ownership and rural pursuits still carried a mystique fitting to a ruling class: the ability to ride to hounds and massacre birds were important attributes of the gentleman.

The third quarter of the century was an age in which the new bourgeoisie enjoyed such a far-reaching dominance that it rarely came under any substantial native-born attack. The accompanying euphoria was not totally blind – there were too many reformers about to enable the ruling classes to be unaware of the appalling squalor and poverty in their midst. But then, as now, when the rulers gave their assessment of the state of the nation they were talking about *their* situation. Lord Brougham's definition of the 'people' is instructive: 'By the people I mean the middle class, the wealth and intelligence of the country, the glory of the British name.'[5] This was in 1859. Eleven years later Froude, in celebrating the 1868 Reform Act, made it even more explicit: 'The people have at last political power. All interests are now represented in parliament. All are sure of consideration. Class government is at an end. Aristocracies, landowners, established churches, can abuse their privileges no longer. The age of monopolies is gone. England belongs to herself. We are at last free.'[6] After 1868 the 'people' now included the labour aristocracy – but it did not include the farm labourers or most of the urban poor, let alone *women* – of any class.

Some of the more sophisticated members of the ruling classes, appreciating that subtle means were required to attain the ideological loyalty of the working classes, set themselves up in business as providers of 'useful knowledge'. The Society for the Diffusion

of Useful Knowledge, established in the thirties, was
wound up in 1847. Its publications, in simple and clear
language on every conceivable subject and priced very
cheaply, ran into a circulation of millions. Not a few
of the pamphlets extolled the middle-class virtues and
bourgeois political economy.

The working man had a commodity to sell like anyone else
– his labour – and his only way to prosperity was to
raise its price. This he could do individually by improving
his skill as a craftsman, saving his money, working hard
and living temperately. By this means he would himself
become an article of rare value and his price would rise:
his fellows, by doing the same, would increase the general
wealth and keep goods in rapid circulation. Universal
abundance would result, except, of course, for the idle,
turbulent or debauched. Friendly Societies were prudent
and laudable institutions; Trade Unions, by calling strikes
and violently stopping the wheels of industry, merely
spread desolation and despair.[7]

Floods of similar propaganda, mixed in with
genuinely useful knowledge, continued to be published
in the fifties and sixties by which time the whole
tendency was put on a firmer footing with the establishment of workingmen's clubs and institutes under
aristocratic and bourgeois patronage.[8]

Despite all this, 'worms' were turning. The voice of
the submerged working class was making itself sufficiently heard to revive unease, which was echoed by
Mark Rutherford in 1885: 'Our civilization is nothing
but a thin film or crust lying over a volcanic pit,' and
he wondered 'whether some day the pit would not
break up through it and destroy us all.'[9] When the
ruling classes thought of their subordinates – which
was not all that often despite the work of Dickens and
philanthropical reformers – they almost invariably split
them in two. When Gladstone spoke of 'our fellow subjects, our fellow-Christians, our own flesh and blood,
who have been lauded to the skies for their good con-

duct', he was thinking of the labour aristocracy who on being given the vote had faithfully supported the Liberals. The other, larger part, was the 'volcanic pit' of squalor and poverty.

Broadly then, ruling-class strategy toward the working classes followed its realistic distinction. The articulate, literate, and more prosperous part was co-opted into citizenship: it was given the vote and its great institution, the trade union, was given certain legal immunities thus bringing it within the pale of respectability. The poverty-stricken part, showing no inclination for political activity, could be left to its own devices. That their physical condition did improve through urban improvements such as the clearing of some of the worst slums, the paving of streets, and provision of drainage etc., was due more to the fear of epidemics than to human concern and the need for political concessions.

The hey-day of the labour aristocracy

By the middle of the 1870s the skilled workers, along with the cotton spinners and the coalminers, stood unquestionably and unchallengeably at the head of the working classes. Even in the late forties '. . . the craftsman . . . had his status in the community, wore his top hat, stood apart from the mob, and had no thought of using his union for political ends: he often identified himself with the actually governing classes sufficiently to join one or other of their camps, and he did not want the division between them to split his union . . . the craftsman had a stake in his country.'[10] If this characterisation of E. Phelps Brown overdraws the situation, it does have a general accuracy. While there may have been no *inevitable* reason why the sons and nephews of the practitioners of the illegal traditions of the unstamped press, trade societies, and corresponding societies should have come to be regarded by Gladstone as 'our own flesh and blood', there are plenty of good reasons why they should. But let's be clear: by no means all of those associated with the earlier radical and revolutionary stirrings found themselves and their descendants in top hats in the new era. '. . . (The) continuous flow of new casualties (obsolescent tradesmen) declined into the residuum, where, increasingly concentrated in urban slums, they passed from the sight not only of the middle class, but of the more successful part of the working class.'[11]

It is not difficult to see why people such as George Howell – an archetypal working-class opportunist[12] – should have seen the political salvation of the working class as lying nestled in the austere bosom of the Liberal Party and been militantly opposed to the formation of a labour party. Nor to see why Robert Applegarth of the Amalgamated Society of Carpenters and Joiners should have told his conference in 1869: 'Opposition of masters and men does not arise from a desire to oppress each other, but rather from ignorance . . . I look to education to teach all parties better.'[13] Nor again why the Portsmouth lodge of the Ironfounders should have proposed in 1849 not only the cessation of strikes, but the abolition of the word 'strike'! A mere glance at the employment situation of the labour aristocrat shows why it is not difficult: '. . . the skilled worker of the middle of the nineteenth century tended to be in some measure a sub-contractor, and in psychology and outlook bore the marks of his status.'[14]

It is not without significance, as Royden Harrison has pointed out, that '. . . the term working classes rather than "working class" accorded most closely with the linguistic conventions of the mid-Victorians. Politicians, political economists and members of the working classes themselves were at pains to spell out the implications of this distinction.'[15] As a member of these classes said himself: 'Between the artisan and the unskilled labourer a gulf is fixed. While the former resents the spirit in which he believes the followers of genteel occupations look down upon him, he in his turn looks down upon the labourer. The artisan creed with regard to the labourers is, that they are an inferior class, and that they should be made to know and kept in their place.'[16] The artisan had very good reason for keeping the labourer at arm's length – his prosperity was largely dependent upon the extent to which he could keep his skill in short supply.

The artisan was generally much approved of by the more far-sighted members of the ruling class. Small surprise when: 'The cotton spinners invested their personal savings and trade union savings in the cotton mills. The skilled shipyard workers in Jarrow and Newcastle did the same in their industry and the boilermakers sent their officials to become officials in the employers' association.'[17]

Because the artisans were literate and articulate, and because the ruling class took a great deal of interest in them and their organisations, we know a lot about their political attitudes and their way of life. On the other hand precious little is known about that incomparably larger section of the working classes – probably a full 85% of it – the labouring masses. This was not an undifferentiated mass, at least in London. But the character of London as a national and international capital city, with its 'fashionable' seasons and its concentration of the wealthier classes, meant that it had a highly distinctive labour market, distinguished by its incredible array of separate occupations, and the seasonal nature of most employment. Seasonal unemployment was not, however, unique to London, even though its special features exacerbated the condition of the casually employed poor. London employment was typically labour intensive and conducted in small workshops; in the provincial cities it tended to be more capital intensive and growingly concentrated in factories. This meant that in the provinces employers had a greater incentive to try to iron out seasonal fluctuations so as to keep their capital employed; in London it meant lay-offs. The absence of a concentration of the ruling class in the provinces meant the absence of a proliferation of trades catering to its multitude of whims and fancies. The immense sub-divisions of the London labour market, and its ultimate dependence on the 'seasons' and personal idiosyncrasies of the wealthy, apparently gave rise to a highly ambiguous state of mind among the casual poor, superbly caught by Stedman Jones:

At a political level, the most striking characteristic of the casual poor was neither their adherence to the right, nor their adherence to the left, but rather their rootless volatility. Casual labourers who had swelled the ranks of Chartist demonstrators in 1848, were howling down high churchmen at the behest of the vestrymen of St. George's-in-the-East in 1859; the disinherited who turned out to cheer Garibaldi in the 1860's, could with equal fervour support the Tichborne claimant in the 1870's; the dock labourers who were to strike under the radical leadership of the Labour Protection League in 1871 had applauded Tory gentry promises of winter bread and coals in 1867; those who had forgathered in Trafalgar Square on 8th February, 1886, to hear Conservative-inspired demands for protection as a solution to unemployment, could riot the very same afternoon under the banner of socialist revolution; those who had participated in the great Dock Strike of 1889, fell with little resistence under the spell of protectionists and anti-alien propaganda in the 1890's.[18]

It does however seem likely that this form of political consciousness, if given particular emphasis by conditions peculiar to London, was widespread throughout the country. It is, after all, precisely what one would expect where one class is ideologically dominated by another and yet finds itself periodically hard up against the exploitation of which the ideological dominance is but a veneer. As Genovese has said of slavery:

All forms of class oppression have induced some kind of servility and feelings of inferiority; failure to induce these means failure to survive as a system of oppression. The slavish personality represents the extreme form of this servility and expresses itself, among other ways, in a longing for the master, for this other represents superiority in strength and authority and perhaps even virtue. But this other . . . must, in reality, prove unattainable to the slave. The act of love is therefore frustrated, collapses into hatred, and generates, at least potentially, great violence.[19]

Ideological dominance, however, cannot be alone and of itself sufficient explanation for the apparent quiescence of the bulk of the working classes with respect to trade unionism. Nor can it be enough to accept the reasoning of John Burns (one of the leaders of the 1889 London dock strike): 'The great bulk of our labourers are ignored by the skilled workers . . . (so that) ostracised by their fellows, a spirit of revenge alone often prompts men to oppose or remain indifferent to unionism . . .'[20] Perhaps it could usefully be more often remembered that by no means all of the skilled workers were unionised – if Mayhew's estimate of 10% would not have borne examination in 1874 when the TUC alone claimed just over a million members, the fact remains that a majority remained outside the unions. To account for this, as for the non-unionised state of the labourers, we need not resort to such relatively fragile categories as 'subservience', 'revenge' etc., but to the very same set of factors that account for the artisans' acceptance of the bourgeois view of the world: namely, the structure of employment – small factory and workshop, sub-contracting, casual and seasonal labour.

The unions of the skilled workers, and indeed those of the coalminers and cotton spinners, positively reeked of respectability. Gone was the political adventurousness that had marked earlier years. Thomas Cooper, an old Chartist, reported in 1863 on a visit to Lancashire:

In our old Chartist time, it is true, Lancashire working men were in rags by thousands; and many of them often lacked food. But their intelligence was demonstrated wherever you went. You would see them in groups discussing the great doctrine of political justice – that every grown-up, sane man ought to have a vote in the election of the men who were to make the laws by which he was to be governed; or they were in earnest dispute concerning the teachings of socialism. *Now,* you will see no such groups in Lancashire. But you will hear well-dressed working men talking, as they walk with their hands in their pockets, of 'Co-ops', and their shares in them, or in Building Societies. And you will see others, like idiots, leading small greyhound dogs, covered with cloth, in a string![21]

Making due allowances for exaggeration, it is hard to dispute the general direction of Cooper's observation. If it is more than doubtful that a thought-out political position was ever a widespread phenomenon amongst the mass of the workers, few workers in the industrial areas could not have been touched to some extent by the abundance of conflicting and competing ideas in the Chartist years. *Now* there were no divisive issues of a fundamental nature that caught up large numbers of workers in a mass movement. There were, naturally, still plenty of old Chartists around and the new ideas of Marx and Engels were slowly percolating through to the 'advanced' men;[22] but these people were marginal until the socialist revival in the 1880s. The trade unions, the co-operative movement, and single-issue movements such as the Reform League were all dominated by the same people with essentially the same views of their society. The co-operative movement had been sheared of its Owenite connota-

'... like idiots, leading small greyhound dogs, covered
with cloth, in a string!'

tions as an alternative society in the making. Large numbers of producers' co-ops rose and fell, particularly during and after strikes and lock-outs, but they were motivated less by utopian socialist aspirations than by a desire for a place in the sun. Only the 'soundly financed' retail co-ops survived.

It is true that one may point to Applegarth's membership of the First International alongside Marx as indicative of remnants at least of socialist thought; but his association was more concerned with spreading British ideas on trade unionism to European colleagues than with making an international revolution. Likewise with the labour establishment's help for the Paris Communards in 1871. George Potter and other labour figures formed a committee, in company with Baron Rothschild (!), to:

. . . set up a fund so that the Parisian workmen might get their tools out of pawn. Across the Channel this philanthropic gesture was being rendered superfluous by the Parisians themselves who were abolishing the pawn-shops! Most of the English trade union leaders seem to have supposed that the Commune could have been averted by a timely translation of *Cassell's Encyclopaedia of Useful Knowledge*. The Bookbinders Secretary, T. J. Dunning, was speaking with the authoritative voice of the Trade Union oligarchy when he announced that economic categories were immutable and that the Communards must be mad since they dared to contemplate the abolition of rent.[23]

By the 1850s circumstances had sufficiently changed to make it possible for renewed attempts at forming national unions to have a limited success. The building of a fast and efficient railway system in the 1830s and '40s enabled the creation of a national market for a much wider range of commodities than hitherto. And this had the effect of encouraging a tendency toward the equalisation of wages within industries and between localities. The railway system also facilitated the rapid communication of messages and bodies between the regions. All of these factors made it much easier for workers to perceive an identity of interest going beyond that of the immediate community.

More or less enduring federations of trade societies made their first appearance in such industries as printing and engineering in the 1830s and 1840s, but these were regionally based and left autonomy on all major questions in the hands of the local societies. What was significantly different about developments from the 1850s onward was the welding of regional federations and local societies into national unions, with a growing centralisation of powers at national level. These new formations, ever since the Webbs wrote their *History,* have been conventionally called the New Model Unions: a somewhat misleading title since they were little more than logical continuations of a long-standing tendency.

Still, the change was significant enough. The union generally accorded credit for it was the Amalgamated Society of Engineers (ASE), formed in 1851 from an amalgamation of some 120 or so local societies. Its distinctive feature was the creation of a central bureaucracy (of one man initially) on a salaried basis, and the centralisation of finances. It was also characterised – as were its forerunners – by high subscription rates to enable the provision of a wide range of welfare benefits and a strike fund. Since the main attraction of the union was its friendly society function, strikes were frowned upon because they consumed valuable assets. If the ASE provided the model, other unions followed – notably the cotton spinners, and the Amalgamated Society of Carpenters and Joiners (ASCJ) after the disastrous London builders' lock-out of 1859.

The turn toward centralisation had nothing whatever to do with collective bargaining on a national scale; bargaining remained a local function until the end of the century, indeed it did not become widespread until the years between the two world wars. The impetus came from the lessons of bitter experience of previous decades. What had been learned was that unless timing was absolutely right with regard to market conditions, strikes and other aggressive actions were doomed to failure so long as they were undertaken on a narrowly local basis. Changes in the structure of the national economy, due in part to such things as the creation of a railway network, made it possible to develop forms of organisation that could begin to come to terms with previous deficiencies. This patently did *not* mean that the working class was at last providing itself with highly effective fighting machines. The New Model Unions were *craft* based rather than *class* based, and in any case were many decades removed from the time when they could claim to have in membership a majority of those eligible. These unions only organised the most highly skilled workers, men who were proud of their craft and conscious of the status that their scarcity bestowed on them. They were men who were aristocrats of labour. And they knew it.

The New Model Unions were, above all, *trade* unions. Exclusive combinations of tradesmen, they sought to regulate the market for their labour by exclusionist policies. Applegarth of the ASCJ even went so far as to try to exclude all but the very best tradesmen, thereby persuading the employers of his desire '. . . to replace the previous conflict of employers and employed by a harmonious co-operation . . .'[24] By no means all of the old trade societies reconstituted themselves on an amalgamated basis. In fact the large majority remained on a local or regional basis, engaging on an occasional piratical foray into the sphere of interest of other societies in other localities and regions. Some went halfway toward the amalgamated such as the Stonemasons: power remained largely in the local lodges, but they retained a central corresponding secretary who had it as his duty to keep lodges informed as to their various activities. Those unions that did not accept the New Model were either subsequently to do so later in the century, to be merged into other unions, or in very rare cases to survive until the present day as anachronisms devoid of power or importance.

The New Model gave the labour movement what it had never had before – a stable and relatively permanent leadership. This period saw the beginnings of a 'labour establishment'. Then, as now, relatively few men found themselves in those positions that gave them an opportunity to acquire the skills necessary for the day to day management of union affairs. And when one man, or a small group of men have knowledge and expertise not possessed of others, they *appear* to be in a position to manipulate others. Thus we see in this period the growth of the modern phenomenon of large numbers of rank and file trade unionists persistently complaining of the high-handed autocracy of their leaders, or resisting amalgamations on the grounds that 'tyranny' would result. Once amalgamations did take place they were invariably either accompanied or followed by attempts on the part of the rank and file to impose checks on their leaders. So marked was the reluctance to delegate powers that provision was made in some cases for the oversight of even the most minor of administrative matters. In the case of the ASE for example, the consequence was that a national delegates' meeting could literally go on for months at a stretch. The ideas of what the Webbs patronisingly called 'primitive democracy' remained strongly entrenched: as they still do today.

The Webbs described the early trade society as 'a democracy of the most rudimentary type, free alike from permanently differentiated officials, executive council, or representative assembly. The general meeting strove itself to transact all the business, and grudgingly delegated any of its functions either to officers or to committees.'[25] When it became apparent that this particular pattern of government could not be reproduced in the larger amalgamations, it nevertheless remained the model that trade unionists carried in their minds, their ideal of what a democratic constitution should look like. Thus whenever circumstances indicated constitutional renovations there was an almost universal inclination to try to get the best possible approximation to the form of the local trade society.

When, because of amalgamations, the need for the appointment of a full-time officer became irresistible, attempts were made to contain him by the device of the 'local executive'. The executive was typically drawn from one of the larger branches in one of the important regional centres of the trade. Then, to try to ensure that no single branch could enjoy continuing dominance, the head office would be moved around from time to time and from town to town. A good example of this was the wanderings of the head office of the United Society of Boilermakers: for twenty years or so it moved around from one port to another, and it was not until 1888 that it finally settled in Newcastle-on-Tyne.

It did not take trade unionists very long to discover that a part-time executive, relatively unskilled in the trade of officialdom, was no match for a practiced general secretary or equivalent. Hence the advent of written constitutions, delegate meetings, and the use of the initiative and referendum. The typographers adopted the referendum as their means of legislation in 1861, and in 1860 the United Kingdom Society of Coachmakers simultaneously put forty-four propositions to the vote. The referendum, however, created more problems than it solved, for it was not exactly unusual for contradictory propositions to be carried simultaneously: the Webbs suggested that many bankruptcies followed from motions to both *decrease* subscriptions and *increase* benefits! As time went on executive power was deployed against the use of the referendum. Some executives refused to put certain motions to the vote, others specified time limits as to the amendment of rules – ten years in the case of the Operative Bricklayers Society after 1889. Others abolished the referendum altogether – the ASCJ in 1866. Yet others vested the power to initiate a referendum in the executive where it became a formidable instrument of central control. As the Webbs put it, it greatly enhanced the power of the general secretary '. . . who drafted the propositions, wrote the arguments in support of them, and edited the official circular which formed the only means of communication with the members.'[26]

Throughout the period of 1850–90 there was a strong, persistent and irreversible tendency for powers to be concentrated at the centre. Tenaciously held popular views that power properly belonged to the locality, and attempts to enforce those views, were progressively overcome. That the ideas continued to persist and that they were never defeated without a struggle meant that leadership 'victories' were never total, and ensured, furthermore, that leaders were always looking over their shoulders to see if the troops were following.

These years saw the birth of the crude and naïve theory which had it (and lamentably still has it) that the rank and file is all virtuous and the leadership composed of traitorous 'sellers-down-the-river'. A theory by no means the sole property of socialist and militant critics. If it was true that the leadership was starting to develop separate and distinct interests of its own, it was also true that many of the clashes between it and the rank and file had their basis in the sectional claims of the latter rather than the 'power aspirations' of the former.

Revolts of one form or another were a commonplace in any union that attempted to organise on anything beyond a purely local basis. Indeed it is fair to say that the leaders of the new 'amalgamateds' probably spent most of their time trying to strike a balance between the often-competing interests of different sections of the membership. The ways in which the balance was struck, the conceptions as to the nature of that balance, and the forms of expression of the sectional interests all reveal that the union leader was neither villain nor hero; rather was he an incomplete prisoner of impersonal historical forces. Nowhere was this clearer than in the experience of the miners' unions after 1860.

Challinor has summed up the situation as follows:

. . . In studying the coalminers, the tension between the leadership and the rank and file is one of the most vital factors in reaching an understanding of how the movement develops. MacDonald and the militants – the lap-dog or the lion? Did one get a lump of sugar through begging like a well-trained poodle or a hunk of meat by showing the lion's fangs and being prepared for bloody struggles? That was the question.[27]

This is a considerable over-simplification. While it is undeniable that attempts to federate local and county miners' unions were constantly bedevilled by conflicts between those who wanted a militant policy of confrontation and those who wanted a conciliatory policy, the ideological conflict was a secondary effect and not a primary cause. *That* conflict was but a reflection of the economic differences between the various coalfields: different fields produced different sorts of coal for different purposes. Coking coals, steam coals, domestic coals – each had different markets with differing fluctuations in demand and therefore prices. Different prices indicated different wage rates and hence differing necessities for wage struggles. Patterns of ownership varied as between fields – a small number of large firms dominated some, a large number of small firms dominated others. Geology mattered, too – the accessibility and workability of seams varied from county to county and this meant that payment systems also varied. Yet another complication was the employment relationships – sub-contracting was prevalent in some fields, wage-earning in others; trucking, i.e. payment in kind through company owned shops, became extinct in some areas and persisted in others. Add all these together and it is easy to see that grievances in some areas could be non-issues in others. Given this, it becomes readily understandable that clashes amongst different leadership factions should focus around the question of collaboration or confrontation – especially when it was so apparent that some leaders were cosy with some coal owners to the point of corruption.[28]

While coal mining may have been unique in the range of possibilities it provided for sectionalism, other unions in other industries were in broadly comparable situations.

The Amalgamated Society of Engineers organised in a variety of industries, each with its distinct characteristics and problems. Where in the 1840s and '50s engineering shops were general in that they undertook a wide range of jobs, from the 1850s onward there was growing specialisation. Some firms confined themselves to textile machinery, others to locomotives, others to armaments, and so on. By the 1870s some engineering work was becoming repetitive assembly work and so new branches of the industry appeared – the sub-contracting firm making components for the larger firm assembling the complete machine. The use of new tools, machines, and raw materials all furthered the degree of specialisation of production and labour. 'Separate shops for the various operations replaced the general shop in both large and small factories. The turnery or machine shop, the fitting and erecting shop, the pattern-maker's shop, the smithy and press shop developed as separate units under the same roof.'[29] This increasing division of labour both within factories and between branches of the industry provided ample scope for sectional conflict. New unions sprang up in some of the new specialisms – The Pattern-Makers, and Amalgamated Brassworkers in 1872 – and bitter local struggles developed: it was at this time that demarcation disputes became a commonplace. Differences in wage rates and methods of wage payment provided further opportunities for conflict. Thus, as amongst the miners, the ground was well-prepared for battles beween rank-and-file and leadership. The leaders, having to contend with a growing volume of routine business and needing to have an eye on the overall needs of the union, were increasingly suspicious of the independent activities of the branches and districts. The rank and file in the branches, faced with immediate and specific problems, were just as resentful of the leadership. Mutual recriminations resulted: Allan, the ASE secretary, was complaining in the early seventies of unofficial strikers, while the strikers for their part condemned the leadership for its tardiness in paying dispute benefit.

A common cause of contention was the growing practice of arbitration and conciliation. The idea of arbitration had been around for many years: an Act of 1824 enabled arbitration on wage issues if both parties agreed, but the Act was never applied. It became fashionable again in the 1840s, and a Nottinghamshire lace manufacturer petitioned parliament in 1845 for establishment of Courts of Conciliation and Arbitration – unsuccessfully. In the 1850s there were a number of attempts to establish permanent boards of arbitration, but all were short-lived. By the 1860s however the number of arbitration and conciliation bodies started to increase, and there developed a 'corps' of arbitrators. 'By 1875 there was barely a trade where trade unions existed which did not have either a standing joint committee of employers and workmen to settle disputes, with provision for arbitration, or the experience of settling disputes through arbitration on an *ad hoc* basis.'[30]

Though part of the impetus for conciliation came from such Liberal employers as Mundella and Morley, it could not have been successful without a parallel enthusiasm on the part of the unions. J. H. Porter has argued that:

The formation of the boards appears to have taken place when the unions had sufficient strength to convince employers that conciliation and arbitration were necessary, but insufficient power to make an openly militant policy more attractive for themselves. This point was usually reached on the upswing of the trade cycle when membership was increasing . . . The experience of unsuccessful strikes in part explains why union leaders were prepared to accept arbitration and conciliation when their bargaining power returned.[31]

Thus the leadership's desire for conciliation involved them in making concessions in boom conditions in order to ensure the continuance of the machinery in slumps. This was a sure recipe for trouble, and so it proved: innumerable unofficial strikes were the direct consequence of the rank and file's unwillingness to accept their leaders' reticence to fully exploit their strength when they had it.

The leadership preference for conciliation had its roots in two factors. Insofar as conciliation avoided strikes, it involved a minimal drain on union funds. Since the leaders depended on those same funds for their salaries they had a vested interest in financial solvency. They could also claim, with no little justice, that solvency was a prerequisite for survival of the union in the long run and that was in everyone's interest. Basically though, the liking for conciliation was a function of the ideology of the union leader. He did not cast himself in the role of revolutionary, either actual or potential. He was not out to change the world but to make it slightly more bearable. In this respect there is no good reason for believing that he differed markedly from the outlook of his members. If the rank and file were not always approving of their leaders' *tactics* as exemplified in organisational practice, few disputed their overall *strategy*.

In the third quarter of the century, as in earlier years, the labour movement attracted support from some members of the ruling classes. Christian Socialists, Positivists, Liberal and Tory manufacturers, while perhaps regarded as slightly or even extremely eccentric by many of their fellows, were not completely beyond the pale. Some of them indeed were very much within it: Thomas Brassey the railway magnate, Samuel Morley and A. J. Mundella, both wealthy hosiers, Michael Bass the brewer, Lord Elcho the coal owner and ironfounder, all helped the trade unions in some way or other. The more intellectual supporters were drawn from the growingly important professional middle classes: Professor Beesley, Frederic Harrison, Henry Crompton – all three Positivists who enjoyed an importance and significance far beyond their number. The support of these was both symptomatic of the new respectability of the craft unions and important in consolidating it. With their influence in parliament and friends in the Civil Service, these people played a crucial mediatory role by bringing the unions imperceptibly into the councils of state.

The response of the provincial bourgeoisie to the annual congresses of the TUC after 1868 is also significant: 'The Anglican churches and Nonconformist chapels of the locality celebrated by religious services the opening of the Congress . . . The mayor of the city, wearing the insignia of office, gave the members a civic welcome. . .'[32]

The years 1850–90 saw an increasingly closer relationship between the trade unions and the Liberal Party – although in the same period the process of disintegration of the alliance also began with the tentative revival of socialism in the 1880s. From the 1850s the trade unions were staunchly parliamentarian, ostentatiously avoiding flirtations with anything more adventurous. First they had to get the vote, and in pursuit of this they had the support of such radical Liberals as Cobden, who had written despairingly of the working classes in 1861: 'Have they no Spartacus among them to lead a revolt of the slave class against their political tormentors?'[33] They had not – for which Cobden must have been quietly relieved. They had the National Reform League instead. The Reform League, despite its Chartist ancestry, wanted manhood suffrage and not much else by the mid-sixties. Closely involved in it, directly or indirectly, were most of the trade union leaders of the day. By 1868, one year after Disraeli had stolen the Liberals' clothes by enfranchising a large slice of the urban working class, the League became part of the Liberal election machine. In 1871 Applegarth of the Woodworkers was secretly in the pay of Glyn, the Liberal whip; three years earlier a number of other prominent trade unionists were being paid by Glyn to prepare reports for him on how the newly enfranchised working class was going to vote in the 1868 election.[34]

If there was no immediate pay-off in terms of legislation favourable to the unions, it did eventually come – and in a contradictory parcel. Following on a report of a Royal Commission on the trade unions, the Trade Union Act of 1871 gave protection to union funds (hitherto unions had been unable to sue those officials who ran off to the latter-day equivalent of South America with the funds), and ruled that unions could not henceforward be regarded as criminal because they acted in restraint of trade. The Criminal Law

Amendment Act of the same year took it all away with the other hand by enabling imprisonment for even contemplating a strike, and by making peaceful picketing effectively illegal. This led to a brief rupture with the Liberals: in the election of 1874 they were opposed by trade unionists. The Tories were elected, and the Criminal Law Amendment Act repealed. For the next twenty-five-odd years the unions rested in the belief that they had exacted from the State almost all that they needed and wanted. Disillusionment with the Liberals did not endure. Indeed after the brief break – which had never been total – the unions moved increasingly closer, particularly when the Liberals agreed to the election of a limited number of union nominees in certain constituencies. With an enlarged proportion of the working class now voting, the time had passed when its aspirations could be suppressed or ignored.

In spite of the unions' quest for respectability, which led them to abhor strikes and prefer arbitration and conciliation, strikes did not disappear. Neither were all employers as convinced as Messrs. Mundella and Morley of the utility of trade unions: Mundella's view that trade unions amounted to a barrier to social revolution was unusually sophisticated at the time. Both strikes and lock-outs were lost and won, but the defeats of the unions less frequently entailed their collapse as organisation and discipline improved.

In the age of the 'top hat', the trade unions had come to terms with capitalism. If they were not always ardent devotees of all aspects of the new order it did at least seem, to the artisan anyway, to have something concrete to offer. Times were generally good until the mid-seventies, and a wide range of legislation seemed to welcome them into citizenship. Practically all trade unionists had the vote after 1868 and most of them used it in support of the Liberals. The establishment of the TUC on a permanent footing after 1870, when the leaders of the London-based amalgamateds condescended to join what had been started by the Manchester and Salford Trades Council in 1868, provided an excellent medium between the individual unions and the government of the day. By 1890 a number of trade union officials had been elected to parliament as Liberal MPs (there were ten in 1886) and one of them, Henry Broadhurst the stonemason, '. . . was made an Under-Secretary of State, . . . was invited to stay at the Palace, and the Prince of Wales stoked his fire'(!)[35]

Their place in the order of things seemed to guarantee a reasonable future in which they would no longer go unrecognised. The structure of their unions changed fairly rapidly in line with this new spirit. Mass participation in union government remained an issue but was rarely paramount: issues such as closure of the labour market, political citizenship, social legislation and the defence of benefit funds were those that counted. And since these went hand in hand with an acknowledgement of the status quo, it followed that the means of attaining them should be attuned to the institutional means now available. And the means best suited were those of backstairs lobbying in parliament and administrative efficiency in the union office. So then did the union respond to the mode of adaptation to the wider society.

Bearing in mind that William Allan of the ASE had told the Royal Commission on Trade Unions in 1869 that the interests of labour and capital were incompatible, it is legitimate to ask *why* the new model unionists should have come to accept the new order. There are a number of reasons for this. First, there was the prolonged period of rising prosperity from 1850 to 1873 which gave the artisan a wholly unexpected place in the sun. Second was the fact (to which I shall be returning) that trade unionism as such only confronts the basic contradiction of capitalism –

the exploitation of labour – at the point of production. That is to say, trade unionism only experiences exploitation as an economic fact, and not as a *politico-economic* fact. Third was the seemingly disastrous model of Chartism etc. to look back upon: 'It was the younger generation, reacting against their disastrous Chartist and Owenite elders, who laid rough hands upon the existing unions and founded others upon new principles . . . it was a revolt in favour of prudence, respectability, financial stability and reasonableness, and against pugnacity, imagination and any personal indulgence.'[36] Related to this was the tendency toward oligarchy amongst the new union officials, itself made possible by the limited economistic aims of trade unionism. Fourth was the lack of a clear distinction in status between many trade unionists and their employers – masters moved down into the ranks of the artisan, men moved up into the ranks of the masters. And finally there was the fact that in this period it was still possible for the rising bourgeoisie to give the impression of being a politically progressive force: what was good for them was to some extent also good for the artisans, the partial mutuality of interest thus tending to obscure their irreconcilable differences. By the 1890s the industrial bourgeoisie was entrenched and no longer a progressive force. No wonder then that the labour movement generally and the trade unions particularly should have shown signs of moving toward socialism. In 1886 the TUC debated nationalisation of land, and in 1887 the President said in his address: 'Gentlemen, socialism has lost its terrors for us. We recognise our most serious evils in the unrestrained, unscrupulous and remorseless forces of capitalism.' A new era was in the offing, new forces emerging.

Unemployment was high in the 1880s, and wages had ceased increasing after the mid-seventies. If the condition of the unskilled labourer remained appalling, he was showing signs of organised revolt: his first unions started to appear in the seventies and eighties. Furthermore there was the socialist revival, heralded by the formation of the Marxist Social Democratic Federation in 1884. When the SDF organised a demonstration of the unemployed in London in 1886, it turned into a riot of the London poor who smashed windows and looted shops. London had seen nothing like it since the bread riots of the 1860s. The riot was rightly seen by the ruling classes as symptomatic of a new belligerence.

3. Gunboats in the Mersey, Soldiers at Tonypandy, and Knee-breeches at Buckingham Palace, 1890-1926

Trade Unionists are beginning to realise that so long as the capital and the machinery are in the hands of a small class . . . no real progress can be made toward bringing about our social emancipation.

The Friendly Society of Ironfounders to the 1893 TUC[1]

The immense display of working-class solidarity in the 1926 General Strike brought to a close a remarkable era in the history of the labour movement. The working class rose to a position of political prominence of such magnitude that it could no longer be ignored. Nor was it. The advance of the trade unions and socialist organisations provided innumerable occasions for the ruling classes to be afraid for their future. Their fear was *partly* justified for there were many people about who were distinctly ill-intentioned toward them. But it was not wholly justified as events were to prove. Magnificent though the General Strike may have been, it was also a political fiasco.

Still, considerable advances had been made. Trade unionism in 1926 touched upon almost every occupation of any size: where in 1892 there were about 1½ million union members, by 1926 there were 5¼ million. Where in 1890 there was little more than a whiff of a possibility of a working-class political party, by 1926 there were 151 Labour MPs and there had already been the first Labour government.

Tests of agility for the new ruling class

John Saville argued that: 'Through all the decade of the nineties and well into the new century, a hostility developed toward trade unionism in general and new unionism in particular that bordered at times on the hysterical . . . This whole period after 1889 is one of a developing counter-attack by the propertied classes against the industrial organisations of the working people.'[2] This seems to be a reasonable judgement. Troops and cavalry, police baton-charges, warships, all became a familiar feature of many large strikes from the 1890s to the 1920s. Not since the years of Ludd had the State found it necessary to so extensively deploy and use its instruments of violence. Striking miners were shot at Featherstone in 1893 and Tony-pandy in 1911. Gunboats were anchored in the Humber during the 1893 dock strike and in the Mersey during the Liverpool general strike in 1911. Frightened police going beserk in baton charges was almost a commonplace during a large strike. The courts, more augustly and with great solemnity, were also running amuck: a series of court decisions in the nineties, culminating with the Taff Vale judgement in 1901, eroded the legal status of trade unionism. All this in the context of a growing ruling-class anxiety about the power of the new unions of the unskilled.

What frightened them was not so much the willingness of the new unions to stage militant strikes accompanied by mass picketing, as the fact that these unions were organising the 'volcanic pit', the 'people of the abyss', the 'dangerously volatile' urban poor which Mark Rutherford had feared would rise up and swallow the likes of himself. Their fear was being concentrated powerfully by the revelations of the Charity Organisation Society, Charles Booth, and Seebohm Rowntree of the condition of the poor. What could be more alarming than the sight of the new unions and the socialists apparently organising these very same people? It was this generalised fear and alarm which came to be specifically expressed in legal judgements and in local and national government decisions to use troops and police. It needs to be remembered though that the separate arms of the State do have a limited autonomy. And the courts, though an arm of the State, very rarely receive explicit instructions from governments on individual cases. This was certainly the case in this period, for while the courts were engaging in frontal warfare, governments were making concessions.

The kernel of government strategy was disarmingly simple. When Bonar Law told the Cabinet in 1919 'Trade union organisation was the only thing between us and anarchy, and if trade union organisation was against us the position would be hopeless',[3] he was reiterating what had been a guiding principle for nearly thirty years: co-opt the unions. And by 1919 successive governments had had a lot of practice. They were determined to be as conciliatory as the delicately balanced forces within their respective parties would allow. Even in the years immediately before and after the First World War when fears of working-class revolution were at their height and force most resorted to, governments trod remarkably softly. If this were not the case one would be hard put to explain the appointment of working-class magistrates, the appointment of trade unionists to the Factory Inspectorate, the Factory and Workshops Act of 1891, the Arbitration Act of 1896, the Workmen's Compensation Act of 1897, the reversal of the Taff Vale decision by the Trades Disputes Act of 1906, an Act limiting the hours of work for adult miners in 1908, the establishment of Trade Boards in 1909 to regulate wages in certain sweated industries, the beginnings of state social insurance in 1911, the payment of MPs from the same year, and the legalisation of trade union political action in 1913.

The British ruling class are renowned the world over for their sophistication. If there was ever a period in which they earned their fame, and in which their skills were put to the test, it was this one. Very broadly the ruling class were presented with two political questions, one major and one minor. The major question was that presented by the working class. The minor one was related to it: which party, Liberal or Conservative, was to be the ruling-cass parliamentary expression?

When Lord Randolph Churchill said in 1892 that if Labour could obtain its aims within the constitution all would be well, and that it was therefore incumbent on the Tories not to adhere to '. . . unreasoning and short-sighted support of all the rights of property . . .',[4] he was speaking as a Tory but expressing a view commonly held by intelligent members of the ruling classes regardless of party. But if all factions of the ruling class *cognoscenti* were agreed that concessions had to be made to the working classes – and most particularly to their strongest instrument, the trade unions – the issue remained as to whether it was going to be the Liberal faction or the Tory faction that was going to do the conceding. In the early nineties the advantage seemed to be with the Liberals. They, after all, had had twenty years' experience of co-opting labour leaders, and furthermore had shown themselves willing to implement the least onerous of labour's demands. The Tories on the other hand were bereft of these qualifications. Apart from connections with the Lancashire cotton unions the Tories had little contact with organised labour. By 1918 it was clear that the Liberals had lost, for in the election of that year the Labour Party polled almost as many votes as the Liberals.

The eventual Tory victory over the Liberals was less

a function of the actions of the Conservative Party and more a function of the contradictions within the Liberal Party. In the early 1900s the Liberals were swimming against the tide in two respects. While the economy was coming to be dominated by the large firm, the Liberal Party drew most of its support in parliament from an amalgam of middling and small businessmen and middle-class professionals. The larger businessmen were throwing in their lot with the Tory landowners: unlike their smaller brethren they were not so convinced of the virtues of competition. In the country at large the Liberals were dependent upon the working-class vote – a vote which, after the advent of the Labour Party in the 1906 elections, was expecting more radical policies. The Liberals therefore were confronted with trying to reconcile the demands of two groups of 'consumers', each basically hostile to the other; at the same time they had to face the awkward fact that one of the customers, labour, was showing signs of opening shop on its own account. The Liberal government of 1906–10 tried hard to prove its radical credentials with a strong reform programme including a number of taxation measures highly unpopular with the rich. But it could not do what it needed to do – improve the living standards of the working class. Indeed throughout its tenure living standards continued to fall. The Liberal Party had shot its bolt, though the intervention of the war was to obscure this fact until the election of 1922, when the Labour Party supplanted the Liberals to become the second largest party after the Conservatives.

The Conservatives had had to do rather more than wait for the outcome of the struggle between Labour and Liberal, yet not much more. The division within the Tory ranks was between those who wanted to take a hard line with labour and those who wanted to appease. The appeasers, epitomised in Stanley Baldwin and shrewdly led by him, eventually won.

Leading Tories, seeing after 1918 that future electoral struggles were likely to be between themselves and Labour, were anxious to conceal their hostility toward socialism. It was imperative for the party not to present itself as an instrument of the rich against the poor. What made this possible, as Maurice Cowling has said, '. . . was the belief that the trade union leaders were paper tigers.'[5] Their judgement was to be proved to the hilt in 1926.

The failure of the struggle for socialism

While the politically active sections of the ruling class were making their bid for the trade unions, the politically active sections of the working class were doing likewise. Throughout the period the unions provided the terrain on which the struggle for socialism was fought, being pulled first this way and then that. The Social Democratic Federation, especially active in London and Lancashire in the second half of the 1880s, proved a training ground for a new generation of working-class activists. That throughout its life it suffered a high turnover of membership was not so important. What counted was that those who passed through its ranks added to the numbers of working men becoming familiar with socialist ideas. Indeed, in the early years it seems likely that most socialists were not members of a party at all. Some were isolated individuals working in trade union branches and trades councils, others were members of small and intense discussion groups who spread the word at work and moved in on strikes.[6]

Though the main aim was the conversion of the trade union movement as a whole, agitation necessarily went on at all levels and seized what opportunities presented themselves. Those who could tried at union delegate conferences and at the annual meetings of the TUC to commit their unions to socialist policies.

The TUC throughout the nineties saw a constant struggle between the 'old guard' of trade union leaders, who wanted to continue their attachment to the Liberals, and the socialists who wanted the TUC to sponsor a labour party. The delaying tactics of the TUC Parliamentary Committee (the rough equivalent of today's General Council) were successful for the best part of a decade. Not until 1899 did the TUC set in motion the discussions that led to the formation of the fore-runner of the Labour Party, the Labour Representation Committee. That did not mean that the old guard had changed its mind; it did mean that the new unions of the semi- and unskilled workers, when allied with the growing number of socialists in the old unions, were now strong enough to form a majority.

The general context which brought about the change in attitudes through the nineties was, as the Webbs put it:

With capitalists ready at any moment to suspend a profitless business, collective bargaining proved as powerless to avert reductions as the individual contract. In face of a long continued depression of trade, marked by frequent oscillations in particular industries (traditional) trade unionism, it seemed, had been tried and found wanting. These were the circumstances under which the disillusioned working class politician or trade unionist was reached by the lectures and writings of the socialists. . . .[7]

With the formation of the Independent Labour Party in 1893 a roof was provided for those trade union socialists up and down the country who found the Marxist and more revolutionary Social Democratic Federation a little hard to take. The ILP, with a strong reform programme, was not far distant from the Liberal left-wing and was tailored to the limited outlook of the trade unionist but recently wooed away from Liberalism. The TUC, in accepting in 1899 the need for a Labour Party on the lines advanced by the ILP, was not going much beyond Gladstonian

liberalism. Yet if the step was a timorous one, it was
to have profound consequences. With the trade union
movement now committed to its own party, and in
the name of socialism, it was able thereafter to beat
off all attempts to push it in the genuinely socialist
direction of dispensing with capitalism.

Despite the objective timidity of the step of setting
up the Labour Representation Committee in 1900,
many trade union leaders did not see it in that light.
At the founding conference the previous year delegates representing rather less than half the TUC
membership were present, and it was not until 1909
that the last big union, the Miners Federation, finally
dissolved its links with the Liberal Party and signed
up. The fact was that, from the union leaders' pragmatic point of view, the founding of a Labour Party
was a distinctly risky business. They had grown
accustomed to working with the Liberals and had a
settled pattern of relationships with them. It had taken
them decades to get into a situation where they could
rely on being consulted on labour questions, and they
did not want it all undone by what they saw as a
bunch of visionary, irresponsible young hotheads.

The Social Democratic Federation, long a thorn in
the side of the trade union establishment through its
influence in the London Trades Council, left the
Labour Representation Committee in 1903 disgusted
with its unwillingness to proclaim itself for militant
struggle. In 1911 the SDF joined up with seceding
branches of the ILP to form the British Socialist
Party, subsequently to be the nucleus of the Communist Party when it formed in 1920. In 1903 the
Socialist Labour Party had been founded in Glasgow,
a Marxist syndicalist party and a direct off-shoot of
the party of the same name in the USA. Revolutionary
in spirit and objectives, the SLP was violently opposed
to trade unions on the grounds that they propped up
the capitalist order, and that it was quite impossible

to convert them to socialism by 'boring from within'.
As De Leon, the American SLP leader, said: ' "Bore
from within?" We tried it. We went into the unions
and bored from within. We tried to teach the class
struggle . . . We struggled and we struggled with the
labor lieutenants of the capitalists; it came to hand
encounters; finally, we landed on the outside . . .'[8]
The British SLP, never numbering more than a few
hundred members though extremely influential on
Clydeside, hewed to the same line. The Industrial
Syndicalist Education League founded by Tom Mann
in 1910, while believing with the SLP that the capitalist
order could be overthrown by a general strike, also
believed that the trade unions had to be organised
as industrial unions before the big slam could be
delivered. The League accordingly worked within the
unions trying to persuade them of the virtues of
industrial unionism. The following year – 1911 – saw
the formation of the Guild Socialists who advocated
the transformation of the trade unions '. . . into great
workers' corporations which should demand and secure
from a reorganised State the whole responsibility for
the conduct of industrial affairs.'[9] 1920 saw the
creation of the Communist Party in the wake of the
Bolshevik revolution. Committed to working for
socialism on the Bolshevik model through the trade
unions and the Labour Party, this was the only
socialist group outside the Labour Party to survive
through the twenties in any strength.

These various socialist groups, and many other
local and regional ones not discussed, were working
on fertile soil in the 1900s. But as G. D. H. Cole, who
was himself active in the general movement, has said:

The underlying movement was a mass movement of sheer
reaction against the failure of either orthodox trade
unionism or moderate parliamentarism to secure any
improvement in working-class standards of life. The
theorists, working class and middle class alike, who sought

to give this movement form and direction and to interpret its vague strivings into a new social gospel, never
really captured the great mass of the working class. They
might lead it in this or that particular struggle, and might
help to stir up troubles that would not have occurred
without their impulsion. But the mass, as ever, was thinking not of Utopia and not even of the class war, but mainly
of the immediate issues involved in each separate dispute.[10]

Exactly so. Most if not all of the new socialist
parties formed in this period were manned by people
disillusioned with the performance of the new Labour
Party. In parliament the party was largely composed
of men not markedly different in outlook and tempera-
ment from the old Liberal trade unionist MPs –
indeed many were the same men with a new label
around their necks. Being the products of less turbulent years they were quite incapable of understanding
the new ferment let alone leading it. Marx's classic
aphorism about 'the weight of dead generations laying
like a nightmare on the brain of the living' was never
more apt. This did not mean, of course, that these men
were irrelevant. They remained on the scene when the
ever ephemeral strike was but a folk memory. They
retained control of their unions and their hold on the
Labour Party precisely because the labour unrest at
the grass roots was not political in motivation but
economic. This meant that as soon as a strike was
over the established leaders were back in command.
In general political outlook they were much closer to
their rebellious members than were the activists.
Cowling has captured this mood precisely:

As trade unionists they sought a larger share of the
national wealth through trade union negotiation. As leaders
of the Labour Party they favoured the redistribution of
wealth by taxation. They used class slogans to discredit
Lloyd George and the Conservatives by whom he was
surrounded. But they were neither syndicalists nor revolutionaries. They neither wanted nor sought more than *co-
operation* between worker and management.[11]

Trade unionism defeats socialism

Insofar as the new unionism of the early nineties was merely the organisation of semi- and unskilled workers, it was not 'new' to all. Numerous and short-lived attempts to form just such unions had been made in the previous twenty years. The renewed attempts from about 1889 succeeded where the others had failed primarily because changes in the economy and structure of employment made the terrain more amenable to organisation, and secondarily and derivatively because of the growth of aggressive socialist ideas.

From the 1890s onward the large firm became increasingly prominent, largely as a result of mergers undertaken as defensive operations against shrinking profit margins, being designed to eliminate competition in domestic markets. Monopolies or near mono-polies were formed in sewing-cotton, textile dyeing and finishing, glass, cement, wallpapers, tobacco, and chemicals. Amalgamations also spread across indus-tries as firms in one sought to control the outlet for their products in another: three large Sheffield steel firms – John Brown, Vickers, and Cammell – bought shipyards on Clydebank, at Barrow, and on Mersey-side respectively. In the field of banking, a rush of amalgamations reduced the number of private banks from several hundreds to fewer than twenty. In insurance too there were similar changes. By 1926 the structure of industry and finance looked much tidier. If small private companies were in a numerical majority, the bulk of capital was securely tied up in the large joint-stock company with shares quoted on the stock exchange. The credit system was stream-lined, and the names of companies and banks, hitherto having only local connotations, came to be household words. The concentration of ownership tended to lead to the concentration of production. Certainly this period saw the growth of the ever-larger factory and the decline of the workshop. In 1913 there were 3,000 more factories and 2,000 fewer workshops than in 1912, and the factory population was seven times that of the workshop. In London in 1898 – *the* centre of small-scale production – there were some 8,500 factories but 56% of workers were in 750 of them.

Most of the adherents to socialist ideas in the working classes were craftsmen, the men who were to play crucial roles in the development of the new unions. All over Britain members of the old craft unions played an important part in the new wave: Tom Mann and John Burns, both ASE members, in the London Dockers Union; Glasgow and Liverpool dockers were organised in a union started by a printer and an engineer; an ironmoulder was prominent in the Knights of Labour in Liverpool, and a working jeweller in the same city helped organise the tramwaymen; in Leeds Tom Maguire, a photographer, was important in organising a spate of new unions. It seems unlikely that the new unionism was the result of spontaneous organisation on the part of the unskilled in many places. If they were responsible for the initial impetus by going on strike, the subsequent organisation was typically the work of those with the vision of a different future and equipped with the all-important skills of numeracy and literacy. These highly necessary attributes were supplied by craftsmen, semi-skilled workers who had learnt from them, and occasionally by middle-class sympathisers.

The key presence of the craftsmen – members of the 'labour aristocracy' – strongly suggests that new unionism, far from being a radical break from the old craft exclusivist unionism, developed in part from its womb. This becomes especially clear when one tries to account for the extraordinary propensity of members of the ASE to work in and with the new unions and socialist organisations.

For two decades the growth of specialisation,

technical change, and concentration of ownership had been working to undermine the privileged position of the skilled engineer. New machine tools meant that what once was skilled work was now semi-skilled; specialisation of product separated groups of engineers with competing interests; and concentration of ownership of the means of production opened up a gap between the worker and his master. As Hobsbawm put it:

. . . As production concentrated and the owner-manager gave place to the joint-stock corporation . . . (so) a whole set of novel managerial, technical, and white-collar grades wedged themselves between the 'skilled man' and his 'master' . . . Step by step the labour aristocrat found himself forced into the ranks of the working-class; and, on the whole, he moved to the left.[12]

These changes meant that the traditional practices of the ASE were becoming ill-adapted to the economic circumstances, as forceful critics like John Burns were pointing out when they attacked the union's unwillingness to fight for fear of prejudicing the sick and superannuation benefits. Other craft unions like the Boot and Shoe Operatives and the Ironfounders, whose members were also being forced into the ranks of the working class by technical and economic change, were also under attack. 'Send for John Burns' was the call from the floor at a turbulent meeting of the Boot and Shoe workers in London in 1889. In the same year the Glasgow iron-moulders joined a demonstration in support of Corporation Tramway workers, and sent donations to strikes of unskilled workers. In 1894 the Friendly Society of Ironfounders, a staunchly traditional craft union, elected a militant to be assistant general secretary.

Change was everywhere broadening the horizons of the craftsman, forcing him to look beyond the boundaries of his trade. No wonder then that those with the broadest vision acquired socialist theories and,

once equipped, sought to put them to practical purpose
by reforming their own unions and helping the unskilled to get their own off the ground. What was *new*
about the new unions owed much to these craftsmen
for they could see, from their own experience in their
own unions, that the old practices were as ill-suited to
the labourer as to the craftsman. If the fact that they
were also socialists was hardly irrelevant to their readiness to help, it was almost certainly irrelevant to the
people they were helping. As one commentator said
at the time: 'There is no doubt whatever that those
Socialists who took part in the (1889 docks strike) were
welcomed not because of their Socialism, but in spite
of it; not on account of their speculative opinions, but
for the sake of their personal ability to help.'[13]

In the years 1889–90 there was hardly an area of
Britain untouched by newly unionised workers. Rising
with an incredible flourish of militancy, spreading with
an infectious energy and enthusiasm, the time was
absolutely right. The economy booming, employers
were in no position to resist with the reserve army of
the unemployed no longer available for a reservoir of
blacklegs. There were limits to the strength of the
workers however – the Liverpool tramwaymen for
example did not dare engage in strikes because the
tram companies retained a large labour reserve in
readiness for such an eventuality: the union collapsed
in seven months in face of the repressive activities of
the employers who used the time-honoured devices of
the 'document' and dismissal of known union men.[14]
Elsewhere the men showed themselves temporarily
invincible scoring small local victories through strike
action: dockers, building labourers, shipyard labourers,
gasworkers, corporation workers, merchant seamen,
semi- and unskilled engineering workers, clothing
workers, woollen textile workers. Almost everywhere
the pattern was the same: one section of workers
strategically well-placed, and perhaps with some pre-

vious history of attempted trade unionism, would stage a strike, organise a union, and gain concessions. Other groups of workers would then follow their example and take the same route. Typically then the formation of a union would take place once the strike was under way. The strikers would then call in assistance in the establishment of their union – the Rotherham stove-grate workers sent for a small businessman from Walsall who had a reputation for performing such services. Other strikers might call for help from the craft-run trades councils or have services offered them by socialist activists. This general movement also did the craft unions a power of good with many non-unionists joining the ranks – the ASE picked up 14,000 new members between the end of 1888 and the end of 1890. Other established unions, like the Amalgamated Society of Railway Servants with a decidedly anti-militant history, got caught up too. After a near total stoppage of railwaymen in Scotland in 1890–91, it was transformed from a friendly society patronised by middle-class Liberals, to a militant union.

It need hardly be said that in every case the workers had grievances of astounding magnitude. Liverpool tramwaymen worked as much as a 103 hour week, railwaymen could work thirty-six hour shifts, dockers twenty-four hour shifts. Wages were frequently only a little above subsistence level, and security of employment almost non-existent: most labourers were employed by the hour, and by the day if they were lucky. Hundreds of thousands of families were dependent upon the man's odd days of employment and the pitiful earnings of the woman scraped together through some sort of domestic work such as dressmaking, sackmaking, or assembling matchboxes. Yet further indignities were added by the autocratic and dictatorial attitudes of employers and supervisors. The ship owners' journal, *Fairplay,* viewed the docker as little more than a beast of burden:

The simple docker alone, for whose purpose a turnip would answer for a head, and a round of beef for brains, must have everything regulated for him, so that he, the ignorant and sometimes drunken, may be raised by the state, at the expense of the ratepayers, to the level of beings as superior to him in intelligence as can possibly be.[15]

Such a view was far from unique. The railway owners treated their workers as if they were in the armed services: those who protested against their conditions were regarded as mutineers and, no doubt, would have been shot had the law allowed.

With renewed depression from 1891 many of the new unions crumbled completely while others were forced back on to their original basis of strength to wait upon a more favourable economic climate. In 1900 the state of unionisation amongst dockers was little better than in 1880 – although the decline was not uniform, the position varying between ports and between groups within ports. In some places unionism was destroyed, in others only weakened. In Hull the union was destroyed by the employers in 1893; in London there was a slow but inexorable process of decay; in Liverpool it survived in some sections of the docks.

In general, the employer's ability to completely crush the unions depended upon the level of skill of his workers. If skills could be adequately learned by green labour then blacklegs could be brought in when there was a labour surplus. However, the successful deployment of blacklegs was also dependent on the employer having sufficient resources to hire and transport them. The ship owners' association, the Shipping Federation, was especially well-placed to use blacklegs and was in the vanguard of the anti-union 'crusade' of the 1890s. With ships used as mobile dormitories to move blackleg labour, the Shipping Federation was independent of local labour markets and successfully broke strike after strike, and weakened trade unionism in the docks and the shipping industry to the point of insignificance. The railway owners used similar tactics to break strikes. Owners of lines not struck supplied labour to those that were. On the railways, however, the unions were not driven out of existence, despite the intimidation of individual members. Blacklegs, who were other railwaymen, could be used to break strikes but not the unions. The skills of most railway workers could not be readily learned by green labour: throughout the nineties the Amalgamated Society of Railway Servants steadily grew in membership.

The whole story of the nineties, after the first brave flourish on the crest of boom conditions, was a story of the elimination of many gains, for with the onset of depression the employers counter-attacked. While the unions as a whole experienced an increase of membership of nearly a million between 1892 and 1910, it seems likely that the craft unions and others which organised labour with some scarcity value were those which gained. (In this period the Railway Servants (ASRS) more than doubled its membership, and the ASE grew by over 60%). The new unions either disappeared altogether, clung on as little more than paper organisations, or shrank to small groups clustered round a relatively sheltered trade. The unions with the greatest survival value were those like the Gasworkers and others organising semi-skilled workers. Those with the least had organised general labourers and transport workers. A good example of these tendencies was the Dockers Union – originally based on dockers in London, by 1908 the Newport (Mon.) tinplate-workers branch of the union had an income nearly nine times greater than that of the metropolis.

But membership figures were as unstable as economic activity generally. With the up-turn in trade from 1910 went a new resurgence of unionism that went on until 1920 and dwarfed the previous rising into insignificance. A total membership of 2½ million in 1910 expanded to over 8¼ million in ten years, and although the onset of depression in 1920–21 eroded these gains there were still 5¼ million paid-up unionists in Britain in 1926. All unions shared the overall gains – the ASE trebled in size between 1910 and 1919; the ASRS (by 1920 the National Union of Railwaymen) increased by nearly six-fold to a position of near saturation of its potential field of recruitment by 1920. In the same period the Gasworkers' membership increased by 1,430%, the London Dockers by 500%, the Workers Union by 8,900%, the National Amalgamated Union of Labour by 790%. They all lost membership again after 1920 but in no case was a union's survival really in question. The Workers Union, for example, was one of the worst hit: it lost 69% of its members but still had a total of 140,000 in 1923.

This *second wave* of new unionism, though more aggressive than the first, was operating in a new environment which was largely of labour's making. At any time, given the level of employment and economic activity, trade unionism is dependent for its existence upon the willingness of employers to concede recognition and the absence of State harassment through the law. In the years 1911–14 and 1918–20 such was the ferment among the working classes, and such the fear of revolution among the ruling classes, that government and employers fully appreciated the wisdom of A. J. Mundella who had told the House of Commons in the 1870s that the trade unions constituted a barrier to social revolution. Realising that the socialist revolutionaries prominent in the second wave made the socialists of the first look tepid reformers, employers became much readier to treat with union leaders. In 1912 the Shipping Federation, hitherto the group of employers most ruthless in their opposition, recognised the Seamen's Union. The railway owners, running the ship owners a very close second, were bullied by the government into recognition of the unions in 1911. That recognition was already widespread in many other industries was indicated in a House of Commons debate in 1911 over the national rail strike, when a Liberal MP said: 'We . . . see in the coal trade, in the cotton trade, in the iron trade – the great masters of industry welcoming trade unions, co-operating with trade unions, working with trade unions, and we do not understand why the directors of the railway companies decline to follow what seems to us this wise plan.'[16] The growing, if often grudging, willingness to recognise trade unions as permanent bargaining partners was not, however, merely a sophisticated response to the perception of the working class as a potential revolutionary force. It was mainly politicians who possessed that degree of awareness, and they were only willing to bludgeon their more stupid colleagues in industry when the industry concerned was of strategic importance. What finally made the ship owners and rail owners capitulate was the strength of the unions. The unions, now much better organised and on a national basis, were able to pre-empt the employers' tactics of breaking strikes and unions by the use of blacklegs: if stoppages were national in scope the source of blacklegs just dried up because most of the potential blacklegs were themselves on strike or in employment. Where in the early nineties the new unions made a pretence of being national in scope, the first few years of the second wave made that pretence much more of a reality.

The 1911 revival of new unionism began, like its predecessor, with an astonishing outburst of spontaneous strikes from the rank and file. Beginning with the seamen in Southampton, it proceeded to take in almost every group of workers. By 1912 even the badly depressed farmworkers were caught up in the turmoil. The revival looked similar in another way too – once again socialist militants came to the fore to provide leadership, this time with the doctrines of syndicalism and industrial unionism. Yet despite the similarities to the nineties there were some important differences that made the second wave quite distinctive and nothing like as threatening as it appeared.

The years 1911–14 did not see a rapid formation of new unions – the reverse, for the number of unions actually declined. The new wave was therefore capitalised upon by existing unions. Those that had remained on paper since the nineties were revived, and those that had barely lived through the lean years started to thrive again. It was this latter group that was most important because the struggle for survival had made the puppy an old dog who had learned a number of organisational 'tricks'. The constituents of this group had, in the nineties, to learn how to adapt their organisations to their environment at a time when the very level of activity made it impossible to devote much attention to organisational problems. If his organisation was thin in members it was now firm in its structure and methods of working, and capable of channelling the new energy and numbers into established patterns. This meant that where the socialist agitator in the nineties was right at the centre of union activity, leading it, directing it, from 1911 he was outside the union structure having the ephemeral role of strike leader. When the strikes were over, the established union leaders assumed control. From henceforward the socialist agitator was to be, to the leaders of the new general unions, what he had been to the leaders of the old craft unions in the nineties: 'a disruptive influence out to undermine properly constituted authority for ulterior political ends.' From the twenties onwards, with the Labour Party having made itself the 'authorised' spokesman for the trade unions and the working class, left-wing socialists active in the unions (particularly members of the Communist Party) were regarded by trade union leaders in the same way that the early trade unionists were regarded by employers. They were 'outsiders', 'troublemakers', who disturbed the masses who were really content with their lot.

By 1910, after two decades of the new unionism, it had become clear that in most matters of substance the new unions were no different from the old. Certainly they were more outward looking than the craft unions in their readiness to accept almost anyone into membership regardless of occupation. They had lower subscriptions, avoided friendly society functions of making available a wide range of welfare benefits by providing only for strike pay, and tended to have far more paid officials. But all of these things that set the new unions apart from the old were directly related to the labour markets in which they operated. Lacking the possession of scarce skills as a bargaining counter, they had to try to organise into membership all those who could possibly be used as blacklegs against them. Organising low-paid workers they had no choice but to charge low subscriptions, and low subs could not bear the cost of benefit funds for pensions, sickness, unemployment, etc. They had to retain a large staff of full-time officials to keep up with the shifting employment so characteristic of the general labourer. If their only benefit tended to be strike pay this was because it was the one benefit that *no* trade union could survive without. That the new unions at first often had socialist leadership was of little lasting importance. In the first place such men soon learned to be as canny as the Liberals at the head of the old unions in carefully husbanding resources and frowning upon unofficial strikes. And, in the second place, many of the old unions were electing socialists to leading positions from the mid-nineties.

In matters of substance, to repeat, the new unions once organised showed themselves quite as cautious as

the old. This was not because their leaders were mere
place-seekers or 'traitors' to the cause of socialism,
even if a minority were both. On the contrary. The
plain fact was that they had to contend with the
same sort of problem that confronted the craft union
leader only writ large: the sectionalism of the membership. Added to that they had to contend with two
factors that most of the old unions did not have to
contend with: the dedicated, fanatical opposition of
the employers, and large numbers of members un-
accustomed either to work discipline or to trade union
discipline. When it is further considered that the new
unionists had to face '. . . the prejudice, ignorance,
and apathy of important groups in their own class who
were not prepared to accept the need for, or the
decisions of, the unions',[17] it is easy to appreciate the
magnitude of the new unions' problems. Where the
trade union leader was also a socialist dedicated to the
overthrow of the capitalist order his problems were, if
that is possible, yet more compounded: his socialism
demanded implacable hostility to the employers while
the survival of his union demanded that he restrain
his members and establish a workable relationship with
the employers. Since limited trade-union aims such as
wages and working conditions were what attracted
men and women to the unions and not the waging of
class war, the leader had to be a trade unionist first,
and a socialist in his spare time.

After the heady days of 1889–90 had passed and the
new unions found themselves faced with an adverse
economic environment and expanding employer-
hostility, the question of organisational survival
became paramount. Many of the leaders were not
equipped with the experience to cope with that sort
of issue for they had risen to prominence as leaders
of strikes which were taking place in economic conditions conducive to victory. Thus, as in the Workers
Union between 1910 and 1914:

Central direction . . . was limited in scope; the main issues requiring decision at this level were the appointment of organisers and the administration of benefit funds. Industrial relations remained very much the prerogative of the rank and file at local level . . . Where a local full-time official existed, his task was to recruit new members rather than to control existing ones; he would normally be involved in negotiations only after deadlock had been reached domestically, and often after the members had stopped work.[18]

Once the strikes were settled, the expansive phase over and the most accessible areas of new membership mopped-up, there was a need for central government to consolidate gains and provide for the future. Hence the growth of a central bureaucracy; from its inception in 1898 until 1910 the Workers Union employed but one official at its head office, by 1914 there were two dozen, and by 1920 a complex machine employing a hundred people. In 1919 the rule book was extensively revised so that the 'Executives' monopoly of authority was established unambiguously.'[19] Subsequent attempts to restore local powers to district committees were invariably defeated.

Other unions, established somewhat earlier, had gone through exactly the same process. By 1891 the Gasworkers and General Labourers Union had suffered a number of set-backs after initial success – the employers had counter-attacked and a number of costly strikes had been lost. In that same year the union altered its rules: 'all labour disputes (should be settled) by amicable agreement or arbitration wherever possible.'[20] Two years later Will Thorne, the general secretary, was telling his members: 'Strikes, through whatever causes, should be avoided wherever possible. Some employers think that many of us live and thrive upon strikes. What can any leader gain through a strike? Look at the worry, anxiety, and responsibility they have to contend with during a strike.'[21] Even

Tom Mann, unquestionably the greatest agitator of the period, as a leading official in the Dockers Union attempted from time to time to restrain various sections of the membership from striking in 1891. The trouble was, as Lovell has said: 'The efforts of Mann and others to give the Dockers Union a real rather than a paper existence was not without its ironic side. Wherever a section of the men established a vigorous unionism, it manifested the greatest opposition to central direction.'[22]

As amongst the dockers, so elsewhere. New unionism invariably started after the spontaneous action of a small group of workers who then constituted themselves as a branch under the umbrella of a union. The new unions therefore were little more than federations of a host of small unions based on a localised occupation. Thus where the horizons of the members were bounded by the locality and perhaps only one employer, the horizons of the leadership tended toward the whole trade and a wide range of employers. This meant of course that the continued livelihood of the union was ultimately dependent upon the leadership's ability to weld together a membership that was unable to look beyond its own immediate interests. The resultant tension between a union leadership trying to centralise control and the rank and file trying to retain local control was a perpetual source of conflict.

Faced with a persistence of militant, localised, and unofficial action throughout the nineties and the early 1900s which often proved unsuccessful, the new unions found their strength being progressively whittled away in area after area. Their response was the inevitable one of imposing more and more central control by gaining freedom of action for the full-time officials. The main stumbling block to the attainment of that end was the 'local executive', a governmental device inherited from the craft unions. Given the unquestioned belief in democratic control in the trade unions, there remained the issue of how it was to be achieved. In the early days it was simply resolved – the district in which the union was situated would provide the executive committee of lay members to determine national policy. But it was a method of resolution which suited neither the officials nor the members in the outlying districts. The officials were unhappy because it meant that their actions were subject to constant scrutiny and sometimes dispute: 'The local executive of the National Amalgamated Union of Labour tried to keep elaborate checks on the work of their officers by means of diaries which recorded their work and were subject to regular inspection by a "Diaries Sub-Committee".'[23] And the members were unhappy because they had no representation on the national committee. The Gasworkers settled the problem by redrafting the constitution in 1908 – thenceforward the executive was to consist of the general secretary plus two representatives from each district, one of whom was to be a lay member and the other the full-time district official. Since the new executive was only required to meet quarterly, the day to day business became the province of a sub-committee of the national executive dominated by full-time officers. No union was untouched by similar developments in the period 1890–1926 though the issue was settled in a number of different ways. The ASE for example imposed severe checks on its leadership by electing a full-time executive composed of delegates from each district, and then, to keep a check on the executive, had an elected General Council which met annually to hear appeals against executive decisions.

The changes in internal union structure were not *just* dictated by the need for organisation survival in the face of hostile employers and a volatile membership, for changes in the structure of industry also indicated new patterns. The gradual rise to prominence of the large firm now made it possible for the employers to form their own associations. From the late eighties they grew in such numbers that by the outbreak of war in 1914 there was hardly an industry of any importance without one. Formed almost invariably to deal with labour questions, the logical consequence was bargaining on an industry-wide scale. The cotton industry had industrial agreements from 1893, the boot and shoe industry from 1895, the engineering industry from 1898, the shipping industry from 1912, the railways from 1911. These developments, as the Webbs were very quick to realise, '. . . transformed the trade union official from a local strike leader to an expert industrial negotiator, mainly occupied with the cordial co-operation of the secretary of the Employers Association and the Factory Inspector, in securing an exact observance of the Common Rules prescribed for the trade.'[24] This development had a number of consequences for the structure and practice of trade unionism. By bringing the trade union leader into close and regular contact with employers and by tieing him to written agreements it increased rank and file suspicion of his activities. In the engineering industry where the agreements had to be flexible to embrace the diversity of trades within it, there followed a rapid growth of the numbers of shop stewards who were in a position to focus and direct rank and file suspicion.

Since unions were only in very rare cases coextensive with their fields of operation it followed that different unions had to sit down together and thrash out a common policy. And this created yet another series of problems for individual unions, because fratricide rather than fraternity was the characteristic relationship between many of them: the shipbuilding and engineering industry was rife with demarcation disputes; the Railway Servants Union, mainly organising the semi- and unskilled worker, was constantly at loggerheads with the more aristocratic footplatemen's union, ASLEF. Further, insofar as national negotiations implied national strikes, a national strike of such key workers as miners, dockers, seamen, railwaymen, etc., could result in the laying-off of tens of thousands of other workers not involved in the dispute. National strikes were also, and necessarily, political phenomena since they could disrupt the entire economy. This meant that governments started to show a keen interest in the conduct of industrial relations and that trade union leaders started to develop continuous contact with the ministers and civil servants of some ministries.

Shop stewards first rose to national prominence in the war years although they had been active for many years previous. The Tees district of the NAUL reported in 1892 that shop stewards had settled disputes, and an organiser of the same union told a conference of union officials in 1901 that the key to successful organisation was the shop steward. In 1896 the ASE had empowered its district committees to appoint shop stewards (suggesting that they had already been operative). And in 1897 some employers were complaining of '. . . "Forms of interference . . . surreptitiously and continuously exercised by shop stewards." In the same year a Clyde firm complained how shop stewards "repeatedly checked one of their turners for turning out too much work".[25] By the mid-war years they were a serious force to be reckoned with in the ASE. With their officials firmly committed to support of government policies with respect to allowing semi-skilled operatives to do what had been skilled men's jobs, the shop stewards came into their own as shop-floor leaders.[26] Just how powerful they had become was revealed in 1915 when Lloyd George visited Clydeside to treat with them.

The shop stewards' movement of the First World War was extremely important, if only as a harbinger of the strength of shop-floor organisation that was to develop after 1945. Solidly anchored in the engineering shops, and led by left-wing socialists, it at once showed its economic strength and its political weakness. The power of the shop stewards lay in the potency of the workers' grievances. Engineering work had been going through a process of 'de-skilling' for thirty years, and the war-time proposals for dilution of skill by the admission of semi-skilled workers to what were regarded as skilled mens' jobs, were seen as an unconcealed attack on job security. The shop stewards articulated these fears and at the same time tried to place them at the heart of a critique of capitalism. Their bargaining strength was unquestionable for all their basic demands were met: it was agreed that dilution would be for the duration of the war and no longer. Their political strength was transitory. Attempts to form a national opposition within the trade unions collapsed ignominiously with the onset of depression in 1921: '. . . in many districts there were large-scale dismissals of shop stewards. This happened particularly in some English districts where it had a fatal effect on some (shop stewards') committees.'[27] In Sheffield sackings did not even result in shop-floor sympathy action: the sacked stewards had to fall back on the union for support and accept union discipline. The ideas that had informed the shop stewards' movement did not die for they passed over to the Communist Party, taken to it by those shop stewards who were so influential in its formation in 1920.

Despite disputes between unions over 'spheres of interest' as the general unions in particular competed for membership, the growth of employers' associations did start to force some unions into federations and eventually into amalgamations. The most important federation to emerge was the National Transport Workers Federation in 1911: it linked more than twenty unions organising dockers, carters, omnibus workers, and general labourers. The main unions involved in the Federation, the Gasworkers and the Dockers, were subsequently to engage in mergers with other member unions to form the Transport and General Workers Union in 1921 and the National Union of General and Municipal Workers in 1924. The ten-year life of the Federation was not conspicuous for its harmonious relations for it was as bedevilled by sectionalism as were the internal relations of the separate unions. Union leaders showed themselves quite as intransigent as their own dissidents in their unwillingness to cede sufficient autonomous powers to give the Federation's executive enough bite to be thoroughly effective. The same story attached itself to the even more abortive Triple Alliance, formed in 1915 out of the National Union of Railwaymen, the Miners Federation, and the Transport Workers Federation.

The Alliance aimed quite simply at a situation where each of its constituents would negotiate its 'contracts' so that they all terminated simultaneously; that is to say, creating a situation where it could threaten both government and employers with such vast disruption that its claims would have to be conceded. On the face of it then the Triple Alliance amounted both to a significant step toward 'one-big-union' and toward industrial action of such a magnitude that it could pose a straightforward challenge to State power. Potentially indeed it did carry both of these threats. But only potentially.

Sectionalism ensured that it had fatal flaws: it had no separate organisation of its own, no constitution, preserved the autonomy of each member union, and gave each the right of veto. It remained firmly in the hands of the national officials who constituted its executive: it had no regional or district organisation. It was exactly as Allen has characterised it: 'The elements of surprise and spontaneity, and the facility to take action at the moment when the workers were emotionally prepared – matters vital in industrial conflict – were impossible under the (rules).'[28]

The Alliance never did go into action. The NUR never even consulted its partners in the Alliance before their national stoppage in 1919, and the only time it was called on for support – by the Miners in 1921 – the other members withdrew at the last minute. The fact was that some of the Alliance's leaders, especially Thomas of the NUR, could not face up to its political implications. The government, with its Emergency Powers Act of 1920, had already made it clear that it viewed the Alliance as a potential threat to the State. Although the Alliance did limit itself to economic objectives, the leaders were always aware that industrial action could easily escalate into political action. This was something they were not prepared to face. When the government called their bluff in 1921 the railway and transport workers' leaders ran for cover. Bevin had '. . . warned a delegate conference of the Triple Alliance (in 1920) that unless they overhauled the organisation to make it capable of speaking with one voice it would be revealed as a "paper alliance" when the testing time came.'[29] There were never more prophetic words. The unions had been cheerfully going their own sectional way. Only when crisis threatened was the Alliance resorted to – and the normal sectional ways then stood across the path of united action.

The failure of the Triple Alliance exposed the internal weaknesses of the trade union movement. The failure of the General Strike exposed its external weaknesses. By 1926 the unions had divided up the world into two separate spheres of activity. There was the political world which was to be taken care of by the Labour Party, and there was the economic world which was their province. It was an unrealistic division, but it was serviceable. What it meant was that the trade unions did not see themselves as a political force in either the parliamentary or the revolutionary sense. They saw themselves primarily as negotiators of treaties with employers, and secondarily as negotiators with governments. They took both for granted – which is another way of saying that they had no *articulated* theory of their role in a capitalist society. Their leaders, both locally and nationally, talked (generally with sincerity) of socialism. But they talked of it as though it were something far beyond the horizon. Because they lacked a theory they lacked also a strategy – hence socialism lying hull down over the horizon. They did have tactics though. A world that refused to stand still required from them some response. And respond they did. They took the world as they found it, 'waited' for it to impinge itself on them, and then developed tactics to cope with situations as they arose. Trade union leaders, like most of their members, lived in and for the present. They had a philosophy right enough. The philosophy of 'we'll cross that bridge when we come to it.'

In 1925 the Miners, facing the possibility of a wage cut in an already badly depressed industry, appealed to the TUC General Council for help. It obliged by asking the Railwaymen and the Transport Workers to black the movement of coal: both promptly agreed, believing that a successful attack on the miners would be followed by another on them. The mere threat was sufficient to get government intervention and the impending crisis was postponed for ten months by the payment of a government subsidy to the coal owners' profits. It was well-understood by government and unions that the subsidy would expire in May 1926 and that the consequence would be yet another reduction in the miners' wages. That is another way of saying that both knew that there would be a General Strike in 1926. The unions, preferring the fool's paradise of the present, were jubilant at the concession

of the subsidy and gave no thought to tomorrow.
Tomorrow was another day; a bridge yet to be crossed.
While the government used its ten months to make
elaborate preparations in readiness (by an amazing
set of 'coincidences' all the members of the Communist Party's central committee, bar one, were
imprisoned in that period for terms which ensured that
they would be behind bars for the month of May,
1926) for a general strike with revolutionary implications, the TUC General Council did precisely nothing
until a week before the day; that is, until it was
absolutely certain.

The dilatoriness of the TUC had nothing to do with
lethargy, for idleness was not a characteristic of union
leaders, least of all of Citrine, the TUC's General
Secretary. The TUC had adopted the defensive tactic
of a readiness to negotiate. Unable (or unwilling) to
believe that the cessation of the subsidy was non-
negotiable, they wanted to do nothing that could be
characterised as belligerent, yet – knowing of the
government's preparations – implicitly ceded to the
State the right to use its coercive force against the
trade union movement.

The TUC knew from the outset of the Strike that
it was well hooked on to a paradox. By conceding to
the State the *right* to use force against it, it was saying
that the Strike was devoid of revolutionary import. On
the other hand it thoroughly appreciated that a general
strike, being an attempt to coerce the State, could only
be viewed by a government as being at least potentially revolutionary. What was ostensibly a national
sympathetic strike in support of the miners, and therefore purely economic in motivation, was in fact a
political strike to the very core. An awareness of this
rapidly passed to the forefront of the collective consciousness of the TUC General Council. Although the
government knew very well that the union leaders
were not personally out to make revolution they under-

The battleship *Ramillies* in the Mersey in 1926 –
Jimmy Thomas, Labour MP, two years earlier

stood clearly what the Strike implied. They knew too that leadership could pass out of TUC hands – that was why some 1,000 rank and file Communists were rounded up during the strike. The TUC knew that too – which was why it insisted on using the term 'National Strike' rather than the syndicalist term 'General Strike'.

As the days passed the TUC got increasingly worried and at least one very influential member of the General Council, Jimmy Thomas, was near panic at the thought of control passing into the hands of much more militant leaders in the regions and localities. After nine days of a stoney silence from the government and rabble-rousing propaganda from the government's newspaper, the *British Gazette* (the TUC's paper, the *British Worker* was studiously moderate), the TUC took flight and hurried with indecent haste to negotiate an unconditional surrender. In calling it off the General Council had done nothing inconsistent and betrayed no ideals. It was composed of trade unionists, not revolutionaries. The members behaved as fitted their character. What the General Strike unequivocally signified was that trade unionism of the twenties and revolutionary politics were incompatibles. It was ironical that the Strike should have ended on that note for a number of members of the General Council had started on their careers with a different view.

The period 1890 to 1926 is difficult to capture for it lacks the simplicity and coherence of the earlier period. If the new unions thrust themselves on to the centre of the stage with a tramp of dissenting feet, they succumbed to the same sort of conservatism that typified the old unions. If there was an employers' offensive beginning in the early nineties, successive governments were making placatory noises. A veritable flood of socialist ideas of various complexions made an enormous impact at various times – and faded away. There were odd times when the ground was ripe for revolution and governments prepared themselves for it, but the threats were contained with extraordinary ease. A period more liberally strewn with paradox and contradiction would be hard to find. But there was a pattern.

The key is the character of the 'new unions'. Nothing obscures an understanding of the period quite as much as this term. It has been shown above that they were 'new' only in the sense that they organised classes of workers hitherto left unprotected. In all matters of substance they were quite as conservative as the old unions. Indeed in some respects they were even more conservative for their constitutions provided for fewer checks on full-time officials than those of the old unions: in that sense they were less democratic. That the leaders of the new unions waxed strong with socialist rhetoric ceased to mark them off from their colleagues in the old unions by the outbreak of war. By then such rhetoric was the stock-in-trade of any self-respecting trade union leader.

The stirring speeches of labour leaders may well have taken in the working class, but the ruling class was not deceived. 'A Conservative spectator at the Labour Victory Demonstration after the 1923 election thought it a very tame show. It struck no note of revolution but rather of respectable middle class nonconformity. They sang hymns between speeches, which were all about God!'[30] Stanley Baldwin was quite happy to assure anxious middle-class investors as to the safety of their savings after the formation of the Labour government in 1923. Others more concerned with the maintenance of traditional rituals were relieved to find most of the new Labour Cabinet prepared to don court dress of knee-breeches and kiss the monarch's hand on being sworn into office. While snobs may have been appalled at Mrs Clynes' (wife of the NUGMW leader) letter to *The Times* expressing the view that daughters of prominent labour leaders should be presented as debs at Court, they must still have slept soundly. Tory leaders '. . . recognised that there were clever men among the trade union leaders . . . (But) there was a feeling that their cleverness was not dangerous, that many of them could be bought, argued or charmed into conformity.'[31] Those bought included George Barnes of the ASE, Will Crooks of the Coopers Union, Jimmy Thomas of the Railwaymen. Those charmed included John Hodge of the Steel Smelters and Will Thorne of the Gasworkers. (Will Thorne reassured King George V in 1917 that labour was not planning revolution: 'This seemed to relieve his mind, and he spoke to me in a most homely and pleasant way. I was very pleased.'[32]) Most prominent Tories had had some experience of labour leaders, both politicians and trade unionists, in the Lloyd George coalition governments: 'Experience at first hand in office showed that Barnes – a Scottish Episcopalian – was "an old-fashioned and very cautious Scottish Whig," that Hodge was a very fat, "rampaging and most patriotic Tory working man" . . . and that many of the leaders of the Labour Party were distinguished from Tories "only by name".'[33]

History does not record whether they were *surprised*, but they certainly must have been gratified. If they were surprised they should not have been. The shrewd politicians leading the ruling class – both Liberal and Conservative – had done much to create conditions in which trade unionism could operate with the minimum of legal harassment. The socialist trade union leaders rapidly discovered through harsh experience that they could not simultaneously be effective trade union leaders *and* revolutionaries – and concentrated their energies on trade union work. The logic of such work, as we have seen, drew them willy-nilly into a complex of relationships with employers and the State. In 1910 seventy-seven members of the Boot and Shoe Operatives held eighty-five positions on statutory bodies and various committees.

By 1912 eighty members held 100 positions. There were now members of Old-Age Pensions Committees, members of National Insurance Act Advisory Committees, a member of a Water Board, and school managers . . . All these changes meant that the Union was . . . becoming more closely knit both with society and the state. It was building up an increasingly complex network of links with other voluntary organisations, and it was co-operating with state machinery to administer new and complicated social legislation.'34

Some, but by no means all, employers were rather slow to see that from the mid-nineties the unions were out to control rather than to exacerbate industrial conflict. But with the growth of industry-wide bargaining and regular contact with trade union leaders, more and more employers began to see that trade unionism had certain positive virtues from their point of view. This became even more apparent in the war years when the government made arbitration compulsory, and a host of joint committees of one sort or another obliged trade unionists and employers to sit down together. Symptomatic of the climate induced by war was the National Alliance of Employers and Employed established in 1916 to harmonise capital-labour relations. It had joint committees in most industrial centres and organised country-wide conferences to disseminate its ideas. While the two post-war years of 1919 and 1920 saw another resurgence of militancy – there were nearly three million disputes in those years – it was a revolt induced by the rank and file rather than the leadership. Union leaders, while forced to take over the leadership of many of the strikes started by their members, were wanting to continue the close relations established with employers in war-time.

In the latter sphere much of the co-operation that had marked the war years did continue, though there cannot have been many examples of such extreme collaboration as marked a Boot and Shoe Operatives strike in 1921. The strike was against a group of manufacturers who had seceded from the employers' federation, revoked national agreements, and cut wages. The employers' federation, anxious to eliminate competition in a period of falling prices, actually went so far as to supplement the union's strike pay![35] Extreme though it might have been, it did follow logically from the sort of resolutions that had been passed in the war years: a conference of Bristol employers and trade unions in 1917 resolved in part that 'the unions are not only of advantage to the operatives but to the employers as well.'[36] The rank and file were not continuously persuaded that the unions, as constituted, were advantageous to themselves. On almost innumerable occasions different sections of the working class showed themselves considerably more aggressive than their official leaders.

It cannot be sufficiently emphasised that trade unionism was solidly rooted in the workplace; that the new unions were set on the road by the actions of the rank and file at the point of production; and that the second wave of new unionism in 1911–14 was inspired by a nation-wide outbreak of *unofficial* strikes. The second wave threw into prominence a new generation of socialists, sharply and pertinently critical of their predecessors who were now custodians of the Labour Party and established unions. While G. D. H. Cole was right in characterising the rank and file revolt of those pre-war years as essentially economistic in motivation, the fact remained that the leading echelons were incomparably more sophisticated in their political analyses than the socialists of the nineties. The leading elements of the second wave had had an opportunity to see the new unionism and the Labour Party in action. When they discovered that the new unions were as conservative as the old, and the Labour Party a more virile version of the Liberal Party, it was almost inevitable that they should develop a fundamental critique of reformist politics and traditional trade unionism. Rank and file leaders became then the first theorists to emerge in the labour movement since the first half of the 19th century. That their theories drew to a greater or lesser extent from French and particularly American syndicalism did not mean that they were under 'alien influence'. The origin of the ideas was unimportant. What mattered was that in their general principles they could be applied to industrial capitalism and the role of trade unions within it no matter what its nationality.

The failure of the rank and file leaders to take control of the labour movement had very little to do with mystical theories of the 'innate conservatism' of British workers. Their ability to lead was dependent on the spontaneous volatility of the workers over very specific economic grievances. But the ability of the leaders to generalise economic discontents into political discontents was always foiled by the existence of 'official' leaders who could assume control of the rebellions and channel them into political harmlessness. Bonar Law's assessment of the unions as being the only thing that stood between his class and the breakdown of the established order was essentially correct. If the field had been left to the rank and file socialists in 1919, the Cabinet's preparations for revolution would have been well-justified. Much the same can be said for 1926. Then too the militancy was strong at the grassroots, with rank and file leaders prepared to engage on a political adventure that the TUC was afraid to contemplate.

The lesson of this period – for ruling-class conservative and for working-class revolutionary alike – was that trade unionism could amount to a considerable weapon of social control. It had been used as such and not found wanting.

4. Treaties, Truces, and Frontier Incidents, 1926-1972

The basic issue remains what it has always been:
to advance our struggle against the ruling class and, as
part of this advance, to exert and extend our control on
the shop floor. Despite the difficulties, I welcome
the struggle, it is life; the absence of struggle is stagnation
and death.

Phillip Higgs, a convenor of shop stewards[1]

I think the unions are growing up. They all started
the same way – they had to – with a certain
militancy, but now they're growing up and becoming
very statesmanlike.

A labour relations manager[2]

The trade unions in this period manifested remarkably similar tendencies to those evident in all the previous decades. Sometimes they looked as though they were a lot of artificially contrived Balkan states, each internally unstable and in a state of armed truce with each other. At other times, and much less frequently, they looked as if they collectively amounted to a mass movement prepared to take on the State. In the event neither tendency became a reality.

The Trades Disputes Act of 1927 was an act of revenge for the General Strike. The Industrial Relations Act of 1971 was an attack on the bargaining strength of the trade union rank and file. During the forty-four-year period in between, the State developed and extended its tactics of co-opting the trade union leadership. Citrine, TUC General Secretary, and Pugh, the Steelworkers' leader, were knighted in 1935. *The Times* noted the honours as being a recognition of 'the great part played (in our national affairs) by the Trade Unions'.[3] R. H. Tawney, a prominent Labour intellectual, was rather more acid – 'who will believe that the Labour Party means business so long as some of its stalwarts sit up and beg for social plums like poodles in a drawing room?'[4] The event created quite a stir in labour circles at the time, but by the 1950s State honours were taken for granted: 'To run through the list of leading TUC figures (in the fifties) is not unlike running through a list of leading civil servants: Sir Vincent Tewson, Sir William Lawther, Sir Thomas Williamson, Sir Lincoln Evans.'[5]

State trumpeters of the Royal Horse Guards sounded a special fanfare at the opening of the new TUC headquarters in 1958. The Post Office commemorated the TUC's centenary in 1968 with a special issue of postage stamps, and the Queen attended the TUC's celebratory banquet. These gestures were important. Only those who were unquestionably safe got the ultimate accolade of participation in State ritual, a share in pomp and circumstance.

The period is divided by the Second World War – with high unemployment before and a fully-employed welfare state economy after. It is united by the increasing involvement of the trade unions in the running of the State. Unemployment drew the sting of the unions in the inter-war years – almost half their membership was wiped-out between 1920 and 1933. For their ex-members on the dole the unions were totally irrelevant. It was established by then that trade unionism was concerned with regulating the terms of employment. Since unemployment was not the fault of individual capitalists but of the workings of the capitalist system as a whole, it followed that unemployment was a non-negotiable item. Recognising that unemployment was rooted in the system, trade union leaders acknowledged government responsibility for the workings of the system, and dutifully went through the lobbying rituals. Their further recognition of parliamentary democracy meant that when governments showed themselves incapable of remedying the problem the union leaders merely sat back and hoped for better days. In Skidelsky's words, the unions accepted 'unemployment as the price to be paid for maintaining wages (and this) made them less interested in increasing unemployment benefits . . .'[6]

Even in the matter of increasing the dole the unions showed themselves less than energetic, relying largely on the plaintive speeches of their Labour Party colleagues in the House of Commons. In the early twenties the TUC had jointly organised protest demonstrations with the National Unemployed Workers Committee Movement, but in 1927 severed its connections with the NUWCM on the grounds of its CP affiliations. The TUC attempts to found its own Unemployed Associations in 1927 and 1933 foundered on the rock of union hostility.

The unions' inability to cope with unemployment was not merely rooted in their conceptions of themselves as bargainers with employers. Political considerations obtruded as well. Effective protest at the conditions of unemployment required the mobilisation of the unemployed at the grass roots, and this was something the unions dared not contemplate for it was almost inevitable that the grass-roots leaders would be militants. That being the case, there was the danger that a union-sponsored movement of the unemployed would lead to a confrontation with the State. 1926 was too fresh in memories to make that a bearable thought. The consequence was that throughout the inter-war years the Communist Party, bitterly vilified though it was, provided (in alliance with other left wingers) the only strenuous opposition to unemployment. That the TUC stood aloof and practised moderation with considerable skill was justification enough for the knighthoods of Pugh and Citrine.

Knighthoods, peerages, and other fripperies of State handed out in the post-war years were rewards for different services. The British economy was in more or less continuous crisis from 1945 to 1952 and from 1961 onward. The disruptive effects of war accounted for most of the problems of the first phase of crisis. The 'Indian summer' of the fifties was brought to an end with the re-arrival of West Germany and Japan as powerful competitors with Britain and the USA in world markets, and the extraordinary growth of powerful bargaining units on the shop floor in industry. Between these pincers, profits were squeezed: the workers' push for higher wages meant that increases in the employers' costs could only be passed on to the consumer if other things were equal. Other things were not. Increased competition in international markets made it difficult for manufacturers to pass on to consumers, in raised prices, the full amount of the increases in costs. Manufacturers therefore had the choice of raising prices and losing markets, or of holding prices down and taking a cut in profits. They chose the latter, hoping that a political solution could be found at home to curb the strength of their workers.

The obvious solution of deliberately creating a higher level of unemployment proved unacceptable until the advent of a new Conservative government in 1970. It was politically unacceptable because, despite the apparent passivity of the working class for most of the post-1945 years, fears remained of what it might do if provoked. And it was economically unacceptable because much of British industry was dependent upon mass consumption in home markets. The Conservative government of 1970 risked continuing the rise in unemployment which had started in the last years of the 1966–70 Labour government. But by 1972 it had got cold feet and started to use all the economic devices of re-inflation so familiar to budget-watchers, and some of the political devices familiar to trade union leaders.

Most trade union leaders were aware – in some degree at least – of the nature of the crises, though it is doubtful that over many were worried about the profit-squeeze as such. What did worry them was the level of investment, since the lower it was the worse the employment prospects were for their members. This entailed that directly or indirectly, consciously or unconsciously, they were concerned with profit-ability. At the time of writing investment decisions were still determined by expectations of profit.

Throughout the post-war years governments of various complexions (the variety of colouring was not notable) sought, at different times, to persuade trade union leaders to exercise some restraint on the wage demands of their members: the wage-restraint of 1948; the pay-pause of 1961–62; the incomes policy of 1964–68; and whatever is likely to emerge out of the government sponsored talks between the TUC and the CBI in the summer and autumn of 1972. Every experiment strengthened the links between governments and the trade unions, and those of the sixties cemented them with the creation of new quasi-state machinery. In between experiments governments attempted to control wages by exhorting employers not to give in to 'excessive' wage demands, and by holding down the level of settlements in the nationalised industries and in government employment. Every exercise, with the exception of the one in 1961–62, gained the co-operation of the TUC. Every exercise was undermined by the strength of shop-floor bargaining. Indeed the potency of the latter was enhanced at each stage as more and more workers became wage-militant. Looked at through the sequence of events since the late 1940s, the Industrial Relations Act of 1971 was a perfectly

logical development. Designed to inhibit the strength
of the shop-floor bargainers and enhance the control
of trade union leaders over them, it seemed to the
Conservatives exactly what was needed in the light of
past experience. By the 1970s it was appreciated that
seating trade unionists in the House of Lords, and the
loan of the Queen for festive occasions was not
enough.

The bestowal of honours was never used as a subtle
form of bribery. Honours were conferred on those
who had shown themselves conspicuously ready to be
attentive to the needs of the State. They were for
services already rendered, rather than for services
anticipated in the future. Those trade union leaders
who accepted them – and not all did – signified their
general contentment with the established order. But
contentment with it did not always imply the ability
to maintain it. No matter what some trade union
leaders may have said privately to government
ministers and senior civil servants, as a collectivity
they were being pushed closer and closer to a confrontation with the State. Sidney Greene, NUR
General Secretary, may have got his knighthood but
as he explained somewhat helplessly to the 1964–68
Royal Commission on Trade Unions: '. . . when the
Management puts up some forward-looking proposals,
the difficulty is to get them accepted by our members.
I do not instruct them . . . I may not be opposed to
these new ideas in any way, but the difficulty is trying
to get the members to swallow all these things at
once.'[7]

The TUC's threat of a one-day general strike in July
1972 in support of five dockers imprisoned for contempt of the National Industrial Relations Court was
superficially amazing in the light of its long history of
co-operativeness with the State. In fact it was nothing
of the kind. Every passing year of the post-war period
had made it clearer and clearer that trade union

leaders' clothes were supplied by the rank and file. The real power lay at the base and no amount of hired ermine robes could alter that.

The ruling class goes multi-national

The period 1926-72 saw the continued decline of a ruling class rooted in large landowners. If the political family was not quite extinct – there were seven members of the Devonshire family in the last Macmillan government – the Derbys and the Cecils had come to the end of their centuries-long pre-eminence. If the aristocracy was still to be found at Ascot, Henley, and Cowes in the appropriate weeks of the summer, these 'sports days' of the ruling class were presided over by a new aristocracy of industrialists, financiers, and wealthy professionals. Where for the most part of the nineteenth century the landed aristocracy had acted as custodians for the interests of the bourgeoisie, by the mid-twentieth century the bourgeoisie were running their own affairs. Remnants of the old squirearchy and a few sons of aristocrats were still to be found on the Conservative benches in the House of Commons, but the party was no longer their property. The wealthy landowners that still existed – and they numbered more than a few – were not as a rule politically active.[8]

Robert Boothby, a prominent Conservative, said in 1947: '. . . the Conservative Party . . . must convince itself and the nation that it knows how to prevent a return to an over-privileged and under-employed society . . .'[9] This re-articulation of the traditional Conservative 'One Nation' theme was directed at elements in the party who wanted it committed to policies of non-intervention in the conduct of business affairs.

Throughout the thirties there was a continuing tension within the ruling classes which was mediated by the Conservative Party. One pull was essentially negative – the absence of restraint in the conduct of business. The other essentially positive – calling for a regulated (note *not* directed) economy and the provision of extended welfare services. This later tendency was but a re-statement of the traditional Tory conception of the paternal State: the working class could be assured of protection if only it would accept the established order. It was, if you like, a refurnished version of Disraeli's Young England. The debate was conducted with some vigour: the thirties saw that most unusual phenomenon, a large number of books written by theorising Conservatives. But the debate took place in something of a political vacuum because it was not enlivened by a sense of crisis. The Conservatives had an unassailable majority in parliament, the Labour Party was concerned with re-grouping itself after the Ramsay MacDonald fiasco, the trade unions were quiet in the face of massive unemployment, and the unemployed themselves were largely resistant to attempts by the Communist Party to set them on the march. There was therefore no great impulsion toward radical moves to co-opt the working class. The most that could be said was that with the Baldwinites' capture of the Conservative Party in the early twenties there was never subsequently any determined assault on organised labour. There was, it is true, a general drift in the direction of a new paternalism with state subsidies to private industry and an expansion of state-run industry, but this never spilled over into social policy.

By 1951 with the return of a Conservative government the pre-war debate was settled in favour of the new paternalists. The Attlee Labour government of 1945-51, by opting for regulated capitalism rather than socialism, had provided a working model of a system not markedly different from that proposed by such paternalist Conservatives as Harold Macmillan in the 1930s. In the early sixties the Conservatives re-adopted some of the more radical of the Labour measures that had previously been dropped. In 1962, with the creation of the National Economic Development Council, they were proclaiming themselves in favour of some sort of planning.

What to do about the trade unions was no longer in question. They were recognised as important features of the political landscape that had, of necessity, to be consulted, and sometimes recruited as state auxiliaries. In March 1962, when the TUC had finally consented to take part in the NEDC, Harold Macmillan (then Prime Minister) was sympathising with those trade union leaders who experienced left-wing opposition to participation and held out the hope that '. . . as time went by the NEDC could help to get rid of what had been one of Britain's greatest hindrances: the idea of "the two sides industry" and all this talk of us and them. I prefer the slogan of working together.'[10] The vision of the thirties seemed within reach: the working classes integrated within a new order; the conflict between labour and capital submerged beneath a 'national purpose' and a 'national interest'.

The vision was short-lived. It was once again left to a Labour government in 1964-70 to give it a clarity that the balance of interests in the Conservative Party made difficult. The Prices and Incomes Board, the Industrial Reorganisation Corporation, Industrial Development Councils, Regional Economic Planning Councils were all institutional expressions of the corporate vision shared alike by Labour and Conservative. Harold Wilson's appeals to the Dunkirk spirit and his support of the *I'm Backing Britain* campaign were rhetorical devices to the same end.

The vision was not based on reality – and so it fell apart. As in 1949 and 1950 the trade union leaders could not hold the line. The rank and file, quite unconsciously, was playing the game according to quite different rules. Where ideologically it looked at the world in much the same way as its masters, its daily experiences as workers and consumers pushed it into forms of activity which completely contradicted its political outlook.

Those who said of Britain's entry into the Common Market on the grounds that it meant, in the long run, a surrender of political sovereignty were correct. Entry had precisely that implication – and it was desired by the ruling class. By the late 1960s it was abundantly evident that the traditional capitalist enterprise, narrowly based on the nation-state, had run its course. New technologies required vast markets if they were to be profitable, markets less constrained by the political necessities of small sovereign states. Other considerations pointed to a multi-nationality of the enterprise going beyond the frontiers of a United States of Europe. While the potentiality of expanded markets provided one incentive to multi-nationality, there were other incentives at work too. Labour was both costly and none too malleable in the West – why not, then, set up shop in the backward areas of Europe like Spain and Portugal, in Africa, Asia and Latin America where labour was cheap and repressive regimes kept down trade unionism? What was ironical about it all was that the ruling class, which had always made such play of the 'national heritage' as a means of securing allegiance, were suddenly proclaiming themselves internationalists. In the 1970s the days of nationally-based ruling classes were rapidly drawing to a close.

The short-comings of parliamentary and revolutionary politics

For much of the period 1926-72 working-class politics consisted of an unequal struggle between the Labour Party and the trade unions on the one hand, and the

Communist Party on the other. In the inter-war years it was a case of the Communists trying to push the inert weight of the labour movement in a revolutionary direction. In the post-war years it was a case of the Communists trying to make the labour movement more radical in its reformism. The Communists failed as the whole world knows: the labour movement went steadily rightward. Indeed to such an extent that Harold Wilson, leader of the Labour Party, in 1972 accused the Conservatives in outraged tones of upsetting the agreement on substantial issues which had hitherto united the Labour and Conservative Parties: '. . . we have an administration which rejects the consensus style government we had had under governments of successive parties since Atlee's day. . .'[11] But then this was not really so very far distant from 1929 when Herbert Morrison, then an up-and-coming young man in the Labour Party '. . . was assuring "every business man and business manager" that he wanted to "treat him as a man and a brother, and to help to make his commercial or industrial enterprise more successful than it has been in the past".'[12]

As in the previous period up to 1926 the trade unions provided the ground on which the struggle between the Labour Party and the Communist Party was fought, and it was the trade unions that decided the outcome. Once the Labour Party in the early twenties had refused to accept the Communist Party as an affiliated body it was inevitable that Communists should have concentrated on the unions, though even if affiliation had been allowed the unions would still have been the object of most activity. The Labour Party was never a mass movement in the same way as unions were: it was primarily an electoral machine with its leading cadres concentrating their energies in the House of Commons rather than in the country. Its *campaigning* was carried out in a debating chamber rather than in the country at large. It was not therefore a movement of agitation, and it was only the necessity of elections that periodically forced the party into activity in the constituencies.

For most of the twenties the CP did not work directly within the trade unions. It preferred to work through broader-based front organisations such as the National Minority Movement and the National Unemployed Workers Committee Movement. While both were largely led by party members they drew on support from across the entire left-spectrum, mainly at the rank and file level. The Minority Movement, the direct descendent of the Shop Stewards Movement in the First World War, acted as an opposition group within the unions but with a separate organisation. Its short-term policy was of resistance to wage cuts, reorganisation of the unions on industrial lines and democratisation of union bodies. The long term aim, naturally, was to transform the unions from reformist into revolutionary organisations.

Attempts in the thirties to form a united front with the Labour Party against fascism were constantly rebuffed by the Labour leadership, but CP support for the war after 1941 and of the Labour government until 1947 gave it a temporary and grudging respectability. With the development of the Cold War in the late forties, anti-Communist hysteria reached a new peak, and in 1949 the TUC General Council published a circular advising unions to eliminate Communist influence. By the 1970s anti-Communism was a spent force. A few die-hards remained, unable to exorcise the spectre of earlier years, but the days had passed when a prominent trade union leader somewhere could be relied upon to shout 'Red' at the first sign of unrest amongst his members. Anti-Communism was spent because the party itself was weak. Though it remained sizeable in paper membership its agitational role was minimal – the great resurgence of agitational

pamphleteering in the late sixties and early seventies
was almost entirely the work of the 'new left'. The CP
played the part of twelfth man. Whenever a large
crisis loomed, such as the Industrial Relations Act, its
possession of a central organisation and a wide geographical spread of members enabled it to mobilise
rank and file opposition. When the crisis faded so too
did the party. Committed from the forties to the policy
of the 'parliamentary road to socialism' and to working within liberal organisations, it could not simultaneously act with the verve and vigour that had been
its source of strength and wide-spread sympathetic
support in the pre-war years.

The formation of the CP was a direct response to
the Bolshevik Revolution in 1917, and the party
remained until the late sixties a loyal adherent to the
current Moscow line. The Revolution in Russia acted
as a catalyst. The Comintern, anxious to secure a
revolutionary organisation in Britain, provided money
and agents to bring about the unification of the existing revolutionary parties in Britain.[13] But the people
who joined the CP did not do so lured by Moscow
gold or because of infatuation with the Bolsheviks.
They joined because they could see nothing in the
Labour Party that held out any prospect of far-
reaching change. In this they were, in all essentials,
absolutely right – and had come to the same conclu-
sions as the leaders of the Conservative Party.

After the high hopes of the 1890s and early 1900s
the Labour Party was cruelly disillusioning for the
socialists. The Labour governments of 1924 and
1929-31 showed themselves totally bankrupt in the
face of unemployment and depression, and in the grip
of orthodox political economy to such an extent that
the 1929-31 government fell over the insistence of
MacDonald and Snowden that the dole had to be cut.
In the thirties some of the Conservatives were more
alive to the threat of fascism in Europe than the

leaders of the Labour Party. With the Labour Party well under the thumb of the TUC for most of the 1930s, it could truly be said that the established organs of the labour movement showed themselves timid and devoid of any aggressive or innovatory spirit. It was not surprising then that some of the most able and energetic working-class leaders of those years either joined the Communist Party or were willing to work with it. It was the Communists who kept alive the ideas of socialism, even if some of their tactics were often inept and counter-productive.

In the years after 1945 the Labour Party continued as it had begun in the twenties. Never having been a socialist party, it had no critique, no theoretical understanding of capitalism. Instead it was rich with moral righteousness and indignation, thinking that that alone was sufficient. Lacking any theory it was reduced to palliatives and 'social engineering'. It accordingly competed with the Conservatives on the Conservatives' own terms. The rhetoric between them was more reminiscent of a primary school playground than of sophisticated political thinkers: the Labour Party said 'we can make capitalism work better than you can'; the Conservatives replied 'no you can't'. And so the argument faded into infinity with 'yes we can's' and 'no you can'ts', with charges and counter charges.

In the pre-war period the working class was doubly imprisoned. The Labour Party and the trade unions stood in the way of formal political action in one direction; unemployment and the fear of it barred the way to 'direct action' in the other. The only positive force on offer was the Communist Party, and that suffered a number of handicaps. It urged militancy when it was patently unsafe to be militant; it was denounced as 'alien' at a time when successive generations had been reared on a diet of the glories of the British Empire and the general inferiority of anything not British; it waxed over-strong in its denunciations of trade union leaders who were, if not well-loved, objects of a perverse pride in that they stood at the head of institutions which the working classes had made and still looked to for guidance.

The local and regional insularity of the working class was aided by the differential impact of unemployment as between regions and industries, and by the failure of the one 'legitimate' political organisation – the Labour Party – to provide any cogent analysis of the depression and thus give the working class a sense of political unity. It is doubtful however that, even *had* it been possessed of such an analysis, it could have done very much. Its profound attachment to parliamentary politics would have precluded from it the sort of agitational activity required to generate class unity. Agitating is an extra-parliamentary activity which by implication is *anti*-parliamentary. The Labour Party was serious about its parliamentarism and at no time was inclined to regard parliament as just another platform from which to politicise the masses. The consequence was that from 1926 the working classes were extraordinarily quiet. Dulled into political quiescence, they turned out in their millions to vote for the Conservatives in the elections of 1931 and 1935.

In the post-1945 period parliament became increasingly irrelevant to the working classes, for in years of full employment they were well-placed to determine their own standards of living. On those issues where government – local and national – was seen to be relevant there was a growing tendency in the sixties for direct action in industry to spill over into other areas. This was especially marked in housing where there was a rapid growth of associations among corporation tenants, and in the broad area of urban planning where militant mothers blocked off roads after children had been mown down. Small points these, but they did point to the undoubted growth of working-class belligerence. Yet it was a diffuse belligerence that capitalised on issues. If the range and scope of issues widened as disaffection with government increased, in 1972 the established labour movement showed few signs of being able to build on it. The only people willing to do so were the various sects on the revolutionary left. They were *sometimes* welcomed for their readiness to help in a particular struggle, but their political analyses tended to fall on deaf ears. Deafness in the circumstances was understandable. All they had to offer in the 1972 struggles against the Industrial Relations Act was the slogan *Call a General Strike and Kick the Tories Out*. And so working-class action in the communities, as in the workplace, was securely locked up in sectional insularity.

The rise of the shop steward

Despite the fact that the economic and political environment facing the unions in the inter-war years was radically different from that of post-1945, the problems facing the unions were remarkably similar. If organisational survival was threatened in the depression years by lack of bargaining power, it was threatened in the post-war years by the absence of unemployment and the growth of shop steward organisations as semi-autonomous units within the unions. The years after 1945 saw in some respects a return to the situation of the late 1900s in which national union organisations were little more than federations of a lot of small, localised unions. This is not to suggest that the rank and file was entirely quiet and submissive during the twenties and thirties, thoroughly cowed by unemployment: it wasn't. Indeed if anything it posed *more* of a threat to established leadership than it did in the fifties and sixties.

From 1920 until about the mid-thirties the unions

were mostly engaged in negotiating wage reductions – and they had but little choice in the matter. Such strike action as there was against wage cuts almost invariably ended in defeat. The crushing of the miners in 1926 was the writing on every trade unionist's wall. In the circumstances the most the unions could do, given their political acceptance of capitalism, was to try to minimise the reductions. To do that effectively they needed to negotiate on an industry, rather than a plant, basis.

That the period did see a considerable extension of national industrial agreements owed little, if anything, to the unions, for they had no power to force employers into associations. Despite odd revivals, the entire period from 1921 to 1939 was one of depressed trade – even in 1939 after several years of re-armament unemployment stood at $10\frac{1}{2}\%$. In those years there was a lot to be said from the employers point of view for national agreements covering entire industries. Anything that could be used to ease competition, and thence pressure on profit margins, was to be welcomed. Competition could be minimised by price-fixing agreements and by equalising wage costs between firms. In the growing number of monopolist industries there were different reasons for coming to industrial agreements with the unions. Even if operating with under-utilised plants, their dominance of the home markets gave them some cover from foreign competition. The scale of operation and the capital intensity of the monopolist firm ensured that it was much more oriented to the future than its smaller brethren: largely free from intense competitive pressures, it could afford to look beyond its bank balance at the end of the month. Since labour was one of the volatile elements in the entrepreneurial equation it was eminently rational to look to the unions as a means of stabilising its labour force, and thereby introducing an element of predictability into the course of labour costs. The large firm, furthermore, tended to be headed by sophisticated political animals such as Sir Alfred Mond, chairman of ICI. Such people of necessity had to look very closely at the political environment in which they operated – and they saw in the unions a source of political as well as economic stability. It was not in the least coincidental that the Mond-Turner talks of 1927 were initiated by the heads of some of Britain's largest companies.

The slump in international trade in the twenties and thirties hastened the monopolistic tendency which had been apparent in British industry since the 1890s. The new and expensive technologies of the emerging mass production industries gave it an extra fillip. Mergers and amalgamations in coal, textiles, iron and steel, and shipbuilding were entirely self-protective. Faced with shrinking markets and considerable excess productive capacity, mergers were the only solution to the squeeze on profits. Where mergers proved impracticable because of the proliferation of small firms, price-fixing trade associations became the rule. When none of these measures proved sufficiently effective, governments of the thirties were usually sympathetic to appeals to put tariffs on imported foreign goods that undercut domestic products. The new industries of this period, especially those producing cars and electrical goods, tended very rapidly to become the province of a small number of large firms. The giant Associated Electrical Industries was formed in the twenties. In the motor industry by 1934 there were only three major British firms: Austin, the Rootes Group, and Morris/Wolseley. The Lucas group was formed out of twelve companies to become the major supplier of electrical components to the motor industry. The food and soap industries saw the consolidation of the Unilever empire; chemicals became synonymous with ICI, and oils with BP and Shell.

The State helped along the monopolisation process

not merely by choosing to impose tariffs and by turning a blind eye to the doubtful legality of price-fixing. The 1921 Railway Act created four regional railway companies which subsequent legislation subsidised. London Transport was effectively nationalised in 1933, BOAC became a state airline in 1939, and the Central Electricity Board was established in 1926 with a monopoly of the wholesale supply of electricity. State funds were made available to assist amalgamations in shipbuilding and iron and steel, and the State assumed a monopoly of the sugar beet industry with the creation of the British Sugar Corporation. Given the range of state activity by Conservative governments in the pre-war years, the extension of state control and ownership by Labour governments in the late 1940s amounted to a logical continuation rather than a radical departure.

Although it was the economics of slump that largely indicated national agreements, previously existing institutional practices eased its course of development. As we have seen in the previous chapter, national bargaining across an industry was quite common in the 1890s. The major institutional developments however came in the First World War and in its immediate aftermath. The war-time labour shortage gave employers an interest in national agreements as a means of combating sectional wage demands and competition between employers for scarce labour. The government-imposed compulsory arbitration of disputes meant that the '. . . government encouraged employers and unions to enter into national agreements for the periodic revision of wage rates . . . (in order to simplify the work of the arbitration tribunals).'[14] These considerations led in turn to the government's recommendation of Joint Industrial Councils of which seventy-three were established between 1918 and 1921. Although the JICs were largely consultative bodies, those that survived into the thirties (some fifty or so) were mainly used for wage negotiations.

The movement toward national agreements was not universal. As Flanders has said: 'What happened to collective bargaining during the inter-war years depended very much on whether the industry in question was relatively sheltered or exposed to foreign competition.'[15] This particularly applied to coal mining where the owners were especially resistant to national agreements, although their resistance was not just associated with foreign competition: conditions of coal-getting varied so widely between fields and pits as to make anything resembling uniformity of costs impossible to achieve. Over industry as a whole, the extent to which unions could enter into permanent procedures for the settlement of disputes and the negotiation of wages was crucially dependent upon the cost structures obtaining within industries, and the market situations of particular firms. The effects of foreign competition were at their strongest in the cotton industry. An industry once known for the cordiality of relations between owners and unions, it became a scene of bitter conflict as large numbers of employers sought temporary advantage by reneging on agreements and workers sought to win back what they had lost in previous wage reductions. If the presence of long-established institutions was a factor, it was clearly of marginal importance.

As some of the larger employers were astute enough to see, formal recognition of the unions had quite as much in it for the trade unions as it did for them. Recognition legitimised trade unionism in the eyes of the ordinary worker, it made it safe for him to join a union at a time when previous experience had shown him that to be a union member in a period of unemployment could be a risky business. Recognition also helped to stabilise membership in another way: the information garnered from employers at negotiations enabled the union leadership to spell out in rational argument the 'facts' of the case, and hence endow leadership with intellectual authority. The leader could claim that he had specialised knowledge not available to the rank and file. With the added stature that this gave him, he was in a position to 'refute' critics, label them as 'irrational', and so reduce the possibility of their gaining a following.

Since industrial unionism was rare national negotiations necessarily meant that a number of unions had to negotiate jointly with employers, and this helped to relieve another of the traditional organisational weaknesses. Unions in the past, when faced with declining membership, frequently tried to make good the deficit by poaching members from other unions. Despite the fact that the TUC General Council was empowered in 1920 to regulate disputes between unions, the early twenties saw a rash of poaching. That the General Council was proving an inefficient gamekeeper was revealed in 1928 when TUC standing orders were revised to strengthen disputes procedures. It was revealed again in 1939 when the TUC was permitted to increase its powers still further. By that time, however, many disputes had been resolved through procedural agreements between the unions who were co-signatories to agreements with employers. Amalgamation, the other answer to organisational weakness was not widely resorted to after 1927. The big mergers which had formed the GMWU, the T&GWU and the AEU were over, and for the rest of the inter-war period only some of the small local unions were swallowed up.

While the main trend of the depression years was towards national agreements, local and plant agreements remained common. In most industries there were firms who refused, in the hope of gaining a temporary advantage, to join employers' associations and who continued to negotiate separately with the unions. Within some of the larger firms there was a contradiction between their willingness to negotiate nationally and their introduction of piece-work and time-and-motion study. The new payment systems associated with the latter were almost invariably regulated at plant level so that even in this period there was often a disparity between nationally agreed flat rates and take home pay. In 1934 the Engineering Employers' Federation '. . . countered trade union claims for a national advance with figures of rising earnings due to domestic agreements on piecework, bonuses, or special rates. Although some national advances were granted, the gap between agreed national rates and average earnings began to grow wider each year.'[16]

These developments, largely confined to the engineering industry, gave ample scope for disputes between the rank and file and union leadership. The GMWU leadership:

. . . looked with suspicion on the new shop stewards' movements that were . . . developing, especially in the vehicle and aircraft . . . industry. The 1936 Congress was told that 'in the Aircraft Section there was a Shop Steward's Committee run by the Communist Party, who promoted and advocated claims leading to sectional disputes which the Employers wanted us to say we would have nothing to do with. There was no other answer to give them than to say we would not support any sectional movement of that character.[17]

The association of rank and file militancy with Communism dated from 1924 with the advent of the Minority Movement, although there were much longer-standing precedents for denying the legitimacy of rank and file claims by imputing their inspiration to 'outside agitators'.

The trade unions, being committed to working within capitalism, had to accept capitalist economic realities – which meant a grudging acceptance of wage cuts for resistance was bound to fail unless accompanied by a political movement directed at overthrowing the established order. The trouble with negotiated wage reductions was that they had to be 'sold' to the rank and file who were not notably anxious to 'buy' them. Once negotiated there were the inevitable revolts, given point and focus in a number of unions by the Minority Movement.

Given its limited political outlook the trade union leadership had two courses open to it. It could *negotiate* reductions, and thereby hope to secure small concessions. This course, they knew, would lead to trouble in the ranks and leave them open to allegations of treachery and corruption. To obviate this they often balloted the membership for approval, banking on the fear of unemployment to give them a majority. More often than not it worked, thereby legitimising their decisions as leaders. If there were rebellions they were then in a position to accuse the rebels of unconstitutional behaviour. The other possible course of action was to refuse to negotiate cuts. This had its attractions for it might insulate the leaders from attack from below. It also had its drawbacks because it would either oblige the leadership to call an official strike, accept a lock-out, or leave the rank and file to fight as best it could. The most likely consequence of that was a chaotic defeat which would leave the union smashed in fragments. The choice was a simple one for the leaders: they could negotiate a defeat and preserve the organisation, or they could refuse to negotiate and run the risk of ruining the organisation. In choosing the unpopular course of negotiation they preserved the union and knowingly incurred the price of revolt.

The only people capable of mobilising the discontent were members of the Communist Party. They had the organisation and they had a highly intelligent and capable leadership prepared to make great personal sacrifices. Rapidly earning a justified reputation as people prepared to fight, the Communists attracted the support of other militants and soon had a toe-hold in most of the major unions through their front organisation, the Minority Movement. Large numbers of branches and trades councils affiliated, and the unions had the unique experience of having within their own ranks an opposition movement operating on a national scale. It need hardly be said that the Minority Movement was unloved by the leadership. In 1924 the GMWU executive instructed its branches to disaffiliate from trades councils affiliated with the MM, and in 1928 required all district council members to sign a document denying membership of the Communist Party and the MM. In 1927 and 1928 the TUC General Secretary wrote a series of articles in the TUC journal denouncing the CP. He received support from the executives of the T&GWU and the NUR who instructed their branches to sever connections with the MM, from the AEU who had tried to prevent its branches from paying affiliation fees to it, from Boilermakers who had prohibited CP members from acting as union delegates to the TUC and Labour Party conferences, from the Boot and Shoe Operatives executive who issued instructions that members of the MM and the CP were not to be permitted to hold any elective office in the union. As Graubard put it: 'The trade union hierarchy, pledged to eternal opposition, resisted the Communists by revising union constitutions, conducting "disruption" inquiries, and expelling recalcitrant members.'[18] By 1929 the MM was virtually extinct, and the CP, under instructions from the Moscow-based Red International of Labour Unions, embarked on a short-lived and disastrous policy of forming breakaway unions under direct Party control. When that policy was shelved after a year or so, Party members worked more or less openly in the unions. Under constant watch from the union hierarchies and the state security forces, Communists and their sympathisers were constantly the objects of witch-hunts from the 1920s right through to the 1960s.

Although individual Communists became important figures in the Miners, the Railwaymen, the Engineers, the Electricians and the Transport Workers unions, organised opposition was easily crushed despite its ability. By no means all of the union leaders were *ideologically* opposed to the Communists even if they were not themselves Party members. Hicks of the building workers, Turner of the cotton workers, Conley of the garment workers, Bromley of the railway engineers, Cook of the miners, were all sympathetic to the MM's long-term aims of industrial unionism and the overthrow of capitalism, but few of them could tolerate militant opposition to wage cuts for fear of the consequences for their unions. Tragically, the Communists proved very useful to the unions. Since only they had the organisational capacity to mobilise rank and file discontents they provided the leaders with an ideal scapegoat. So long as opposition could be identified with Communism, accurately or not (and it was often *in*accurate), the leadership could easily discredit militants by simply hanging the Communist label around their necks. A tactic which, with the fear of unemployment as their other trump card, kept the rank and file in line. Thus did the unions survive, depleted in strength, but otherwise intact.

The post-war years (at least until 1969) were characterised by full employment and in this situation the ever-present tension between leadership and rank and file took on a new twist. In the inter-war years employers found the unions useful because they could assist in regulating competition, and because they could also contain those sections of the labour movement that wanted to move in revolutionary directions. With the revival of national and international trade after 1945 and the readiness of the State to regulate the economy, the trade unions became split into virtually two parts. At the national level trade union leaders became an established part of the political process: government economic strategies required the co-operation of the unions. Union leaders were therefore co-opted individually as 'consultants' and collectively as participants in the auxilliary machinery of government. At the local level workers were finding that their strength lay on the shop floor. Union branches, district and shop steward committees were playing the market with all the vigour of nineteenth-century businessmen. Thus where the leaders were trying to help governments introduce an ordered capitalism, the rank and file were following traditional *laissez-faire* policies of taking the market for all it could bear.

Trade union collaboration with government was not a new departure. Neither was it 'immoral' nor a 'betrayal': it was a perfectly logical consequence of the aims of trade unionism. Although it suited the pretensions to grandeur of a few union leaders, at its roots it had precious little to do with the psychological motivations of individuals. Trade unionism was about improving the lot of the working classes in the 'here and now', and to the extent that improvements could be obtained by collaboration with governments, then to do so was an eminently rational course to follow. George Woodcock, the TUC General Secretary, spelled out the logic in 1962 in answering the critics of the TUC's decision to join the National Economic Development Council. The Building Trade Workers' journal in 1961 had said: 'The reply of trade unions to the Tory invitation (to join NEDC) should be an uncompromising no. (The unions) are the basis of the Labour Party. Whether they like it or not any joint co-operation between (the unions) and the Tory government is almost tantamount to forming something like an economic coalition government because we face a crisis.'[19] Two months later George Woodcock noted that some members of the TUC believed it was wrong for a trade union body with close associations with the Labour Party to join anything proposed by a Conservative government and went on to say '. . . frankly that will not stand a second's investigation. That idea carried to its logical conclusion would reduce the TUC to nothing . . . There was another view – the highly orthodox one – which said that a big organisation like the TUC should in almost all circumstances accept invitations to consultation issued by the government of the day.'[20] The same position was reiterated by Sidney Greene, NUR General Secretary, eighteen months later in urging the annual conference to reject a resolution ordering the union's withdrawal from NEDC: 'Mr Greene stated that he was the only NEDC member who represented a union catering solely for the workers in a nationalised industry, and if the resolution went through they would be unrepresented on a body which might have an important effect on their lives.'[21] These arguments were well-rehearsed, for they were part of the continuing debate between the 'left' and the 'right'.

But they had not enjoyed such a public airing since the Mond-Turner talks of 1927 and 1928. These were discussions between a group of prominent industrialists headed by Sir Alfred Mond, Chairman of ICI, and members of the TUC General Council headed by Ben Turner, TUC president. The initiative had come from the employers who, disturbed by the General Strike, were willing to try to negotiate a peace treaty with the unions. For the union leader's part:

Collective bargaining was no longer enough. If the unions wanted to exercise some influence over the decisions which determined wages and hours, if they wanted to reduce unemployment and forestall the effects of rationalisation, they had to go further than meeting the employers' representatives to negotiate new wage agreements. They had to talk to the men at the top who took the decisions, and talk to them about wider questions than rates of pay and length of shifts.[22]

When the talks were attacked by the left at the 1928 Congress of the TUC, they were justified by the majority of the General Council on the grounds that since the movement had rejected revolution there was a choice of either sitting back and letting the employers take the initiative, or the unions involving themselves in the formation of economic policy and seeking to improve material standards in the immediate future. It was not without significance that the same Congress authorised the General Council to conduct an inquiry into 'disruptive elements and activities.'

As it happened the talks did not lead to the prompt despatch of any goods to the unions beyond an admission from the employers that it was in everyone's interest for workers to belong to trade unions. The long term consequence however was that '. . . personal friendships were formed between businessmen and union leaders which were to be of great importance when collaboration between them again became possible.'[23] It is worth emphasising that collaboration only again became possible with the recovery of trade union strength in the war and the years of full employment afterward, i.e. with the unions committed to parliamentary reformism in the inter-war years, *economically* they had little to offer. Only with a recovery of bargaining strength were the employers interested in talking serious business.

The twenties and thirties saw no great extension of the network of relationships with government beyond that existing in the 1900s because very little new state machinery was created that required the services of trade unionists. The war years of 1939-45 naturally saw the widespread co-optation of trade union leaders on to a host of committees concerned with economic planning and development. After the war much of the planning machinery was retained for several years, though the 'bonfire of controls' in 1948 marked the end of attempts to *plan* the economy in any sort of detail. It did not, however, mean the end of attempts to regulate the path of the economy. For the entire period to 1972 successive governments used the devices of price controls, wage-freezes and pay-pauses, direct and indirect taxation, bank rate, and hire purchase regulations to broadly direct the level of economic activity.

None of these devices could be at all adequately used without a firm basis of consultation between government on the one hand and unions and employers on the other. The institutional developments necessary to effective consultation, already broadly adequate in 1945, became more so in the ensuing years. With respect to business and finance the growing concentration of capital in large firms meant that individual companies wielded such economic power that there was never any question of them being ignored. Where smaller companies were concerned governments encouraged them to speak through representative associations. As J. P. Nettl put it, business divides into two: those firms large enough to deal with government direct, and the atomised world which can only speak through an association. Furthermore, since large firms are also members of associations they may be persuaded by government to play the role of 'uncle'.[24] Small wonder then that Nettl '. . . found that members of . . . Main Boards move socially in Whitehall circles to a remarkable extent.'[25] Had he looked at the trade unions he would have found a comparable picture.

George Woodcock:

When I first went to the TUC in the thirties if I rang a government department I would be treated with the utmost suspicion – nothing but defensiveness. Then came the war and closer co-operation became necessary. By the end of the war we had the position that exists today where we can telephone any of these officials and exchange the most extraordinary information. I would tell them what our sticking point was and they would do likewise. In many cases we could fix it on the understanding that they never let me down and I never let them down – a sort of 'secret diplomacy' which can only be done through mutual confidence. Our prestige has gone up with most government departments, particularly the Department of Employment and the Treasury.[26]

The co-operation that governments required of the unions was their moderation in wage demands. In the late thirties ' "the Ministry of Labour argued with a growing insistence that wage control was unthinkable, that reliance must be placed instead upon the realism and moderation of organised Labour." '[27] As we have seen, that reliance was misplaced: trade union leaders were prepared to be moderate, but their members were not. As H. A. Turner rather carefully put it when talking of the failure of the 1964–9 incomes policy; 'To the extent that the policy restraints were more real at the national or industrial bargaining level, it was natural for a greater concentration on negotiations at the enterprise level to develop.'[28]

This did not mean that national negotiations were either dead or unimportant – for example the GMWU in 1964 was represented on 145 permanent negotiating bodies spread over sixteen different industries. Despite the steady growth of workplace bargaining there was no parallel fall off of national and industrial bodies. Neither was there any indication that shop stewards and others bargaining at local level wanted a cessation of national negotiations. An attempt by the Engineers (AUEW) in the spring of 1972 to give up national negotiations and force them at plant level was less than a roaring success. Pressure was put on the union's executive from branches and district committees to resume national negotiations – which it duly did in mid-summer. The union's policy, activated at a time of considerable redundancies in the industry, showed just how dependent was shop-floor power on boom conditions.

Local bargaining, especially in the sixties with the advent of productivity deals, spread out far beyond its original stronghold in engineering. Even so, it was still largely confined to manufacturing industry at a time when the proportion of the working population engaged in it was steadily decreasing (in 1931 23% of the occupied population were white-collar workers and 70% manual workers; by 1961 the figures were 36% and 59% respectively). This meant that a large and growing proportion of workers were dependent for the bulk of their earnings on national negotiations. Their jobs allowed them little opportunity to vary their output so they had little scope for local bargaining. This particularly applied to white collar workers in public service and manual workers in public utilities. The inevitable corollary of this was that such workers tended to lag behind their fellows in manufacturing, and accordingly forced union leaders into greater shows of militancy at national level – producing the interesting phenomena of strikes by teachers and bank clerks.

While trade union leaders were nearly always willing to collaborate with governments, that collaboration was never total and at no time ever approached the point where the leaders effectively became government functionaries. In 1950 the TUC virtually gave up its attempts to restrain wages; it boycotted the 'Cohen Council' of 1957, the National Incomes Commission of 1962, the Industrial Relations Act of 1971. The fact was that no matter how receptive individual leaders might have been to government blandishments – and some were quite immune – they could not rely on their members to follow them. As in the period of 'wage restraint' from 1948 to 1950 '. . . the unions could only give the government the industrial peace and economic co-operation it desired on condition that the government allowed the unions sufficient economic concessions to keep their members from growing too restive.'[29]

Rank and file sectionalism was not a dominant characteristic of the pre-war years. Opposition to leadership was, as we have seen, economic in basis but mainly political in expression.* Opposition to leadership in the post-war years was typically economic in basis *and* expression. (It was particularly noteworthy that one of the very few opposition movements – the Reform Movement in the National Union of Seamen – developed in an industry where there was literally *no* scope for local bargaining and where wages were notoriously low.) This did not stop some union leaders – especially during the Cold War period – from denouncing some unofficial strikes as being the work of 'Communist agitators'. In the late sixties, with the Cold War but a distant memory, the anti-Communist rhetoric faded away and the TUC General Council declined to buy Harold Wilson's line that the 1966 seamen's strike was Communist-inspired. The new baddies were 'Trotskyites', 'Maoists', 'Anarchists' and other ill-defined and ill-understood left-wing groups. Naturally there were parties, sects, and groups approximating to those labels which were growing in strength: none of them in 1972 had the quality of organisation of the CP in the pre-war period. The most that could be said was that through their pamphlets, newspapers,

*Not invariably though: 'An unofficial movement in the BISAKTA held a conference at which 61 branches were represented, drew up a programme for democratising the union, reducing officials' salaries, and issued its own duplicated newssheet. A Members' Rights Movement appeared in the AEU, a Reorganisation Committee among the Boilermakers, and a Rules Revision Committee among the Furniture Workers.'[30]

and leaflets they were having an undoubted influence on the thinking of rank and file leaders.

Throughout the post-war years the unions experienced nothing remotely resembling the challenge of the Minority Movement in the twenties. The CP came near to something resembling it in some unions in the late forties, but considering the period as a whole it was never much more than a pipe-dream of pockets of isolated individuals. The opposition that leaders *did* experience was latent rather than actual, and short-lived rather than long-term.

Its characteristic expression was the unofficial strike which ignored union authority and side-stepped established procedures for wage and dispute settlement. If many unofficial strikers found themselves emulating their fathers by ignoring union officials' pleas to return to work, not a few union officials found themselves emulating *their* fathers by tacitly supporting the strikers. It was not invariably true that unofficial strikes were willingly led by shop stewards. As the Donovan Report noted:

. . . The shop-floor decisions which generally precede unofficial strikes are often taken against the advice of shop stewards. Thus shop stewards are rarely agitators pushing workers into unconstitutional action. In some instances they may be the mere mouthpieces of their work groups. But quite commonly they are supporters of order exercising a restraining influence on their members in conditions which promote disorder.[31]

Breakaway unions, the expression *par excellence* of a discontented rank and file, were sparse on the ground. There was a small rash of them in the late forties as a more or less direct consequence of the unions' acceptance of wage restraint in 1948, and an unusually large one was formed in the wake of the rather unique circumstances of the Pilkington strike in 1970,[32] but they were more often talked of as a

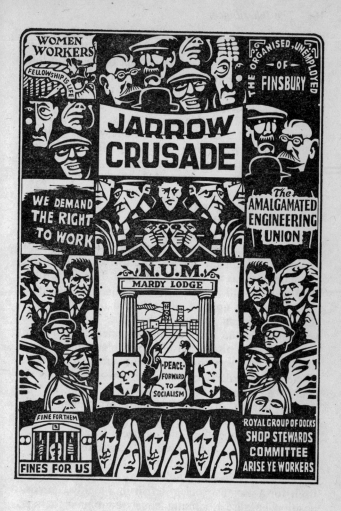

possibility than actually established. The main reason
for their relative absence was at once an explanation
of the form that intra-union opposition took. So long
as most everyday grievances and earnings supplements
could be settled by a shop stewards' committee effectively free from union control, there was little point
in forming an alternative union. The stewards, furthermore, could use the union machinery to legitimate
their positions by securing elective posts within it and
thus influence the unions' national policies. Only shop-
floor leaders who concentrated on the plant to the
exclusion of working within union structures left
themselves open to retribution if they got themselves
into a position where management, abetted by the
union, seized an opportunity to get rid of them.[33]
Given the possibilities of gaining a fair degree of local
autonomy within the unions, the formation of breakaway unions was an archaic response. In a sense then,
they had learned from their dads.

The growing upsurge of rank and file militancy as
seen in unofficial strikes in the fifties and sixties revealed within the trade union movement the inherent
strains of reformism – but did not explode then. Where
the leadership was in intermittent pursuit of a tight,
efficient and orderly organisation directed toward the
goal of a 'rational' economic order, the rank and file
was in pursuit of the immediate attainment of its
sectional interests within which it was difficult to
retain any conception of an overall economic and
political strategy. This division between leaders and
led smacked of an inevitability.

The leadership's unreadiness to positively proclaim
itself for a socialist society left it in a highly equivocal
position because it simultaneously continued to assert
the belief in the incompatibility of labour and capital.
The resolution of this dilemma was perpetually postponed. The knowledge of the ultimate irreconcilability
of labour and capital was pushed to the back of their

minds while they concentrated on producing temporary compromises.* The compromises were necessarily couched in the *general* terms of an outline of policy which frequently cut right across the very *specific* nature of existing rank and file demands and grievances. Leaders were thus constantly placing themselves in almost impossible positions. They were anxious to conciliate governments because they were afraid that if they could not, legal restraints would be placed on union activities. While on the other hand, if the State was going to interfere, the union activities that it would be concerned with were those of the rank and file. If the law was going to try to make the leaders responsible for the actions of their members, that meant the leaders would have to try to discipline them. That prospect did not enthral the leaders for they feared that attempts to rigidly control the rank and file would lead to breakaway unions and (perhaps more important) a simple drop in subscriptions.

The rank and file's sectionalism was part of the daily round of trade unionism. Although it was unlikely that many workers were well-versed in the tenets of classical political economy, collectively they nevertheless acted in accordance with them and adopted the time-honoured strategy of exploiting their

*The Donovan Report represented an excellent statement of the trade union position. The Report took for granted the necessity of an incomes policy and then proceeded to say what form trade union practices needed to take to make such a policy operable. It identified the main obstacle as shop-floor bargaining which, since it was relatively uncontrolled (except by general market forces), gave rise to pressures on profit margins. The prime need therefore, for Donovan, was to develop means by which plant bargaining could be brought under the administrative umbrella of the established union machinery. In sum, all it wanted was a more orderly negotiating process in which the union secretariats had some measure of control over what went on at local level. If that could be achieved then union leaders would be able to act at national level with greatly enhanced authority.

market strength. If that meant that the membership often acted 'unconstitutionally' in union and management terms, then so much the worse for constitutions. This was a hard world unimaginable to the Marquess of Queensberry. The members' attitude was that constitutions were historically dated since they were expressions of what the *past* had decreed were legitimate grievances and procedures. Refusals to operate those constitutions were therefore, implicitly, claims for a recognition of new definitions of what was 'right and proper'.

Sectional bargaining was a direct consequence of two factors. There were the pressing grievances of daily life in the factory, pit or wherever. These could often be resolved by quick and decisive action – such as what came to be called in the motor industry 'the downer'. There was also the failure of the trade union movement to hold out to its members a longer-term prospect of a radically transformed society. Without that prospect the movement was less of a movement and more of a collection of separate organisations looking toward the interests of particular groups of people. Without that prospect the unions could offer nothing to unite its people regardless of income, occupation, skill, etc. Insofar as reformism meant gradual change through piecemeal reform, the rank and file could have quite legitimately claimed to have been working as effectively toward that end as their multitude of critics.

Sectionalism *within* any particular union did not as a rule create major organisational problems for the leadership. Certainly long drawn out unofficial strikes led to grumblings by the rank and file at the union's failure to make the strike 'official', but these complaints did not often shake the union concerned. There may have been a falling-off of membership after the strike or a desertion to another union*, but turnover

*The GMWU virtually lost its entire membership at the Ford plant in Liverpool after the 1969 strike. The GMWU was

of labour was often such that resentment lived but a short time in any particular plant. There was though a cumulative effect of a generalised dissatisfaction with union leadership. In the 1960s large numbers of workers could be heard assenting to the view of previous generations: 'the union officials and the bosses are all in it together.' Neither was it unknown for the same sentiment to include shop stewards.

These views, widely held as they were, never gelled into sizeable opposition movements. The continued effectiveness of sectional bargaining (with or without union help), a rising standard of living (as measured by consumption of commodities), and a relative absence of unemployment all combined to make discontents manageable and to make it difficult for the left to gain a large following. There was no imperative working on the leadership to make them want to change their rules so as to enhance their powers. The only union in the post-war years to launch major constitutional changes was the Electricians, and in that case the changes followed from the leadership's unique obsession with 'left-wing disrupters'.

From another perspective there *was* an incentive for rules revision. Sectionalism had the effect of making the union leaders appear as if they had no clothes when negotiating with governments. They could never make any hard promises because they had no ultimate control over their members. We have seen that the Industrial Relations Act and the Labour government's ill-fated predecessor *'In Place of Strife'* were deliberately designed to strengthen their hands. But it was a strength that they did not want. They were no more anxious for the government to extend their powers for them than they were to try to obtain them for themselves. Their view was – and in all essentials it was correct – that their position *vis à vis* the rank and

the only major union that refused to give the strike official recognition. The ETU, though having only a handful of members, similarly declined recognition.

file was quite delicate enough as it was. Much as some leaders personally may have liked an extension of their powers, they did not welcome the anticipated consequences for internal union politics.

Although there were few *constitutional* changes the general tendancy toward greater centralisation continued. The merger movement in industry in the sixties was paralleled in the unions with the two largest, the Engineers and the Transport Workers, prominently involved. More and more union head offices became accustomed to the labours of intellectuals as graduates were recruited to form corps of experts. Where in the simple days of the thirties the numbers of graduates working in the unions could be counted on the fingers of one hand, by the seventies they were numbered in dozens. The TUC, without acquiring any new powers over its constituents, nevertheless grew in authority as the scope and depth of consultations with governments increased. There were even occasions when the TUC acted voluntarily as an arm of the State, as in 1969 when it agreed to vet the wage claims of the member unions and act as mediator in intractable unofficial strikes. Yet as the edifice became more imposing, it simultaneously looked as brittle and fragile as ever. The central contradiction of British trade unionism remained unresolved. The pursuit of the politics of reform drove trade union leaders into the arms of the State. The rank and file's pursuit of control over the disposal of its labour power ensured that those arms could never form an embrace.

Part II

Living on a Legacy

The first Henry Ford told a Chicago court that
'history is bunk'. A perverse remark from a man who
was patently a child of his epoch. History everywhere
invades the present, for the raw material of thought
is the events of the past: it is only possible
to think on what is known. There are, therefore,
'lessons' to be drawn from history. But there is no
guarantee that they will be learned or even noticed.
There are those who deny history. They are the
more certain to be its captives.

5. The Rank and File in Ragged Order

You've got to keep your feet on the ground. If you
go around the world with rosy ideas about things,
about the members, they'll pretty soon come unstuck
because the members can be bastards . . .

We are the union!
A Ford shop steward[1]
Dutch printing workers

In the early days of trade unionism it was 'natural'
that the focus should have been on the locality and
particular workplaces within it. Before the advent of
the railways and the telegraph the centre of the world
for most of the people was the immediate community.
To a Liverpudlian, London or Glasgow would be
almost as foreign as Paris or Marseilles. Only members of the bourgeoisie and a handful of artisans
had any adequate knowledge of a social order that
extended beyond the boundaries of the parish. It was
a bit early for Marx and Engels to have exhorted in
1848: *Working men of all countries, unite!*

Such consciousness of class and rank as there was
could not be generalised further than the local gentry
and the mill or mine owner. If there were nationalistic
sentiments, they drew their inspiration from conceptions of monarchs locked in struggles with each other.
Nationalism, that is to say, was an identification with
kings and queens rather than with the common characteristics of 'whole peoples'.

As the nineteenth century progressed frontiers everywhere expanded. The city, the metropolis, was rapidly replacing the parish as the centre of social life. As geographic boundaries moved outward under the impetus of economic development, so likewise did social and economic boundaries. Local markets became regional and then national. Local politics became totally subordinate to national politics in all important matters. Local trade unionism became – nominally at least – national trade unionism.

The world expanded, too. Australia ceased to be merely a prison hulk floating in the Pacific, and the USA was transformed from a rebellious colony to a 'refuge' for hundreds of thousands seeking escape from the miseries of famine and the industrial revolution. Europe bred a new nationalism – fed by the revolutions of 1848 and the subsequent creations of Italy and Germany as nation states. British imperial expansion in Africa, the Middle East and Asia brought vast new territories within the orbit of what by the end of the century had become an international system of capitalism.

Knowledge of this expanding world filtered through to the localities where the great majority of the population remained firmly rooted. The extension of the vote to the working class invited it to consider national and international issues. Newly arrived national newspapers tried – and with no little success – to impose on the working class a bourgeois way of looking at the world. New generations of working-class pamphleteers did their best to put the record a little straighter and set limits on the inroads of ruling-class propaganda. In this situation horizons broadened. Vague conceptions of class developed which went beyond the bounds of pit villages and cotton towns: an awareness that in the last resort labour was labour no matter where it was based.

Yet this dawning of class consciousness was ill-nurtured and ill-fed from the beginnings to the present day. The trade-union created vehicle of class advance, the Labour Party, though using class rhetoric for electoral purposes, declined to practise the attack on capitalism that was implicit in its speeches. Its insistence on parliamentarism cut it off from its roots and forbade it an educational and agitational role. Unable therefore to politicise the working class, the working class remained unpoliticised. Other attempts – such as those by the Communist Party from the 1920s – to do what the Labour Party neglected to do, were forestalled by the Labour Party's assumption of the role of the working class's legitimate voice. Politically, the working class remained badly educated and was largely left to cope as best it could with the propaganda daily launched upon it by the mass media. Although the media had a certain degree of autonomy, its objective position as an instrument of class rule was at its most evident in its reportage of the 'state of the economy' and industrial disputes.

This did not mean however that the working class was firmly and unresistingly in the grip of ruling-class ideology. There was a continual process of education through collective struggles which kept alive the 'us' and 'them' consciousness of the workplace, which ensured that the under-developed consciousness of the nineteenth century was never extinguished – even if it did not advance. Like the ruling class, the working class had its political families. So new generations learned about past struggles and acquired some of the skills of political analysis.

The failure of the Labour and Communist Parties to mobilise the working class had the consequence of concentrating the latter's energies in that situation where it was best equipped to resist – the workplace. Only there did it experience itself as a class for there was no other location capable of bringing it together. In no other place was an identity of interest among workers so apparent or so apparently necessary. Outside the workplace all was divided – the collectivity of producers was dissolved into a fragmented mass of consumers where the individual was exalted. Thus strikes were often as bitterly denounced from within the working class as from without: a strike of one section inhibited the ability of others to consume. And the fact that today's complainants were often tomorrow's strikers seemed in no way inconsistent – nor was it in the circumstances. To the extent that one group of workers could affect the ability to consume of other groups, the others had little choice but to emulate them if they wanted to retrieve their situation.

That the working class was divided into a large number of competing sectional groups meant that working-class organisations had failed to overcome *politically* what were *economic* facts. This is to say that sectionalism was the direct outcome of a labour market differentiated by industry, by variations among firms within industries, and by the division of labour within particular workplaces. The product of a division of labour, labour was accordingly divided within itself. While in general terms geographically scattered groups of workers had similar sorts of problems, the problems of any specific group were unique. They were bound in time, revolved around particular people, and were confined to a particular workplace or section within it. Thus while the division of labour within the national labour market ensured sectionalism between broad industrial groups, the division of labour in a workplace ensured sectionalism between groups housed under the same roof. As Clack said of a Midlands car factory: '. . . a sense of solidarity amongst workers in the factory was of a tenuous, limited, or even grudging kind. There were attitudes or feelings not merely of apathy but of antipathy towards other groups of workers.'[2]

It is not difficult to see why this should have been the case, especially in large plants where work groups were isolated from each other and did different sorts of work for different rates of pay. With respect to everyday working, the problems of the boilermakers in a shipyard were not those of the fitter, any more than were those of the face-worker in a pit the problems of the surface-worker. The strongest loyalties therefore attached to the work group and were there enforceable by the social processes within it. Loyalty across groups within a plant was much more fragile and was dependent for its achievement over a much narrower range of issues such as increases on basic pay, the dismissal of a mate, or general redundancy. Solidarity across industries was even more fragile – indeed, almost surprising. Yet it did occur, and with no little frequency. Sympathetic strikes, the blacking of goods by one group of workers on behalf of another's dispute, collection of monies for strikers, assistance on picket lines – all were as familiar features of the industrial scene in the seventies as they were in the 1900s, and were nothing if not manifestations of class solidarity.

Sympathetic action or support of varying kinds was of course dependent upon the extent to which one group of workers could capture the emotional identification of others. And that identification was in turn dependent upon whether or not the specific issues could be seen as potentially threatening to workers everywhere. Since workers characteristically thought of their collective strength primarily in trade union terms, few things were better calculated to mobilise inter-industry solidarity than issues related to union bargaining power. An excellent illustration of this was the aftermath of the imprisonment of the five London dockers for contempt of court in the summer of 1972. The day before their imprisonment London dockers and lorry drivers – all members of the same union – were involved in an unusually bitter sectional dispute. Picketing dockers were turning away lorries from container terminals. This hit at the livelihoods of the lorry drivers, so they in turn picketed the docks in retaliation. But on the day that the dockers were imprisoned the lorry drivers called off their pickets and announced their support for the dockers: what had been a family quarrel had developed into a threat to trade unionism and that demanded a closing of the ranks no matter what the differences. Broadly comparable action during the miners' strike in the late winter of 1972 had been effective in seeing it through to a successful conclusion. The miners were seen as a low-paid group of workers who had a legitimate claim for a large pay rise, but who were being resisted by government. Other workers who suffered because of the strike – power-cuts led to lay-offs and dislocated domestic routines – nevertheless contributed heavily to the miners' strike funds, helped man their picket lines, and cut off supplies of oil to the power stations. Once again an external threat brought to life a limited form of class consciousness.

Sympathetic action did not contradict the general tendency toward sectional action. On the contrary, it was an extension of it. If the immediate basis of sectional action in a work group was a highly specific grievance, the context of that grievance was part of the general conflict between employer and worker. It was, so to speak, a 'miniature' example of the fundamentally hostile relationship between labour and capital in which only collective action by labour had any prospect of success. Thus the first and very quickly learned lesson of workers was that their only strength lay in unity: a unity of themselves *against* employers or their shop-floor agents. Now although the lesson was learned in localised situations of some intimacy where all the principal actors on stage were familiar figures, it could still provide the basis of generalisation to other *unfamiliar* situations because its essential feature was the alien character of 'them' – the bosses, the gaffers. Workers could, that is to say, generalise from their own bosses to other people's. They might have talked about good bosses and bad bosses, but bosses were bosses for all that. It was precisely because working-class consciousness was boss-orientated that given the appropriate issues, i.e. those that challenged its ability to act collectively, it could apparently explode the limitations of trade unionism pure and simple and *unconsciously* engage in activity of considerable political moment.

Once workers went beyond the boundaries of the workplace trade unionism that they knew and understood, they had then moved into the arena of national politics of which they had little practice or understanding. They accordingly became reliant on such national institutions as they had – the trade union secretariats, the Labour Party, and to a much more limited extent the Communist Party. Since all three had developed techniques of working within the established order and no workable strategy for going beyond it, upsurges of militancy from the base were promptly confined and constrained to the known and accepted paths and patterns of that order. This often gave rank and file activists and many of their constituents cause to complain of having been 'sold out': little appreciating that working within the system meant, by definition, making compromises with it. The complaint was usually false. What 'selling out' most typically meant (blatant cases of treachery apart) was that opinions differed as to what was a 'reasonable' compromise. That labour leaders were ready to compromise rarely had anything to do with their political morality. Indeed most frequently it was, more than anything else, a reflection of the dilemma that mutually embraced both leaders and followers. It was a reflection on the one hand of the leadership's appreciation that the rank and file's horizons were mostly bound by the workplace, and that expressions of solidarity that occasionally went beyond them were responses to specific

'. . . upsurges of militancy from the base were promptly
confined and constrained . . .'

issues rather than to far-reaching political principles. It was a reflection on the other hand of the inability of the political leaders to generate perspectives that indicated alternatives to piecemeal politics. When it came down to it leaders and led alike looked at the world through the same blinkered spectacles.

Labour and capital: the contradiction

In 1972 there were some eleven million trade union members, a small fraction of whom experienced that membership as being part of a social movement. Indeed the vast majority not only did not see themselves as members of a movement, but did not vest a great deal of loyalty in the various unions either. 'Apathy' was a much-used term by trade union activists at all levels – and invariably deplored right from the earliest days. The people who minded the union machines were as much minorities as those who ran governments and political parties. Apathy was built-in in a number of ways – almost to the extent that it was a self-fulfilling prophecy. Few unions owned their own meeting-halls, and those that did could not have coped with a 50% turnout; union journals did not have a saturation circulation (in 1963 only one out of the eighteen largest TUC unions produced as many copies as members); if by the 1970s larger numbers of workers played some part in the negotiating process (by having the opportunity to vote on agreements), still larger numbers were presented with agreements as a *fait accompli*. Generally then, participation was neither expected nor demanded.

It was interesting that in popular speech unions were talked of as though they were something separate from the workers' experience, as if there were a clear distinction between membership and the continuing organisation of officials and union offices. This was a recognition of a reality, for as a general rule rank and file loyalty was to the principle of trade unionism rather than to trade unions as organisations. Trade unions as such were merely institutional expressions of the felt need for collective action in the workplace. Thus, because they existed independently of any particular workplace, they took on the features of an external organisation. With their conception of trade unionism as being the practice of solidarity in the work group or workplace, they could look upon the trade unions with a jaundice akin to that of a Tory backbencher. Looking upon trade unions as large, impersonal, national organisations that at no visible point touched upon their daily experience, they could and did appear as *almost* alien and sometimes threatening.

In one respect the unions were little more than loose federations of a very large number of sectional interests which, at their most general, were occupational groups, and at their most specific, work groups of perhaps no more than a dozen men. Most unions took into membership a wide range of occupations and, of course, an infinitely wider range of work groups. This diversity inevitably gave to those who ran the union machine as full-time officers an allegiance not shared by the bulk of the membership. Where the members were mainly interested in the union only to the extent that it touched upon their own specific interests, the full-time officer, while looking to particular membership group interests, had also to assess those in terms of overall union strategies. The officials, furthermore, lived a life that was not that of their members. Their world was the world of negotiation and internal union politics. Although objectively it was directly related to the world of the shop-floor, as a species of subjective experience it was altogether very different from the intimacies of life and labour in the place of work. Two things thus combined to give the members a picture of the union as something separate and distinct: on the one hand the workers' interest in the unions as an expression of sectional interest, on the other the actual organisational mechanics of institutional life in the trade union secretariat.

This separateness was frequently enhanced by the ability of the union member to look upon the union's activities as a complete outsider. Since the union was central to him only insofar as it directly impinged upon his specific affairs, when he read his newspaper and watched television news broadcasts about what his union was doing with respect to other groups of workers he read and watched as an outsider. Cut off from his fellow trade unionists in other industries by lack of knowledge and the absence of a coalescing political philosophy, he tended to assess them and his union through the subtle tones of judgement implicit in mass media communications. He tended therefore to look at the actions of other workers and the unions in terms of how they affected him personally (the media invariably discussed industrial action of varying kinds in terms of its effects on other workers and on consumers generally; i.e. industrial reportage was always conducted in tones of regret). Over any extended period of time any one group of workers would rarely attempt to draw on union support for industrial action (with the obvious exceptions of carworkers and dockers), but his media-gained knowledge of events elsewhere would teach him that hardly a week would go by in which his union was not involved with other workers. He would get the impression, that is to say, that his union was continuously involved in action with respect to *other* workers – and in the pursuit of interests that could be seen as running counter to his own. There was then an ever-present tendency to look on other workers' disputes through the eyes of the consumer rather than through the eyes of a fellow worker. That the unions were only doing – or more accurately *appeared* to be doing – what their members required of them, namely separately pursuing their separate interests, could pass almost unnoticed. So concentrated was the worker's consciousness on local economic issues, that the one enduring instrument of working-class unity could at times actually appear foreign and alien.

Apathy then was certainly built-in; not just institutionally in the ways outlined above. Nor for the reasons commonly produced by union activists of all political persuasions – the boring nature of most union business at the branch; the rival attractions of telly and the pub; the 'natural' tendency for interest to be confined to a minority; the need of leadership for a passive rank and file so that it could more easily insulate itself from challenge from below. These factors, though relevant, were only marginally so. The guts of the matter, the basic and underlying reason for apathy, lay elsewhere. It lay in what Huw Beynon called 'factory consciousness': a factory class consciousness

. . . understands class relationships in terms of their direct manifestation in conflict between the bosses and the workers within the factory. It is rooted in the workplace where struggles are fought over the control of the job and the 'rights' of managers and workers. In as much as it concerns itself with exploitation and power it contains definite political elements. But it is a politics of the factory. Implicitly tied up with the day-to-day battle with the boss.[3]

While virtually all workers were possessed of this way of thinking to some degree or other, it was the rank and file leaders who carried it most articulately, who really carried it in the marrow of their bones. It was they who were at the forefront of shop-floor struggles. It was they who were in a position to most thoroughly comprehend the finely-meshed web of management politics. And their role as leader at once entailed and required that they acted as the rank and file's shield. Thus, while the general circumstances of life on the shop-floor ensured the production and reproduction of a factory consciousness, the actual pattern of workers' organisation inhibited its fullest expression among the rank and file. In a situation where it was *possible* for their own leaders, the shop stewards, to appear remote, it was an easy matter to regard the unions as things apart from their members.

Apathy was a common-sense explanation for the rank and file's apparent lack of interest. And like most common-sense 'explanations' it was not an explanation at all. Common sense alights on the obvious, delights in the cliché – and deplores explorations that tunnel under the surface of things. It gives psychological 'explanations' for things that cannot be explained in terms of personal characteristics. Common sense is a refusal to come to terms with the social and political. It is a refusal to see that what appear as personal shortcomings are in fact merely individual representations of defects in the way the social environment is organised. In the particular case in question apathy was an elementary consequence of the mode of consciousness to which trade unionism inevitably gave rise. Trade unionism was rooted, fundamentally based even, in a factory consciousness. And that was a way of looking at the world that pointed to certain definite ways of coping with the world – ways of coping that could not but fail to generate passivity.

Certainly a factory consciousness tended to generate passivity. Certainly it tended to generate sectionalism. Yet it must be emphasised that they were only *tendencies*. There were, as we have seen, circumstances in which the tendencies could be stood on their heads, circumstances in which workers united as workers rather than fought each other as consumers. If consciousness of class was weak in the sense of a collective will to political action, there remained class sentiments. And prominently featured amongst them was the sentiment that the unions, no matter what their deficiencies, were still in the last resort for 'us'. This was most well-advertised in the case of the huge demonstrations against the Industrial Relations Act in 1970 and 1971, and the TUC's threat of a one-day general strike in the summer of 1972 in protest at the imprisonment of dockers who had infringed the Act. It was also well-advertised in much less obvious ways. Disaffection with a union's conduct was typically followed, not by 'feet-voting', but by desertion to another union or, in extreme cases, by the formation of breakaway unions: both being forms of action indicating that disaffection was with a particular union and *not* with the principle of trade unionism. Desertions and breakaways were indeed very positive affirmations of the deeply felt need amongst workers for the protection of trade unionism.

These latter cases, i.e. of desertions and breakaways, merely demonstrated the most limited aspect of a factory class consciousness: its rootedness in an understanding of the need for a collectivity of 'us' the workers to confront the collectivity of 'them' the bosses. The former cases on the other hand, i.e. of political demonstrations and of threatened massive sympathy strikes, pointed to ways in which the 'us' and 'them' consciousness of the workplace could point to a class consciousness of a more developed form. On those occasions when the State made blatantly obvious attempts to curtail the working class's only organised power base, it was relatively easy for workers in separate workplaces to generalise from their own boss to all bosses and mobilise accordingly. On questions of trade unionism the working class could organise itself for mass action, for the class had the necessary organisations and was equipped with the necessary sentiments. Opposition to other attacks on the class were most likely to crumble (as for example in the story of the implementation of the 'pay freeze' in 1972–73), for on the broader political front the class had no appropriate organisations.

The rank and file on the shop floor

In respect of the rank and file's claims on union resources the variations were as wide as those among industries and firms. Some groups of workers, often for quite long periods of time, made remarkably few calls on their union's resources. Agreements were drawn up periodically and that was the end of the matter, except perhaps for the odd call to pursue a claim for accident compensation. Other groups of workers called disproportionately on the union's services. They used up more of the strike fund, consumed more of the officials' time, and had more officials attendant upon them. In the Transport Workers Union for example the carworkers and dockers were much more 'expensive' than the members who worked in chemicals and electrical supply. In fact, given that at any moment resources were fixed, and that some groups of workers were strategically better placed to use collective action effectively, the inequitable distribution of resources between membership groups was primarily determined by factors outside union control.

The importance of the union to the rank and file depended upon the general conditions of the industry in which the latter worked. If the industry was in the process of rapid decline, rapid technical change, or unusually prone to variations in output with fluctuations in market demand, then the union tended to assume a more than ordinary significance. Where social factors, such as the communal solidarity of miners, and political factors, such as the ability of dockers and power workers to affect the overall workings of the national economy, were overlaid upon the more basic economic considerations, union activity became a more or less continuing object of concern. In exceptional cases where the union organised in isolated single-industry communities, it may even have become the fulcrum of community life. Listen to Will Paynter who talked of the South Wales Miners in the thirties:

. . . It was a lot more than a trade union ; it was a social institution providing through its local leaders an all-round service of advice and assistance to the mining community on most of the problems that could arise between the cradle and the grave. Its function became a combination of economic, social and political leadership . . . After all, these communities existed in narrow valley concentrations, were dependent upon a pit for their existence, and were tightly bound together by this common interest. The leaders of the local miners' lodges were very much more than representatives dealing with problems of wages and conditions of employment in the mines. They were acknowledged social leaders called upon to help and advise in all kinds of domestic and social problems ; they were indeed the village elders to whom people went when in any kind of trouble.[4]

This sort of situation was, and to the extent that it still remains is, unique. The modern car factory, by comparison, was the complete antithesis. Typically situated in, or on the fringe of, a densely populated urban area, drawing its workers from anywhere within a twenty-mile radius and organised by a number of unions with different practices, the unity of the pit village was a blank impossibility. The same applied of course to virtually all occupations. Although many working-class urban areas did develop a distinctive ethos partially based on common occupations, there remained occupational diversities within them and too many links with adjacent areas to allow trade unionism to develop into a form of 'local government'. The unity of the workplace was dissolved into its constituent atoms at the gates.

The sheer variety of the range of economic, social, and political factors meant that at any moment there were a large number of permutations of possible rank and file relationships to their unions. It also meant that over a *period* of time the same groups of workers could experience a range of different relationships. In the 1930s for instance, London Transport workers were never far from the thoughts of the Transport Workers Union while carworkers rarely obtruded; in the 1930s, for instance, London Transport workers fact that a section of workers might be the continuing object of the union leadership's interest did not necessarily mean that the interest was reciprocated, for full employment often meant that the rank and file was able to cope with its own affairs. In situations of relative labour scarcity many agreements and disputes would be settled at the workplace without them ever coming to the attention of the union secretariats. Only in the case of intractable disputes were union officials drawn in as a sort of long-stop. Thus Clack could say: '(Full-time officials) were rarely observed at the factory, and almost never on the shop-floor. Most factory workers probably saw their union officials only at strike meetings – at which it was more likely that they were being exhorted by the officials to return to work . . .'[5] The union official then could be cast in the role of the meddling outsider who wanted to play policeman. An important part of the 'training' of every union official was going through the experience of being jeered, cursed, and shouted down at meetings of angry strikers. In other words, at times when the rank and file needed their unions most they could appear to be alien in *fact* by urging an unpopular course of action on their members.

Quite apart from the general processes working to drive a fissure between the rank and file and the people of the union machines, there were others rather more specific. The rank and file experienced the consequences of the sale of its labour power at the point of production in highly *specific* situations. The union experienced its members' sale of labour power in a quite separate and different way. The rank and file worked in a particular place, for a particular wage, under a particular system of supervision. The way that wage was made up – so much overtime, so much bonus etc. – was, in its detail, unique. If in outline that wage was largely determined by national negotiations, the traditional customs and practices of that workplace ensured that in subtle (or not so subtle) ways it differed from other workplaces even if they were engaged in producing, extracting, or refining the same commodity. The same went for supervision. If it was widely accepted that in principle the foremen and supervisors were bosses' men, tradition ensured that the way the principle was expressed and experienced varied both within and across industries and between plants owned by the same company. It was for those reasons that a worker new to a workplace could not immediately feel 'at home': he had to learn 'the way things are done here'. In short, while labour power in itself was freely transferable, the social knowledge and skills that were associated with its exercise were not.

The trade union by comparison was much less concerned with particular circumstances, and much more with generalisations. The trade union wanted to create categories, or slot 'particular circumstances' into categories that already existed. Simultaneously, the union was aware that not all particularities could be totally generalised. It acknowledged the necessity of recognising areas of discretion, some of which it would attempt to control loosely, others of which it would remain quite ignorant. In any event most discretionary areas inevitably evaded union control. They were so numerous, varied and complex that they were only susceptible to supervision if the shop stewards were rigidly tied into the union machine; the rank and file were mere automata; and management prepared to sign agreements that tied their first line supervision to detailed formulae of labour 'control'.

The ultimate concern of both union and rank and file was of course identical. Both wanted to maximise the price of labour power and the conditions under which that labour was utilised. But the manner in which this concern was articulated diverged. The union attempted to regulate the price of labour power alone; the rank and file wanted additionally to regulate the amount of effort expended and workplace discipline. The union's *general* concern with price entailed treating labour power in the abstract. The rank and file's additional concern with *particularities* – because it, rather than the union, was the embodiment of labour power – meant that its disposal, far from being abstract, was an intimate part of its life experience. The upshot of this discrepancy was that the range of what the rank and file considered legitimate was wider than the range considered legitimate by the union.* For the union, wage issues were eminently legitimate because they lent themselves to negotiations in abstract arithmetical terms. Issues related to managerial authority could not be reduced to pounds and pence and tended therefore not to be negotiated. (Since 1898 agreements between the Engineers and the Engineering Employers Federation contained clauses to the effect that the 'union accepts managerial prerogatives'.) This did not mean that unions regarded managerial questions as illegitimate in principle: it was merely a recognition that the

*Long-standing exceptions to this generalisation were the craft unions in the shipbuilding industry: they had, since the nineteenth century, entered into agreements which specified in detail which workers were to do which jobs. The generalisation was further undermined with the advent of 'productivity bargaining' on a wide scale in the 1960s: they were attempts to buy off traditional customs and practices.

subtle patterns of plant politics were not amenable to closely worded agreements. It was thus tacitly recognised by the unions that managerial issues were subjects for rank and file negotiation. It could not have been otherwise – unless the unions had been attacking the entire fabric of capitalism – since the rank and file alone was in a position to understand the nuances of workplace politics. Yet workplace politics did not revolve *only* around questions of authority, for authority did not exist for its own sake. Authority was about work arrangements, about how to extract the maximum return for the wage. Disputes over supervisory matters were essentially disputes as to who should decide what amount of labour power was required in return for a given wage.

The labour force in any workplace was sectionalised by the dictates of technology, and management's need for political control, into groups that developed their own different customs and practices. Most workers in large establishments had little or no opportunity to move around, and did not as a rule work periodically in different sections: their intimate knowledge of plant politics was thus confined to its effects on the affairs of their own sections. Even in the works canteen men did not readily mix with other workers from other sections. Very few workers then were in any position to have the knowledge relevant to an understanding of the political system of the entire workplace as distinct from the politics of their own sections. For their knowledge of 'foreign affairs' they were dependent upon the 'bush telegraph' and their links with other workers who were mobile – foremen and supervisors, shop stewards and maintenance men. This isolation of workers was superbly described by Peter Currell Brown in his novel *Smallcreep's Day*:

I had worked here in this section of the factory for sixteen years; and yet in all that time I had not been very far from my machines in any direction. There was never any need to, you see; besides, we were busy and I had never had the time. Some of the men, I know, found important-looking pieces of paper from time to time in the wastebins and would go walking off carrying them, to show anyone who might stop them. They often came back with strange stories of what they had seen in various parts of the factory, and one or two never came back at all.

Given this isolation and the differences as between sections in job content, it was well-nigh inevitable that sectional interests were what mostly activated the rank and file. Because the focus of interest was on the job there was a built-in centrifugal tendency for different groups of workers to fly-off in pursuit of their own specific claims. It was neither grotesque nor irrational. It was the reverse. Given the nature of the work environment and the tendency of the unions to deal in generalities, it was perfectly logical for sectional groups to take independent action.

Sectional action was not however merely a part of the continuing process of work group politics, a process sealed-off from other processes: broader economic and political considerations intruded upon it. Miners were affected by government fuel and wage policies; carworkers and building workers were affected by government credit policies; shipyard workers were affected by the level of world trade. These 'impersonal' forces were interpreted by employers until their effects reached right down to the smallest group of workers. The differential operation and impact of those forces over time, and between industries and firms, meant that the 'mood' of the component forces of the rank and file varied similarly.

The rank and file then was never in a continuous state of ferment. The readiness to follow a course of militant action at a sectional level was most typically dependent on a 'crisis'. Although there were no fixed definitions of what consituted a crisis that were applicable to all groups of workers, in very general terms potential crises existed whenever changes occurred in work arrangements. Such changes were usually attempted when employers were subject to pressures on profit margins. Thus the motor industry, for example, because it produced a commodity particularly prone to variations in demand, had groups of workers going through a cycle of crisis which closely followed the cyclical demand for cars. This suggested that the market-induced crisis entailed militant action of a defensive kind – a holding action against intrusions into work practices established at some previous point on the cycle. The motor industry was peculiarly prone to such crises for few other industries were subject to such a short cycle of change. The rapidity of change made it extremely difficult for workers to develop any great sense of security in their control over work practices – which meant that they were never for long too distant from the threshold of crisis. What had been gained at one point on the cycle soon came under attack on another.[6]

Employment not subject to rapid change was much less susceptible to sectional militancy. If some workers were brought to the threshold of crisis by the advent of new managers or foremen anxious to justify their appointments, generally speaking the customs and practices of work arrangements were well understood and respected by workers and supervisors in stable industries. Nevertheless, since custom and practice was never fixed and always changing, there remained areas of potential dispute at what C. L. Goodrich called the 'frontier of control'.[7] Frontier issues were the customs and practices of the future. They were the issues where legitimacy remained to be fixed, where the rank and file took a tentative, experimental step forward in enlarging the area of control over work arrangements.

Frontier issues arose in all branches of industry, although their liability to give rise to disputes largely depended on how questions external to the workplace affected daily life within it. A declining industry – unless it remained of strategic importance – was likely to have a demoralised labour force unwilling to fight on almost any issue. Industries sheltered from external pressures by their absolute indispensability – such as the public utilities – tended to be relatively undisturbed in respect of their 'ways of doing things'. Other industries – such as chemicals and refining – though subject to bursts of technical change, were saved from dispute by their near monopolistic structures and a history of secure employment. Even so, events of the 1960s and early 1970s showed that hitherto undisturbed areas could be quickly transformed.

Attempts at national regulation of wages and a growing rate of inflation started to draw in, in pursuit of pay increases, workers once known for their quietude – action which had unforeseen consequences for workplace politics: wage militancy gave rise to cost militancy which meant tightening up on labour practices. In some cases cost militancy preceded any show of militancy from the workers. Local authorities, confronted by rising costs and the political unpopularity of rate increases, looked for ways of reducing expenditure. Thus corporation dustmen had their well-regulated routines turned upside down by the introduction of job evaluation and bonus incentive schemes. These opened up to dustmen what had previously been closed to them: the possibility of sectional wage bargaining and an enlarged role for shop stewards.

Cost militancy by employers and wage militancy by workers were both disruptive of workplace practices in a widening range of industry. When, after the 1970 strike, Pilkington workers and managers alike said that 'things would never be the same again' they meant that well-established practices and attitudes would be reviewed. There was no reason for supposing that in

TUMUS —G

that respect there was anything unique about Pilkingtons. A strike in a workplace hitherto free from large-scale dispute did more than merely halt production. The longer it lasted the less was the likelihood that the old political system would survive untouched in the 'new era' heralded by the end of the strike. On the other hand, there were no forces at work to ensure that the new systems of plant politics were any less sectional than the old. New systems meant new issues and new struggles – but on the same basis as before. Labour was still labour and capital still capital. With the collective consciousness of labour largely confined to the work situation, and with trade union structures reinforcing that confinement, everything seemed to change – yet everything seemed to stay the same.

6. The Shop Steward: The Man with Two Masters

This is the shop steward's dilemma, he always has two masters. He has the employer, who can use all sorts of undetectable victimisation that doesn't necessarily mean dismissal, and he has to satisfy the members.

Hugh Scanlon, in an interview with New Left Review 1967

Who is the worst paid man today?
With haggard look and hair turned grey,
Who's blamed when things do not go right
Who gets no rest by day or night?
Though never having been to college
He must possess the widest knowledge
On rates of pay and hours of labour
And how to keep peace with ones neighbour.
Of income tax and how to pay it,
What's best to say, and when to say it,
The how and why and which and when
Of all the problems known to men.
If with the foreman he's agreed
He's sold the men or been weak-kneed.
When for the men he tries to cater
He's called a blinking agitator.
Who is this chap? What! Don't you know him?
Or how much you really owe him?
This chap, whose torment is assured,
Is no one else than your SHOP STEWARD!

Anon[1]

Trade unions did not invent shop stewards – indeed if anything it was men very much like them who invented the trade unions. H. A. Turner has remarked that in many ways the early cotton unions were very much like the unofficial shop steward organisations of a good hundred years later: 'There is the same basis in the workplace group . . . There is the same federal superstructure – the shop stewards forming the local committee, the represenatives of local committees forming the "movement". And there is the same use of "delegates" to communicate with other groups, and particularly to canvass support for local strikes.'[2] If this was so in the first years of modern trade unionism from 1800 to 1850, it was equally true of the two phases of 'new unionism' in the period 1889 to 1914. Where many of the CIO unions of the USA were essentially created by large organisational drives financed by existing unions from the centre, *all* British unions of any importance – with the exception of the Workers Union – grew out of spontaneous rank and file activity. Although 'outsiders' were often influential in transforming rank and file movements into permanent organisations, the initial impetus came from rank and file leaders, the latter-day equivalents of the shop stewards.

With the growing concentration of capital in the third quarter of the nineteenth century, the creation of the national firm, and the large-scale bureaucratised workplace, the trade unions moved in parallel to create their own national organisations. Trade unionism ceased to be a local affair officered by men who worked by day at the bench or machine. Its organisation grew away from the workplace and the locality as it added new tiers to its superstructure. But what it necessarily left behind at the point of production were the same sentiments and the same sort of men who in previous generations had set the national organisations on the road. The local leaders, where they were not full-time officers of the new national unions, acted as spokesmen for the men on the job, ran the local branches, collected subs and, when circumstances were right, led the men out on strike. The shop steward of the latter half of the twentieth century did precisely the same things. He may have been more sophisticated than his forebearers, he may have had a formally defined place in the hierarchy of union organisation, he may have had a bargaining strength that would have been the envy of his ancestors, but the substance of his position remained what it had always been.

The 'shop steward', even if he was not always called that, existed wherever men worked together. As late as the 1960s there were strikes of men and women in workplaces untouched by trade unionism. Who led those strikes? The ubiquitous shop steward. When observers said that for the rank and file the shop steward was the union, they were saying more than they realised. The very guts of trade unionism was the loyalty and solidarity of the workplace. It was that which the shop steward expressed.

Up in front where the action is

Whatever power the shop steward had he drew from his position as an articulator and tutor of rank and file aspirations. His ability to *use* that power depended on economic factors outside his control. *How* that power was exercised depended on the political sophistication of the shop steward, his constituents, full-time union officials, and not least the managers with whom he came into contact. The shop steward, in short, was the point at which a number of conflicting pressures converged. The rank and file pressed him to resolve their grievances; management pressed him to contain his members' grievances; union officials also pressed him to control his members – though for different reasons than managers. The shop steward therefore was simultaneously a rank and file leader, an unpaid personnel manager, and an agent for his union.

'You can go just as far as they'll let you' was a
characteristic summary by shop stewards of their
relationship to their members. And as a summary it
was accurate enough – although the bald statement
concealed a considerable complexity that at once con-
firmed it and gave it the lie. A shop steward was not
a leader in the military sense that he could give orders
and expect unquestioning obedience. On the contrary his leadership was always on trial and open to
question. Yet if he could lead only to the extent that
the led acquiesced, he was in a position to influence
what it was that the led would find acceptable.

The shop steward was not the sort of leader typical
of systems of 'representative democracy' as manifested
in parliaments. He did not, once elected, pack his bags
and move off to carry out his representational duties
in an institution alien to the experiences of his constituents. Neither was his constituency so large that
he could remain personally anonymous to the overwhelming majority of his electors (the average constituency was of the order of sixty people).[3] The
steward spent the bulk of his time at work alongside
those who had elected him, although some of his constituents were more remote than others since his
electorate usually straddled several work groups rather
than being based on one. Still, he was highly visible,
subject to the same experiences at work as his
comrades, and subject to the same group pressures.
He would be watched in his dealings with the foreman
or supervisor. Not a few stewards took the precaution
of having a fellow worker with them when it was
necessary to 'go upstairs'.

The steward had no *power* over his members
because he had no sanctions at his command, no
ability to coerce. Such authority as he had was ceded to
him by virtue of his performance both as a steward
and as a member of the group. His authority in other
words was a function of his possession of a range of

skills relevant to the group, and his general social acceptability: this could mean in some circumstances that while he was nominally shop steward, he had very little authority. Hence the common expression 'you can go as far as they'll let you'. Authority was not a fixed lump of social capital in the sense that once accumulated it was thereafter indestructible. Like physical capital it had to be continually replenished if it was to remain 'valuable'.

The steward's capital – his skills – derived from his personal style and from his possession of knowledge not readily available to his members. Each was as important as the other. Style was summed up in the phrase 'he's one of us': it was important for the steward that he embodied and acted upon the sentiments and morals valued by his members. The more complete his expression the greater his authority. He had to be free from the taint of personal ambition because social striving was not part of the culture of his members; he could not be a 'rate buster' or a 'money-grabber' for that would separate him from the group ethic of the 'fair wage'; he could not be on close and intimate terms with foremen and supervisors for that violated the morality of 'us' and 'them' and roused suspicions of betrayal – 'if with the foreman he's agreed, he's sold the men or been weak-kneed'; variations in taste and life-style were tolerated, but only within the limits set by the current standards. Political tolerance was high, for strongly held left-wing political convictions were no barrier to election as steward, though they remained an object of suspicion: a left-winger's recommendations would be scrutinised for indications of 'political' motivation. As for the world at large so for the rank and file – only those who wanted drastic changes in the world were 'political'.

The qualities of style determined who emerged as shop steward and reflected upon whatever continuing allegiance he enjoyed. But style alone was not enough. The steward was the main link with other workers in the same workplace and with the world of trade unionism at large. His contacts with first-line supervisors, works and personnel management, other shop stewards, and the inhabitants of the union organisation gave him a breadth of knowledge and experience quite outside the ken of his members. He acted, so to speak, as the rank and file's translator and interpreter. Sometimes almost literally, as Fox suggested:

The shop steward may try to prevent direct communication between management and the individual worker, for this can separate the individual from group norms and values. He may suggest that as the men's representative he should always mediate between management and men. His interest in this arrangement may derive not only from a concern with his own status and functions, but also from the fact that, in order to pursue his . . . obligation as leader and sustainer of group action and solidarity, he needs to screen all communication so that his members perceive it in terms of group norms.[4]

Or, to put it less obscurely, the steward knew – by virtue of his experience in workplace politics – that managerial jargon had to be deciphered and statements of intent translated into their consequences for the workers.

What the steward learned was not merely information, but what that information meant in the context of that labyrinth of compromise and tacit agreements that constituted the political system of the workplace. 'Messages' from management necessarily required translation for they would be read 'cold' by the rank and file and, because of the latter's isolation, would be read in terms of what it meant for them in their separate groups. Management's communications did not so much individualise workers as potentially create divisions (or exacerbate existing ones) between work groups. From the shop steward's point of view management communications were less threatening for their propensity to atomise the workers than for their tendency to sectionalise them.* It was an unsophisticated works manager who did not know the meaning of 'divide and rule' – and it was an even more unsophisticated shop steward who did not recognise a divisive tactic when he saw one. As Carl Dreyfuss, a sociologist, put it with a bluntness unusual for one of his trade: 'The employer is fundamentally interested in preventing the employees of his enterprise from confronting him as a homogeneous group. He attempts to undermine and split their strength through minute subdivision and differentiation.'[5]

It was also possible for the shop steward, to the extent that he was prepared to be a social worker, to be an unwitting cause of fragmentation. The range of 'services' that shop stewards, taken as a whole, were prepared to perform for their members was extraordinary. Tax problems, marital problems, problems with the kids, problems with the school, troubles with HP, the mortgage, the Social Security – name the problem, and the odds were that in a large plant there were always stewards prepared to advise on it and a host of other problems. Their main role as social workers however was inside the workplace: helping out with a spot of form-filling, wage calculation, fixing an hour or so off work for a trip to the dentist or the doctor. Trivial things in themselves but nonetheless important to the individual.

To the extent that the steward was prepared to help out with such questions – and some were not (on the

* Only in the course of a strike would stewards be concerned about the atomising effects of managerial communications to individual workers. Strikes isolated workers in their own homes, cut them off from the *natural* communal pressures of the workplace, and rendered them prone to the 'individual approach'. That was why mass meetings were an indispensable part of strikes. They were reaffirmations of a *community* of interest and of the axiom 'united we stand'.

grounds that group issues were what they were in business for) – he could earn himself the reputation of a 'fixer'. He could become, in certain areas of concern, an expert, the man to go and see, a secular curate who took pride in his 'pastoral' role. There were dangers attendant upon this assumption of the role of kindly uncle – even though there were powerful arguments for the necessity of shop floor counsellors with their roots in the working class. The dangers were two-fold. Insofar as a steward emphasised his 'pastoral' work it led him into a tendency to see issues in personal terms: problems were seen as attributes of individuals rather than as consequences of the order of things. In short, the steward's focus could shift from the collective to the personal. And such a shift could, on critical occasions, amount to unilateral disarmament in the face of an opponent wielding a heavy stick. The other dangerous tendency was that the greater the steward's proficiency as an 'expert' the higher his reputation with his constituents. And that reputation could considerably distance him from the rank and file, enlarge his area of autonomy from group pressures, and ultimately lead to wheelings and dealings with management without any secure basis where it counted. Still, there were other and more important factors that could work to set the steward apart.

The shop steward, through his wider knowledge of workplace politics, was usually in a better position to spell out the causes and consequences of conditions and prospective actions. He could situate sectional concerns in the overall context of the workplace and therefore assess the effects of sectional action for it. He was, that is to say, better equipped to judge the effectiveness of a proposal and to advocate one course rather than another. The shop steward was thus an important barrier to sectional action even if he was not always successful. It did not follow that his recommendations would be uncritically accepted. Well-tried and trusted shop stewards often found themselves left behind by the militancy of their members – or out in front on their own. Industry was littered with the 'corpses' of stewards who, on finding themselves in one of those situations, were unable to retrieve their leadership or decided that it wasn't worth the bother. Hence what H. A. Turner called the 'unofficial-unofficial' strike: '. . . the strike, that is, which has not merely the normal quality that it is not approved by the official union hierarchy, but is particularly not first approved by the shop stewards' leader.'[6]

While the shop steward's ability to influence the thinking of his members was the outcome of his wider involvement in workplace affairs, that very same involvement could at the same time work so as to cut him off from his constituents. Where the steward was engaged in workplace politics to a degree that kept him away from his section, his ability to limit the sectional activity of his members was decreased. It was in that situation that the rank and file was most volatile. On the one hand the extent of the steward's involvement with the workplace as a whole caused him to most favour action that involved the entire work-force, i.e. the sort of action least willingly engaged upon by the rank and file. On the other hand his relative lack of involvement with the section meant that 'shadow' stewards tended to emerge and that the rank and file were more likely to launch into an independent course of action. Experienced stewards were of course well aware of their knife-edge position – but were never able to avoid it entirely.

Effective workplace trade unionism necessitated a form of organisation that went beyond coalitions between a small number of work groups – though these coalitions themselves were sources of strain. (The typical shop steward's constituency spread over several work groups, which meant that even the individual steward would be engaged in trying to balance a collection of potentially conflicting interests.) Everywhere there was a tendency to form shop stewards' committees which, in the words of H. A. Turner: '. . . assumed, in relation to managements on the one hand and the rank and file operatives on the other, many of the characteristics that the official unions once displayed under the earlier development of national or industry-wide collective bargaining.'[7] Without this parallel unionism, workplace trade unionism would have taken on the character of trade unionism nationally – the workplace would have been a mass of competing constituencies each going its own way without regard to the others. While that was roughly workable on a national scale, it was a recipe for disaster at plant level where strategically weak groups of workers could not so readily be ignored, and where the strong were not *so* strong that there were not times when they required the support of other groups. Further, in an integrated workplace, the actions of one group could have immediate and visible consequences for others. Thus joint shop stewards' committees emerged as a means of regulating the otherwise 'free market' of sectional groupings.

The committees, which in large workplaces could have over 100 members, constituted the arena in which attempts would be made to order priorities between competing claims. Shop stewards would learn about the problems of other groups, and receive reports from convenors and senior stewards on the current state of play on matters relating to dealings with management and national union policies. Here, too, long-term plant strategies were developed which in many cases eventually affected the bargaining strategies of national unions. As a member of the committee the individual steward acquired allegiances broader than those of his constituency and which could cut right across his primary ties with his electorate. This meant that the most militant of stewards could at times find himself urging moderation on his members. No wonder then that McCarthy and Parker found that 46% of works managers thought stewards to be *less* militant than their members and another 38% only thought them equally militant.[8] In the final analysis the steward's authority with the rank and file depended on his willingness to lead sectional action when no other course suggested itself and to hold it in check when it cut across committee policies. When therefore shop stewards said of their relationship to the rank and file 'you can go as far as they'll let you', they were thinking of those occasions when they sought to persuade their members to follow a course of action not specifically related to the interests of a group. There were other times when the group was prepared to go a good deal further than its steward.

Shop stewards and managers generally understood one another: 'Four-fifths of stewards thought their work was accepted willingly by managers, and three-quarters of managers thought stewards were efficient as workers' representatives.'[9] This did not mean that they liked each other – only that they came to an understanding. They had to. The employer's need for continuity of production or the provision of services and the shop steward's need for the resolution of workers' grievances meant that both became parties to definite sets of relationships. But they did not do so as equals. Indeed the relationship was inherently *un*equal. Tactical advantages shifted. A tight labour market and a crammed production schedule left the advantage with the shop steward if he was prepared to seize it. A slack production schedule made the employer cost-conscious and the workers fearful for the security of their jobs: vantage employer.

These were short-term considerations. In the long-run the initiative lay with the employer. His fundamental power advantage, as revealed in his capacity to innovate, was reflected in the workplace struggles and coloured the social relationships between the leading protagonists. The shop steward was an insurgent forever engaged in attempts to carve out pieces of territory owned and controlled by the employer. The latter therefore was the 'superior': he made the rules because he owned the instruments of production. The shop steward who tried to modify the rules was, in the last resort, the supplicant, for the livelihood of his members depended on their access to the instruments of production.

Ordinarily however the steward was not powerless – labour, one way or another, could and did place strong short-term checks on profit maximisation. Thus part of what was involved in profit maximising was minimising the resistance of labour. Since the steward was the workers' voice, shrewd employers sought to use him as an instrument of control over the rank and file.

Stewards perpetually sought minor concessions from management – concessions which they could afford to make without great expense and without upsetting anyone. But these were sometimes exactly the issues over which management could afford to be obstructive, for refusal was unlikely to provoke collective action. Unless the firm was exceptionally anti-steward, minor issues were likely to be conceded if the steward's approach was generally non-belligerent. Huw Beynon quoted a senior Ford executive:

It's difficult to say what type of steward does best for his members. A militant may well force a few concessions, but we'll always be waiting to get them back or to make life a bit difficult for him. While a quiet, more reasonable bloke may be less dramatic he'll probably get more for his members because if he's in any trouble we'll help him out. We make concessions to him that we wouldn't make to the other bloke.[10]

Many managements did indeed 'help out' stewards. Clegg noted that 'In one (Sheffield) firm the convenor('s) . . . occasional machine work is carried on for form's sake only, and to safeguard the management lest he should be succeeded by a Communist.'[11] Managements, of course, had a very direct interest in who they had to deal with and often did what they could to ensure they got the men defined by them as 'reasonable'. Concessions were made to stewards who had 'troublesome' members or who were being challenged at election time by someone management thought undesirable, and there were even cases where managers effectively appointed their own nominees to the steward's job. (The author found an instance at Pilkingtons where a shop steward, on being appointed foreman, was asked who his successor was likely to be. Replying that he did not know, it was suggested that X would be a suitable character. X was duly approached and appointed without an election!)

Promotion was a commonly used device for dividing stewards' loyalties.* In many firms it was well understood that service as a shop steward could be a prelude to promotion to foreman, chargehand, or personnel work. Harry Nicholas, acting-general secretary of the Transport Workers Union, told the 1964-68 Royal Commission on Trade Unions: '(We have a fairly high turnover of shop stewards) . . . because (once) they have displayed their abilities and possibilities the employers usually made them foremen. In other words they cream off the best of our shop stewards.'[13] Some particularly ambitious men no doubt became shop stewards with the conscious object of bringing themselves to the attention of management as suitable cases for promotion. Others, less consciously ambitious, would acquire a growing awareness of the possibilities and have hints dropped to them that 'good behaviour' would be rewarded. Either way, there was

*McCarthy and Parker found 45% of their sample of shop stewards were interested in promotion to managerial or first-line supervisory jobs. Only 10% thought service as a shop steward was any barrier.[12]

certainly a powerful incentive at work on aspiring men to accept management's definition of 'responsible' behaviour and act accordingly. This did not mean that a hefty proportion of shop stewards were morally corrupt – although other shop stewards and the rank and file might tend to look at it in that light. (Clack noted that when the works convenor of his car plant was promoted to Industrial Relations Officer: 'There was . . . some degree of indignation on the shop floor generally at the "defection" of the Industrial Relations officer, and a strong similar feeling amongst departmental stewards.'[14]) It was less a matter of 'corruption' and more a question of an under-developed class consciousness. In a society that defined personal achievement in terms of self-advancement in a hierarchy of power and prestige, it took an exceptionally tough and class-conscious character to resist managerial blandishments.

Less crude devices were also employed to co-opt shop stewards, especially convenors. Most large firms, and many not so large, provided convenors with offices, internal and external telephones, typing, duplicating, filing, and clerical services. And on top of that they paid him to devote all his time to union activities. In these respects the employers were making a virtue out of necessity – in those circumstances where it was necessary to keep production going at all costs it was more than ordinarily useful to have a man around who was highly skilled in grievance settlement. In the short run everyone gained: the shop steward's job was made easier, the rank and file might get some satisfaction, and management got their production thanks to the services of a cut-rate arbitrator. In the long run the solid advantages mostly accrued to management. The affording of facilities to senior shop stewards and convenors did not mean that they had been fully integrated into the management structure, but it did mean that the ever present conflict between labour and capital was contained and perhaps even masked. The implications of these arrangements were not lost upon the more politically conscious stewards – but the logic of their role as articulators of rank and file demands and aspirations in the 'here and now' left them with little choice but to seize what opportunities presented themselves. In any case, historically, the management's provision of services to shop stewards developed out of rank and file demands that their stewards be allowed to represent them: which meant that where office facilities and the like were afforded they could be presented as 'victories' for trade unionism.

Particularly sophisticated firms, by agreement with the unions, released their stewards on full pay to attend training courses at technical colleges, polytechnics, and university extra-mural departments. There, on apparently neutral ground, they were taught about the structure and policies of their unions, how to interpret agreements and how to use procedures for settling disputes, legislation governing terms and conditions of employment, management policies and the economics and organisation of their industries. These courses, like the publications of the Society for the Diffusion of Useful Knowledge in the 1830s and 40s, jumbled together genuinely useful knowledge with ideology and propaganda. They taught reverence for procedures, how necessary it was to have an 'understanding of management problems', and above all how important and necessary were all the established institutions on the industrial scene. In fine, they taught that if the labour-capital *status quo* was not perfect it was perfectible. There was nothing odd about that. Nor was it reasonable cause for moral indignation. Managements were hardly likely to pay stewards to attend courses if they were going to be taught how to beat the 'system'.

The various devices roughly outlined above were intended to broadly define legitimate relationships

between managers and shop stewards, to imbue
stewards with a general outlook that embodied an
acceptance of the established order. They were not
therefore experienced by stewards as urgent pressures
that continually closed in on them. The management
pressures that did bear most insistently were those of
ordinary social intercourse. Close proximity to management was in itself a pressure of some magnitude.
People who came into close and regular contact with
each other would tend to try and establish a personal
relationship devoid of the strains of conflict. Shrewd
managers would thus try to disarm the steward by
extending the hand of 'friendship' – and it took an
unusually cool character to remain detached in the
face of such overtures. Every shop steward carried
with him his 'kit' of stories, and one of the invariable
items had the theme of the steward who sat in the
manager's office drinking tea, chummily discussing the
fortunes of the local football team or whatever. If
some stewards saw nothing wrong with this, arguing
like the Ford executive that settled and reasonable
personal relationships had their ultimate pay-off, others
like Gerry Caughey, ex-convenor of the Pilkington
Triplex plant in St Helens, thought: 'You've got to
keep your distance. You can't sit in the boss's office
drinking his tea and smoking his ciggies. It's not just
because the fellers on the shop floor might see you
and wonder what the bloody hell you're playing at.
You just can't have this "pals together" stuff because
you *aren't* pals. You can't let anything stand in the
way of your being able to say NO.'[15] As Huw Beynon
put it:

To know that you are involved in an inevitable economic
conflict, a perpetual day to day struggle with the boss
can take you so far. There comes a point when it bruta-
lises you. Many stewards baulked long before this,
weighed down by the contradiction that management may
be on the other side but they are human 'like us'. These

Manager's man of moderation? . . . or shop-floor
militant super-hero?

stewards just didn't have the stomach for confrontation after confrontation, slanging match after slanging match. They were too nice, too soft, they lacked, as one of them put it, 'the killer instinct'. At certain times in a car plant, however, a steward who lacks such instinct gets into severe difficulties. A humanitarian act in the office can have adverse consequences for the stewards' membership. Management may be pawns but in a car plant they're paid to be lethal pawns. One of the stewards put it this way: 'if you've got one of them down, he's bleeding and everything there's just no point in going over to help him up because as soon as he's back on his feet he's going to start hitting you.'[16]

Shop stewards of course were in a better position than other workers to be aware of the intense pressures at work on the managers, and accordingly to be more sympathetic to their predicament. But the willingness of many stewards to see the other's point of view and on occasion be charitable was not a simple matter of humanitarian sentiments. Apart from the softening pressures at work · on the steward ambitious or hopeful for promotion, much more subtle cultural constraints were at work, too. By the 1970s the meritocratic view of British society as being one in which those most able rose to the top was prevalent in all classes. Objectively false though it was, it was a view widely assented to amongst the working class. This meant that many shop stewards felt themselves inferior to their bosses because of their relative lack of formal education. Although some shop stewards perhaps compensated with shows of belligerence, and others more experienced came to appreciate that ability could not simply be equated with formal education, the fact remained that class-rooted feelings of inferiority often gave the managers a head start. Stewards, that is to say, could be flattered by the apparent willingness of managers to treat with them on equal terms. This flattery could be compounded by yet other class-cultural considerations. Publicly distributed knowledge, i.e. the mass media, invariably conveyed the impression that the political and economic structure of capitalism was rational and that it worked to the advantage of everybody. Since as far as the shop steward was concerned, the principal spokesman of that system was the manager, there was always the tendency for the steward to accept management views as 'rational'. Only the politically conscious shop steward was at all well-equipped to cope. Armed with a *critical* analysis of his society, he was much more able to escape the cultural disabilities that afflicted so many of his comrades.

The politically conscious steward was extremely rare. Most other stewards, despite their limited politics, were not as completely dominated as perhaps the above analysis suggested. On the one hand there did remain residues of class resentment expressed in the simple and 'naïve' form that 'it's always us who take the knocks – never them'. On the other hand there was the rank and file which remained insulated from most of the pressures at work on the stewards. (Not, of course, the general and diffuse ideological pressures; rather the direct pressure toward social conformity that came from close and continuous interaction between stewards and managers). In the round then, while the balance of forces tended to push the stewards in the direction of what management and media defined as 'moderation', the typical relationship was one of mutual detachment; a detachment leavened by a joking relationship which provided a brittle veneer of cordiality, but which fooled neither party. The underlying conflicts were too profound to allow widespread practices of self-deception. Each typically regarded the other as more or less fixed features of the landscape. They may or may not have regarded this as regrettable, but they did see it as a fact of life as far as their daily dealings were concerned. The ploys and strategies that were variously set to work were therefore devoted to managing the *status quo* on the most advantageous terms – not to overthrowing it.

This left the shop steward, no matter how tactically brilliant, in an inherently weaker position because it was management that provided the jobs. Labour power was nothing without the instruments to use it – and it was management that owned the instruments and decided whether or not they were to be put to work. All the wiles in the world were powerless in the face of lay-offs or redundancies. The most the shop steward could expect to achieve in those circumstances was to try and negotiate the terms. Even the militant, deeply and aggressively committed to the attainment of a socialist society, was reduced to the role of a persistent, hard-headed beggar.

A perfect example of this took place in the Liverpool Ford plant in 1970 when the workers were threatened. As one of the shop stewards said: 'The lads were worried and they *expected* me to do something for them. They expected me to attempt to make their jobs secure. So that's what I had to do. Me and Les Moore and Les Brookes went in there cap in hand to our Lord and Master and said "Please, Mr Ford, don't take our jobs off us".'[17] Huw Beynon summed up the situation precisely:

To lay men off or to close plants down permanently, ultimately involves political decisions, and it is at this level of struggle that the conflict between labour and capital becomes obviously biased against the worker. Capital is inherently flexible, machines can be written off, investment switched from one part of the world to another. Against the might of capital the power of the shop stewards' committee is negligible unless backed by a strong international organisation.[18]

For that fairly rare character, the politically conscious shop steward, the cap-in-hand submissive routine involved what could only be described as degradation of a particularly deep and repugnant nature. It was a degradation, furthermore, that revealed yet again the contradictions built in to the shop steward's role in particular and into trade unionism in general. The socialist shop steward had to save his politics for when he was outside the factory gates. His socialism fuelled him in his time at work – but all too often it had little to contribute to his activities as a negotiator. There was just no obvious way in which a particular problem, such as a manning dispute, could be articulated as a political issue.* Although objectively every shop-floor issue was at root political, there was no possibility that ordinarily they would be seen as such. The absence of a coherent and forceful socialist politics in the wider social and economic environment ensured that 'factory' issues remained 'factory' issues.

Part of the union

Within the union machines there was considerable ambivalence toward stewards. When George Wood-cock said: 'To the unions he has been a source of trouble – unless he has been a nice little lad who simply reported trouble and then waited until the full-time officer came along. He was a nuisance other-wise',[19] he was speaking for the national leadership. At the local level of officialdom the response tended to be quite different: McCarthy and Parker reported that 'nearly all the full-time officers interviewed were enthusiastic about the work of stewards . . .'[20] To some extent the difference in attitudes may have been due to age differences between the two layers of officials. Most of the national leaders of the sixties had

*Political activism could be useful in strike situations. It provided the politico with a local and national network of contacts that could prove useful in mobilising wider support if the going got tough.

their formative years in the 1920s and 30s – a period in which shop stewards, as formally defined, were mainly confined to the various branches of the engineering industry and often associated with rank and file Communist organisations. This meant that few leaders would have had a great deal of personal experience of shop stewards in factories – their union careers would usually have started through office in union branches rather than through shop-floor organisations. It also meant, given the association in their minds between shop stewards and the CP, that stewards would tend to be looked upon as actual or potential disrupters of the union organisation. (It was interesting, if not necessarily significant, that the two national leaders most sympathetic toward shop stewards in the late sixties and early seventies – Jack Jones of the Transport Workers, and Hugh Scanlon of the Engineers – had served the bulk of their 'apprenticeship' in the post-war period of rapid expansion in numbers of stewards.) The local officials of the sixties, by contrast, derived most of their experience of trade unionism from the post-war years, and had themselves been shop-floor activists. Many indeed were recruited straight from the shop floor. H. A. Turner and colleagues' study of the motor industry found no less than fifteen ex-convenors to be full-time union officials.[21]

If personal experiences went some way toward explaining the discrepancy in attitude, the heart of the matter lay elsewhere. The apparent affection of local officials for shop stewards was summed up in one statistic: in 1966 taking the trade unions as a whole there was one full-time union official for every 3,800 members. (There were, naturally, variations among unions – in the same year the Engineers had one official to 6,800 members, the Transport Workers one to 2,700 members.[22]) Given the sheer weight of numbers for which each official was nominally responsible, and given additionally that that membership would usually be spread over a number of different workplaces, officials had but little choice to be heavily dependent upon their stewards. They needed stewards to perform that absolutely basic chore of collecting subs; they needed them to keep informed of what was happening in individual workplaces; they relied upon them to settle everyday grievances, and to keep the membership informed of union actions and policies. The stewards, in short, were the crucial link between the union as an organisation and the membership at the grass roots. Without them the full-time officer's job would have been almost literally impossible.

The *tendency* (the emphasis is added to make it plain that it was rarely much more than that) of national union leaders to be somewhat less than enthusiastic was because, as has been shown in the historical chapters, his preoccupations were not the same as those of the local officials even though the latter's primary loyalties were to the union. The union leader was concerned above all else with the survival of his organisation, with binding together all those disparate elements that in aggregate made up the union but which taken separately had a tendency to fly apart – to disintegrate into something closely resembling the local trade society of the nineteenth century. He therefore viewed the shop steward as a potential threat to union stability. More personally, he was often seen as a challenge to 'duly constituted authority' and peculiarly prone to 'external influences' – for which read the Communist Party and other socialist groupings.

As Marsh put it, the unions were '. . . much more concerned that the steward, with his semi-independent source of authority in the work group, will either bring the union into disrepute by persistent unconstitutional action, or will succumb to subversive elements which will break down the solidarity of the union as a whole and weaken its overall leadership.'[23]

Furthermore, amongst the older hands at the head of the unions was the fear that had been expressed by a leader of the Boot and Shoe Operatives in 1918: 'You will get on these (shop) committees men whom the employer can squeeze. If an employer, through his representatives, is smooth tongued, our men will give way every time.'[24] These questions notwithstanding, few union leaders looked on stewards and their organisations with as much understanding as H. A. Turner:

The national unions have so far been unable – indeed, have made small attempt – to develop an organisation to give the detailed guidance that co-ordination at the workplace level would require . . . They have mainly confined themselves to briefing their own stewards on such policies as they had as were relevant to workplace negotiations. At the level, the job of co-ordination had thus to be largely done by the stewards themselves.[25] (Thus) The shop steward organisation (in the motor industry) . . . has developed mainly to fill in the inadequacies of current union structure. . . .[26]

Still, despite their reservations, national leaders slowly accepted the inevitable. Always realistic, they attempted to tie stewards into the union machine. As the Electricians Union said in evidence to the 1965–8 Royal Commission: 'For too long the shop steward has been regarded as a thorn in the flesh of management and often of his trade union too. Changes of attitude and structure are required for the achievement of harmonious industrial relations.'[27] Some of the larger unions established their own colleges and embarked on ambitious schemes for training their shop stewards, and others such as the Electricians organised area conferences of shop stewards engaged in similar industries. In the late 1960s the two largest unions, the Transport Workers and the Engineers, both embarked on a policy of getting shop steward representation on national and industrial negotiating bodies and of ceding to them the formal right of rejecting deals negotiated at a higher level. Everywhere the intention was the same: to the extent that the stewards could be absorbed into the union apparatus it was hoped that they would be less inclined to establish their own autonomous organisations and more inclined to accept union authority.

Much of the hostility of national leaders toward shop stewards was returned in full by the stewards. Their immersion in the detail of workplace politics tended to make them impatient of those union policies that urged upon them restraint and 'moderation'. It was not just that rank and file pressures made them look inwards rather than outwards – though those pressures were real enough. It was rather that workplace issues were made of that finely-woven fabric that came of a situation intimately understood. Union policies by contrast were abstract generalities that could not, of necessity, talk to what was immediately present. Coupled with this was the failure of national and industrial agreements to take the market for as much as it would bear. As the rank and file and the shop stewards came to recognise their strength in the years after 1945, national agreements came to be looked upon as akin to minimum wage legislation; they provided the bread and butter while local strength (where it existed) provided the cake and the icing. Where questions of managerial authority were concerned, the unions as national organisations were *almost* irrelevant.

As Turner said, the inadequacies of union structures and policies tended to send shop stewards off in the direction of establishing their own 'unofficial' forms of organisation. By far the most widespread of these was the workplace's joint shop stewards' committee. Typically consisting of all stewards in the plant regardless of union, it formed a sort of industrial union. It developed its own policies, strategies, and tactics insofar as inter-work group rivalries would allow. It often

generated its own funds through levies on the rank
and file, and occasionally through lotteries. Some were
so well-organised that they ran their own newspapers
though most were short-lived, dependent as they were
on crisis. Less typical, but sufficiently recurrent to be
worthy of notice, were the combine committees.

'The reason combine committees exist is that certain problems cannot be settled adequately on a works
basis and must be tackled within the framework of a
company or a group of companies.'[28] Precisely: in
large multi-plant companies circumstances so arranged
themselves as to give rise to variations in rates of pay,
working conditions, and customs and practices. Since
these variations were actually or potentially divisive –
they gave the employers the opportunity to play one
workplace off against another – shop organisations had
an obvious interest in keeping themselves informed
of events in other plants and of developing concerted
strategies. Combine committees were thus primarily
established to pursue more efficiently simple trade
union ends – and this applied both where they built
confederations of shop stewards' committees across
plants within a single firm, and across companies
within a specific industry. But that was not the way
they were viewed by the union organisations.

Often, though not invariably, the impetus for the
formation of combine committees came from members of the Communist Party and left-wing Labour
sympathisers. If this was to be expected because only
the more politically sophisticated shop stewards would
be so equipped as to see most clearly the need for
going beyond the parochialism of the workplace, it
was usually enough to make the union leaders take
fright. Combine committees, that is to say, were
usually viewed by the union leadership as little more
than subversive conspiracies bent on undermining the
unions as constituted. In fact they never actually took
that form, nor could they have done. Combine com-

mittees, like the stewards who comprised their membership, drew what power they had from the rank and file. Since the latter, as we have seen, was thoroughly imbued with a factory consciousness there was precious little chance of them being led in political directions without the unions being so corrupt as to amount to an effective check on immediate rank and file aspirations. This was not the case as we have also seen.

What made combine committees so feared was that they drew their strength from the same place as the national leaders – the rank and file – but in a different manner. The men who made up the combine committees had what the leaders lacked: a direct and living contact with the membership. What *compounded* the fear was the knowledge that that strength cut right across the leadership's secondary source of legitimacy – its access to, or membership of, the national machinery of the State, and employers' associations and negotiating bodies. That is to say, much of the leadership's credibility was dependent on his relations with what were widely regarded as politically legitimate institutions, and on its claims to speak for the members. Combine committees and the like, constituting as they did rival centres of legitimacy, were therefore threats to union authority and its ways of doing things. However, although the remoteness and inadequacies of established institutions was a potential source of weakness for the union machine, it was also a source of strength in its dealings with shop stewards when formed in 'unofficial' committees.

As soon as stewards started to reach beyond their base in the workplace they ran the risk of isolation from it – and that could prove fatal. Unlike the leadership, the stewards had no secondary source of legitimacy. They 'lived' or 'died' according to the mood of the rank and file. The leadership could afford to take a mauling from one section of the membership because the different sections did not much care about their respective actions unless they impinged on each other. If the steward took a mauling from his members it could prove his destruction – that is why many stewards were almost paranoid about the threat of dismissal from their employment. Where stewards, whether organised in combine or works committees, did over-reach themselves by getting too far in front of their members, they left themselves open to swift retribution from either management, union, or an alliance of both.

Appreciating this danger, many stewards took the precaution of ensconcing themselves in the union machine through the branches and other lay offices; not primarily though as a means of self-preservation. A wedge into the lay apparatus of the unions gave the stewards an additional edge, for to the extent that it could be penetrated, the union could be more finely attuned to the needs of the rank and file and thus confer on those needs an extra legitimacy they otherwise lacked if merely expressed at workplace level. Union expression of rank and file demands conferred the seal of respectability. That unions in the sixties and early seventies assumed increasingly militant postures owed much to the success of organised pressure from shop stewards – though not until the stewards had proved to their sceptical national leaders that they really did speak with the authority of the weight of shop-floor opinion.

The role of the shop steward was shot-through with contradictions. And inevitably so. Where on the one hand, as an articulator of rank and file grievances, he was the living embodiment of the incompatibility of labour and capital, on the other hand as a mediator and arbitrator of those grievances he negotiated compromises that left labour and capital in their respective positions. As H. A. Turner put it:

In a sense, the leading stewards . . . (perform) a managerial function, of grievance settlement, welfare arrangement and human adjustment, and the steward system's acceptance by managements (and thus in turn, the facility with which the stewards themselves can satisfy their member's demands and needs) has developed partly because of the increasing effectiveness – and certainly economy – with which this role is fulfilled.[29] (Thus) . . . in general, the stewards' organisation is under pressures that compel it towards certain responsible patterns of institutional behaviour – 'responsible' at least in the sense that its leaders are obliged to balance a variety of group interests against the particular sectional claims with which they are confronted, and to bear in mind the long-term desirability of maintaining good negotiating relations with management.[30]

The shop steward was not an actor who wrote his own script complete with stage directions. If he stamped his personality on developing situations, the situations themselves were the product of social rather than psychological processes that existed independently of any one steward.

At bottom and in outline the sort of part played by the steward was determined for him by the working class's mode of adaptation to the conflict between labour and capital. The failure of any section of the labour movement to give a clear and coherent account of that conflict, to give an analysis that went beyond its most obvious manifestation in the workplace, meant that the conflict was only a *lived experience* at the point of production in particular workplaces. With consciousness rooted in the factory it necessarily followed that even stewards with revolutionary predispositions were continuously involved in making shifting, ever-changing accommodations to the labour/capital *status quo*. Given this environment then, there was nothing especially odd or strange about some shop stewards taking managerial jobs, or about others who were at once outspoken and forceful rank and file spokesmen and yet unpaid personnel managers, too.

7. Trade Union Leaders: Stuck with the Shabby Compromise

Wee fat full-time union official
waistcoat bursting with status
thirty years off the tools
grovels at the bosses' table
looking for a handout
for a dram
to give him strength
to climb on the workers' backs.

Anon[1]

It is true I do not possess a dress suit, and I do not
attend dinners and banquets given by the enemies of the
working classes and make alleged witty after-dinner
speeches there. (Jimmy) Thomas may think that comes
within the province of a trade union leader, but if
it is one of the 'elemental principles of leadership',
I am not going to adopt it.

*A. J. Cook, Miners' leader, in a letter to the
Daily Herald, 1926* [2]

They're not bent. I used to think they were but
they're not. They're not bent. They're just tired that's
all.

A shop steward recently turned full-time officer [3]

Members of the ruling class do not often sit down to
dinner together, but when a fair sample of them did
so in November 1969 to celebrate the 25,000th issue
of *The Financial Times* they took good care to see
that a clutch of trade union leaders were tucking in

with the politicians, managing directors, bankers, senior civil servants, leading churchmen, press barons and editors, university vice-chancellors and professors.[4] The union men – including the left-wingers Jack Jones and Hugh Scanlon – may not have felt it exactly their idea of a good night out, but they did not feel incongruous or express wonderment at their presence.

In February 1969 *The Sunday Times* assured its readers that Vic Feather, TUC general secretary, 'is never out of place whether he is choosing wine and a cigar in a smart restaurant, making deals with employers and Ministers, or simply chatting to rank and file trade unionists.'[5] In June 1959 the director-general of the Institute of Directors wrote to the *Manchester Guardian,* as if to justify the close association between unions and employers: 'Our annual conferences have been addressed by Mr Frank Cousins and other trades union leaders. The last (two) issues of our journal *The Director* carried exclusive articles by the chairman of the TUC, (and) the chairman of the TUC Production Committee . . .'[6]

Union leaders were no strangers either to the annual conferences of the Institute of Personnel Management and the British Institute of Management, or to luncheons of employers' associations. When Neil Chamberlain said of the American scene that: 'In effect the trade unions have accepted the battleground chosen by management. Satisfied with the social framework within which they operate, they are content to provide an *obbligato* to management's lead. The union's "challenge" to management control is more apparent than real'[7], he could almost have been talking of Britain. It was, after all, Campbell Adamson, director-general of the CBI, who said: 'I know the TUC people well and enjoy dealing with them.' But he also said: 'The CBI's relations with them have been good, but without achieving much.'[8]

The rider 'without achieving much' was extremely

important. Despite the close personal links between some trade union leaders and some employers, trade unionism as such had no more than formal recognition. As George Woodcock said: 'Employers take trade unionism as medicine they have got to take. They keep hoping that they will be fit enough without it. I don't think I know of any employers who would take trade unionism as their daily food.'[9] This sentiment was deeply ingrained in trade union leaders and with complete justification. Incredibly defensive people, they were always expecting to be attacked from some quarter or other. This was particularly clear when they appeared before the 1965-68 Royal Commission. There was, on their part, an almost universally thinly-veiled hostility to being questioned. Even such establishment-oriented leaders as Lord Carron, late president of the AEU, and Sir Sidney Greene, general secretary of the NUR, were notably defensive and sullenly querulous. If some trade union leaders welcomed the latent hostility of employers as an indication that they were doing their jobs, others resented it.

Resentment was implicit in Woodcock's likening of trade unionism to medicine. It was not a personal resentment – Woodcock and other union leaders were too important to be slighted or snubbed socially. As Clive Jenkins said to the Royal Commission: 'We have good relationships with most of the big industrial companies in this country. We are on friendly first name terms with their principal officers . . .'[10] What *was* resented was the view that trade unions were nasty medicine – implying that the unions ought to have been regarded as in some way complementary to the activities of business. This was made especially clear on separate occasions by Lord Cooper, general secretary of the GMWU, and by Les Cannon, late president of the Electricians. Cooper told the Royal Commission:

It is an elementary requirement of our basic purpose that we should do everything possible to contribute towards maximising the revenue of a firm or industry to increase the prospects of obtaining better wages and conditions. This approach is the basis of the fruitful co-operation which we enjoy in many firms in which we have exclusive, or near exclusive organisation of manual workers . . . We consider that industrial relations would be significantly improved if more firms regarded trade unions and collective bargaining as valuable instruments in promoting the objectives of the firm to everybody's benefit.[11]

Cannon told a conference on industrial democracy:

I stand for involvement. That is to say, I want unions to get involved in problems of productivity and efficiency, because unless they do, and unless they co-operate in bringing about a higher level of efficiency, a higher level of productivity, a higher level of profitability, the unions themselves cannot carry out their functions on behalf of their members.[12]

These sentiments were by no means universal – Lawrence Daly, the Miners' general secretary, said: 'I take the view that it would be wrong for the trade union movement to get entangled as partners with big business. The basic aim of big businessmen everywhere is to make profit out of someone else's labour, and that is the whole basis of the capitalist society in which we live. My aim in life is to end that completely.'[13] Hugh Scanlon of the Engineers, and Jack Jones of the Transport Workers were often to be heard making similar remarks. The fact was however that radically opposed as the words of the Coopers and the Cannons were to those of the Dalys and the Scanlons, there was not nearly such a wide discrepancy in deeds. And that did not mean that they were hypocrites. Where Daly was correct in his assessment of the relationship between labour and capital, Cannon's view had a certain logic because it expressed a desire to go further in the direction of what trade union leaders actually practised regardless of their politics. As George Woodcock put it:

As leaders of their particular unions politics makes no difference at all. You must have noticed yourself how the most political, the most militant of trade unionists get along fine with the employers. This was true of Foulkes of the ETU, true of Bill Paynter, true of Frank Cousins. He was constantly the bad boy of the TUC, but all the employers could get along with him.[14]

Although this judgement minimised and over-simplified the effects of differences in politics, it was to the point in one major respect: the leader who hoped for the dissolution of capitalism nevertheless had to come to terms with a capitalist reality in his daily round.

Yet given all this, *some* significance did attach itself to union leaders' politics. Coincidence would not be sufficient to explain the fact that where unions had a right-wing leadership there was a strong tendency throughout the 1960s for union funds to be invested in private companies, and where there was a left-wing leadership that same tendency was non-existent (see table opposite). Particularly noteworthy in this respect was the dramatic shift in the ETU's investment policy after the ousting of the Communist leadership in the early sixties. Noteworthy too was the GMWU's steady accumulation of stocks and shares (including holdings in companies such as BSR and Rugby Portland Cement that did not recognise trade unions!), and the steady refusal of the T&GWU and the AEU to engage in any such practices.

The sort of leadership that a union got was princi-pally an indirect reflection of the industries that the union organised. Left-wing and aggressive leaders came to head unions that were organising in industries that contained militant workers. And it so happened that those unions – mainly the T&GWU and the AEU – both had constitutions that made it easier for lay

Trade Union Investments

*Percentage of total investments held in joint-stock companies (figs. approx.)**

	Years 1960–1969									
Union	'60	'61	'62	'63	'64	'65	'66	'67	'68	'69
T&GWU	Nil	Nil	Nil	Nil	Nil	Nil	Nil	Nil	Nil	Nil
AEU	*Figures not available*								Nil	Nil
GMWU	12	27	28	33	28	36	38	53	77	71
ETU	Nil	Nil	Nil	Nil	Nil	26	42	51	50	48
BISAKTA	Nil	Nil	7	18	24	38	36	47	66	64
Boilermakers	Nil	Nil	Nil	Nil	Nil	Nil	Nil	Nil	Nil	Nil
CAWU (Now APEX)	*Figures not available*								38	42
NGA	*Figures not available*				8	8	13		20	24
ASTMS	*Figures not available*								11	11
DATA (Now TASS)	Nil	Nil	Nil	Nil	Nil	Nil	Nil	Nil	Nil	Nil

* includes holdings in the Trade Union Unit Trust
Source: Annual Returns to the Registry of Friendly Societies

members to be influential. In the sixties it was the influence of the left-wing laity that increasingly came to be heard and felt. And that meant, particularly in the T&GWU after the election of Jack Jones, that there developed the basis for occasional alliances between the leadership and rank and file activists against other full-time officers. (There were a number of T&GWU officers dismissed in Jones' first few years of tenure.) Thus a left-wing leader with strong views about the propriety of having a financial stake in the enemy camp could be confident of strong support from his lay executive.

The politics of the leadership was obviously then of some importance. While it did not alter the fact that a capitalist reality had to be coped with, some scope still remained. The reality did not have to be embraced: it was entirely possible to regard it as provisional. That was why such apparently unimportant things as where the union put its money had such symbolic power. It did at least signal a refusal to regard capitalism as an immutable object – and to that rather quiet extent helped ensure that ideas resembling socialism stayed alive.

Such gestures offered a moral solution to the contradiction inherent in trade union leadership. They merely had the merit of recognising their existence. Like the shop steward, the most militant trade union leader was in a situation riddled with contradictions that as a union leader he was quite incapable of resolving. Trade unionism expressed the contradiction between labour and capital but was not the means of resolving it. This left the union leader standing at the forefront of the contradiction and thus especially exposed to the same pressures as the shop steward except in greater degree. Where the shop steward had the protection of close and immediate contact with the rank and file, the union leader as far as the rank and file was concerned lived in a twilight world shrouded in mystery. Where for the steward the pressures to conform came mainly from his mates at his elbow, the trade union leader enjoyed a greater degree of autonomy. Pressures were more diffuse: emanating from the union as an organisation, from employers, and from government via the deliberations of the TUC General Council. The trade union leader, that is to say, moved in a different world of committee rooms, conferences, hotels. He physically lived in a different world too. Living probably in semi-detached suburbia he was cut off from his roots, from his own kind. It could be a lonely and isolated life if the man came from a tightly knit community such as the valleys of South Wales that Will Paynter knew:

Once you come to London the situation is entirely different. I didn't associate with other trade union leaders, maybe because they didn't want to associate with me. I did

'What you get at the top of a union is the inhibition from the realisation that they can't carry their own people with them. . . .'

become isolated. I did go into the coalfields to speak to
miners and so kept contact. But it isn't the same when
you live in London. There is commuting in the morning
behind a row of newspapers. My neighbours probably
don't know who I am. You live a completely detached
existence. I was going to the 'Green Man' every night
for years, an old habit of mine from Wales. I would go in
as regularly as I could and I wouldn't have to order my
drink. They would pull me a pint as I walked through the
door. I had been going for about three years when the
landlady came up to me and said, 'Are you Mr Davies
of Metro-Goldwyn-Mayer?' I had a Welsh accent. She
knew that, but nothing else. I could stand by the bar
night after night and talk to no one. So it has been an
anonymous sort of existence since I have lived in London.
It doesn't bother me really, except when certain things
happen. Like the visitor I had from South Wales in 1959.
He was a Labour Alderman from the Monmouthshire
County Council and a local lodge leader. He had a little
cigarette case filled with Woodbines and he was most
upset when he saw my packet of Players on the table.
He had put the wrong cigarettes in the case which he had
come to present me with because I was one of them. It
was the sort of gesture that can really upset you, and an
absolutely important one to a trade unionist. But if you
are away from the coalfield any length of time that intimacy has gone.[15]

The union leader sensitised to the consequences of his
position through deep political convictions could
obviously insulate himself from his new surroundings –
but at the price of being cut-off from all social contact
outside the union head-office. Even so, as Paynter
said, 'the intimacy has gone'.

Miners' leaders, insofar as they came from coalfields
other than those situated in urban areas, would
obviously feel the change more acutely than those
other union leaders who had not experienced such
tightly-knit working-class communities, who indeed
had already learned to live in suburbia in the pro-

vinces. Most union leaders, by the time they arrived in London, had long since left behind the patterns of association typical of working-class areas. So the fact that they lived in middle-class suburbs had ceased to have any significance. What isolated him was not *where* he lived but *how* he lived. Not the how of the way in which he spent his money, of the sort of objects he surrounded himself with, but the how of his pattern of activity. And *that* pattern was one of continual mobility from one committee or conference to another. He was, in other words, far too busy a man to allow him to strike any social roots in his locality. His house was a base rather than a home. His social networks were not a function of where he lived, but of the demands imposed upon him by the union machine.

Scurrying from one meeting to another, from one railway station to another, the union leader was constantly on the move. A quick handshake, a reluctantly rapid exchange of greetings with an old comrade. Papers out of the briefcase and down to business. A hasty pint and buttie after – and a sprint for the train to the next destination, where the performance repeated itself. No time to relax, no time to fall back into the easy and comfortable familiarity of the rank and file activist. This was not an isolation that involved an act of choice.

Regardless of individuals, everything conspired to set the leader apart. If he had some choice in his precise mode of adaptation to his new environment, the basic structures of that environment had an unrelenting stone-wall quality that could only be taken for granted. This meant that much of the moralistic polemic delivered at trade union leaders was, in general, hopelessly misconceived.

The *Communist Review* of September 1921 roundly condemned Messrs Thomas and Bevin for their failure to support the Miners, their colleagues in the Triple Alliance: 'When they realised that they could not carry out the demands of the determined rank and file, then they ought to have resigned and made way for the younger, more active and courageous leaders . . . We are now beginning to comprehend the real depths of the rascality that inspired the careerists in the trade union bureaucracy.'[16] In the 1950s, 60s, and early 70s similar sentiments regularly recurred in the pages of the various publications of the left. In that same period anyone at all familiar with the proceedings of trades councils and meetings of shop stewards would have heard the same refrain again and again – 'if only we had the right leadership etc., etc.' Nearly always and nearly everywhere there was the same tendency to blame the shortcomings of the labour movement on the alleged 'moral failures' of leaders. If the critics drew some strength from the undoubted presence of corrupt leaders and of others who, if not exactly corrupt in the financial sense, were nevertheless seduced by the reflected glamour of rubbing shoulders with the mighty, their moralising postures precluded them from coming to an understanding of what leadership involved. The left, instead of coming to terms with the inherent limitations of trade unionism and developing new strategies, insisted in its naïve belief that all that was required was a different set of leaders equipped with a different political philosophy. When on rare occasions it got the sort of leadership it wanted, but found that it did not behave very differently, it reverted to its familiar assertion of 'treachery', and one of the slogans of the sixties – 'fake lefts'. Few seemed to share Hobsbawm's awareness that:

. . . even the most revolutionary must fight the battles for improvement and reform according to the nature of the terrain, which is that of 'realistic' calculation in a capitalist economy and a capitalist state. That is to say they must compromise, make allies, and in general act as reformists. If he is to be effective in a stable capitalist economy, even the communist union leader must do this, whatever his private reservations and calculations.[17]

In, but not of, the Establishment

The union leader's isolation began with his election or appointment to full-time office in the locality when he exchanged the comradeship of the workplace for the anonymity of the office. If his sentiments remained with the 'lads' they lacked the reinforcement that came from continuous personal contact. People became cases rather than Joe or Harry – his primary loyalties became attached to the union rather than to his mates. He enjoyed a security that he had previously lacked – he no longer lived under the ever-present threat of dismissal. He became a man of some substance. The union bought him a car and gave him a loan at a low rate of interest to buy a house; he was paid by the month; he paid superannuation; he had someone to type his letters and answer the phone. If he worked hours quite as long, if not longer, than when he had been a shop steward or an unpaid branch officer, he now had a career if he wanted it. He might be asked to let his name go forward as a potential justice of the peace, he would be asked to sit on the local appeals machinery attached to the social services and would be expected to become a member of the joint arbitration board attached to his industry. He might become a school governor, or be co-opted on to the local education committee or hospital management board. He would get to be on first-name terms with officers of the employers' associations and with workplace managers. He wore a suit and collar and tie. He carried a briefcase and took to reading *The Times* or *The Guardian*. He learned to dictate letters, write memoranda and reports. He developed his speaking skills and techniques of handling meetings. He learned how to turn emotion on and off. He learned a new vocabulary and smoothed out the bumps in his local accent. He became, more or less unconsciously, a different man.

The term 'union bureaucrat', shed of its abusive connotations, was an apt description. Although the union official was a highly unusual bureaucrat because he was also a representative – a servant in a way that the civil servant never was – he was nevertheless an occupant of an office in a hierarchy of offices. The workplace offered but meagre prospects of a career. The union machine was by contrast a field of possibilities. The man who made it to general secretary was generally an extremely able politician, though given the presence of factions within the union machine his rise was dependent upon the balance of forces that already existed. In most unions there was a strong element of sponsorship, so that the success in career terms of an official was not merely a function of gaining a clear understanding of the patterns of alliances but also, to put it crudely, of catching the eye of the sitting incumbent who was always alive to the problem of succession. However, the politics of the union machine was not a process insulated from the rank and file. Certainly advance through the union hierarchy depended on alliances within it; it also depended on alliances with rank and file activists who sat on powerful lay committees in unions such as the Engineers and the Transport Workers. In a union like the GMWU, where by comparison the union machine was much more the 'property' of the full-time officials, rank and file followings were much less important: the GMWU was well-known for its nepotism. Still, even in 'family concerns' like the GMWU, reputations with activists remained of crucial importance for in just about every union of major importance elections were held for the top job. Although it was rare for much more than a quarter of the membership to vote in elections for general secretaries or presidents, elections were usually contested. Elections were nominally decided by the voters, but were in fact decided by the full-time officials and the rank and file activists. With most members not knowledgeable of union personalities and politics, they would naturally seek the advice of their more knowledgeable workmates who would in turn have got their knowledge from their contacts with officials, or through their contacts with men who had served on lay committees. The chain of 'communication' was an extended one with many branch lines, but at every junction and railhead small numbers of rank and filers played important roles in filtering information. And an official on his way up would inevitably get to know a fair number of those gate-keepers.

That officials at various points in their careers built up followings did not necessarily mean that they did so consciously. Very few trade union leaders arrived in their positions through a consuming ambition for self-advancement, indeed not a few often carried with them an air of innocent surprise at their relative eminence. Followings, that is to say, were not as a rule cynically collected with a view to subsequent pay-offs. Had that been the case it would speedily have become known to the lay activists who would then have set a 'price' on their favours. But British trade union leaders, unlike their American counterparts, had nothing with which to 'buy' and 'sell' patronage: with the consequence that to all intents and purposes patronage was a non-existent factor in British union politics. Followings, instead of being based on expectations of favours or other 'perks', were rooted in present and past alliances over policies in committees, and of solid trade union services rendered in tough local negotiations. In some unions, such as the Electricians and the Engineers with strong left-wing traditions, politics was also an important factor with both left and right attempting to organise 'bloc' votes. In general, leaders were selected not for their potential ability to distribute favours, nor because they had such superlative personal characteristics that their choice was inevitable: they were selected because they represented some sort of reflection of the dominant social forces at work at a particular time in the union's history. Their personalities were important, but not decisive. As one union leader said in an interview with the author (a leader who, not surprisingly, preferred to remain anonymous):

I can remember when Frank Cousins came into office in the Transport Workers. Very right wing regional officials almost visually readjusted their thinking processes. A new trade union President or General Secretary, bringing a different philosophy to the job, can and does change the union. I have a theory – which is probably wrong – that every General Secretary, when elected, represents the aspiration of his people at *that* time and unless he is very careful, in five years time, he will no longer be representative of those aspirations. So you do get quite sudden changes of policy, not because the General Secretary changes them, but because he is representative of the mainstream of opinion at that time. And his election, if it is fair, should produce circumstances where he is representative of a very strong current strand of union opinion. When he goes the chances are he won't any longer be representative, but his successor will be. Also, I think, through pressure of work a General Secretary grows away from his members; he becomes unable to stop and talk and think and look at people. There is a relationship between a General Secretary and his membership which can be destroyed very quickly. The trouble is one becomes so preoccupied with big decisions that one can easily forget the worker.

Most trade union leaders served an apprenticeship at the union head office as national officers before assuming the top job: it was rare, once the unions were well-established as national organisations, for a local officer to move directly into the general secretary's seat. The move to London – where most unions had their headquarters – did not constitute a radical break for the local official; it merely severed what remained of his local ties. But the local ties after a few years in the union office had already lost their capacity to bind; they had become sentimental attachments rather than pressures demanding conformity. The essentially middle-class life of the *local* officer meant that when he became a national officer he moved in the rather more sophisticated circles of the metropolitan middle class – the change was one of degree, not of kind. With respect to the union machine however, there were political increments to be gained. When lodged in the locality his knowledge of the state of play at head office, though immense by comparison with the rank and file, remained relatively imperfect. What he knew he learned in odd snatches, for he was not a member of the head-office inner circle. Once in it, he was able to piece together a fully-rounded picture of the entire ramifications of the union – and was probably surprised at its complexity as vague ideas of the outline congealed into a firm grasp both of structure and detail.

With the assumption of the top office the transformation of the naïve working-class youth was complete. He now lived in a world peopled by men in politics and business reared by family and education to the business of ruling, and by other trade union leaders who had hoed the same row as himself. In his new world he would encounter the Establishment types that in his youth he had known only through caricature. He became a man of moment, a man to be courted and sometimes flattered – especially by politicians and businessmen. But not so much because he was seen as a potential ally – more because he was regarded as a man who was in a position to mute opposition to their plans and projects. By the ruling class he was seen as a potential instrument of domin-

ance. If the ruling class could get him to do broadly
what they wanted then that was always to the good.
It was a prime axiom of the exercise of dominance
that it was always better to get nominal opponents
to do what you wanted to do yourself, for dominance was not experienced as such if disguised as
consent.

Trade union leaders were not wanted for themselves,
but for what they might be able to deliver. It was
always understood that no matter how amenable a
given individual was, his ultimate usefulness depended
on his relationship to the working class in general
and to the section of it organised by his union in
particular. This was why courtship of individual
leaders was always backed up with tangible concessions to the class when circumstances made it necessary. The success of these tactics was finally dependent
not on the social ambitions of the leader, but on the
very nature of trade unionism itself. That trade
unionism constantly sought an adjustment to the *status
quo* on the most advantageous terms left its leadership
wide open to seductive whispers. Jimmy Thomas had
some justification for claiming that it was an 'elemental principle of leadership' that he should occasionally don fancy dress and deliver speeches at
dinners held by 'the enemies of the working classes'.
In the light of behaviour of union leaders in the sixties
and seventies, Thomas was a man acting in advance of
his time. What made Thomas so unforgiveable, and
his successors so excuseable, was that the latter did
not so obviously revel in the customs and pursuits of
the ruling class. Few other trade union leaders sent
their sons to public schools and gave their daughter
a 'society' wedding with a Tory prime minister as a
witness – or even aspired to do so. Although Thomas
went beyond what was necessary in his apeing of the
style of the ruling class, the subsequent readiness of
other leaders to attend dinners and conferences did

have a certain compelling logic, especially in the years after 1945 when no trade union leader seriously thought that socialism was at all imminent.

In the decades when socialism was merely a pious word, nods in its direction were little more than gestures to the sacred memories of revered ancestors which even the right-wingers felt obliged to make. The gestures were ritualistic and mostly devoid of meaning so far as immediate action was concerned. Where many of the union leaders of the pre-war decades, despite their accommodations with the system, nevertheless looked upon capitalism as something transient, their post-war successors increasingly came to look on capitalism as permanent. In the circumstances where all governments seemed to be interested in a regulated capitalism, there was every incentive for the union leader to involve himself with those doing the regulating. It was important for the union leader that his involvement should be seen to be serious – and one of the ways of proving that was an observation of the social niceties. If everyone was at the very least tacitly agreed that the system was there to stay it would have seemed crudely insulting to have ignored the social lubricants of dinners and other fêtes.

By the early seventies there was a growing number of union leaders less inclined to think of capitalism as immutable, yet they, like those who did, still joined the social round. And for solid pragmatic reasons. The present was insistent, and it was in that block of time that their members lived and were primarily concerned about. Certainly they were in no position to tell the members to put up with the problems of the day because the morrow would see the dawning of a socialist society. Such a statement would have been met with baffled incredulity – and quickly followed by the sound of feet tramping off in the opposite direction. Clearly then, the union leader needed to wedge himself in wherever he saw an opportunity of reducing the impact of capitalism on his members.

The trade union leader was heavily dependent on the negotiating process, and not just because of his need to produce wage rises or whatever, for how the process *itself* worked determined what was to be had out of it. Negotiations, by virtue of deciding what went out of the till and into members' pockets, simultaneously decided the fate of the union as an organisation and the leader's place within it. If in the last resort what was good for the members was good for the union, practice often fell a good deal short of the 'last resort'. There was, in fact, a tension between satisfying the members and the need for negotiations as V. L. Allen made plain:

The effectiveness of permanent negotiating depends on the willingness of the participants to follow it through without resorting to lock-outs or strike action. Consequently the rules of each joint negotiating body usually contain a clause to this effect . . . Ordinary members, impatient of the delays that procedural settlement of disputes entails, on occasion take matters into their own hands and strike. Union leaders, even though they may sympathise with their members, cannot side with them without threatening the existence of the negotiating machinery. Not only do employers refuse to negotiate under duress; they also tend to lose faith in the usefulness of agreements . . . Once the leaders refuse to recognise the actions of their members, and sometimes even feel it necessary to condemn them, they are placed in the invidious position of involuntarily strengthening the hand of employers and straining their own primary loyalties.[18]

In short, the production of 'goods' for the members depended on the ability of the union to enter into negotiations – which ability could, paradoxically, cut across the interests of the members. In effect, the needs of the moment as distinct from the needs of the long-term involved the union leader in juggling two separate sets of interests: those of the union as an organisation, and those of the members who nominally gave the organisation its *raison d'être*.

The negotiation of compromises was a subtle business which had its own elaborate – if uncodified – ritual. Those who became accustomed to sitting opposite one another across baize covered tables in teams had, through their prominent spokesmen, come to tacit understandings. If negotiations had the semblance of a rational process wherein the respective parties put their cases and then proceeded to score debating points off one another, the reality was somewhat different. Certainly cases were put, and certainly attempts were made to knock holes in them as statistics were bandied back and forth. But the debating was not a species of rational argument with each party seeking to persuade the other of the irrefutable logic of its position. On the contrary: it was a process in which each tried to find out what was the *real* sticking point of the other as distinct from the *professed* sticking point. It was a question, in other words, not of giving up entrenched positions but of mutual attempts to modify them.

Each team had its member who did most of the talking, and on the union side it was usually, though not invariably, a national officer below the rank of general secretary. During the course of the across-the-table negotiations adjournments would be taken as the respective sides withdrew to consider and consult in corridors and ante-rooms. Sometimes they would be adjourned for weeks or even months to enable further discussion in board room or union executive committees. Much, if not all, of this semi-public process provided only a face to the world. Behind the façade were the private meetings and discreet telephone calls between the union leaders and company representatives. Exploratory talks before the 'team games' began would establish the guts of the matter, sort out the substance from the side issues, and tenta-

tively define sticking points. The team performances
sought greater definitional clarity – which then became
the renewed substance for further private negotiating.

This meant that not a few national negotiations that
took place across draped tables and proceeded with
fanfares of publicity complete with television interviews, popping flash bulbs, and pugnacious press statements, though a necessary part of the ritual were
often devoid of substance. The real business had
either been conducted beforehand or during adjournments when the chief negotiators met privately,
thrashed out an agreement, and mutually agreed to
sell it to their colleagues. Stories were told of agreements made in the gents lavatories at the Department
of Employment, and Harry Nicholas, acting-general
secretary of the Transport Workers, told the Royal
Commission: 'I do not know how many times on
Thursday night I have sat in the lounge of the Station
Hotel in York and met my opposite number on the
engineering employer's side and resolved the issue that
was chased all the way through procedure and we
have gone into the "court" in the morning and said a
settlement has been reached.'[19] Of course the technique of the 'private word' did not always work,
neither was it always tried: but it worked often
enough for it not to fall into disuse.

This sort of ritual could hardly proceed without
there being fairly close personal relationships between
certain representatives of the two parties. The people
concerned had to be able to trust each other to carry
out their privately made commitments. They had to
rely on each other to be discreet and not to leak
stories to the press. However it was not always as
furtive as that for colleagues were often knowing
parties. Perhaps the lay members of a union on a
national negotiating committee were relatively innocent and were overawed at rubbing shoulders with
the 'great'. Perhaps the career prospects of a junior

official would be threatened if he crossed his seniors. Perhaps some leaders were anyway firm believers in the back-door technique. Perhaps others found themselves in situations where they thought they had little choice – like Jack Jones and Hugh Scanlon in the 1971 Ford strike. After nine weeks of strike and deadlocked negotiations, they by-passed the negotiating committee of which they were not members, secretly concluded a deal with the Ford Chairman, and presented it as a *fait accompli* to the official negotiators.

The secret negotiations that led to the conclusion of the Ford strike were not enabled by pre-existing friendly relations between the Ford chairman on the one hand and Jones and Scanlon on the other because the meeting was arranged by a third party – Vic Feather, TUC general secretary. The 'quiet settlement' then, if sometimes dependent on personal acquaintance, was also a function of a much wider network of people which could be relied upon to provide go-betweens. These people might be called upon because their formal status rendered them appropriate: the TUC general secretary; the Secretary of the Department of Employment or his conciliation officers; other union leaders; prominent businessmen known for their willingness to occasionally perform 'public services'; or indeed anyone who 'knew somebody who knew somebody else'. Thus an unconscious activity of every union leader was building up a list of contacts who might prove useful at some later date – *un*conscious because his work inevitably brought him into contact with a wide range of people of power and influence. The use of the network was not necessarily straightforward in the sense that a union leader made direct approaches himself or through an intermediary – he might just quietly make it known to someone who could be relied upon to pass on a discreet message that he was available for an informal and 'off-the-record' chat . . . a necessary ploy in the high politics of negotiation where no one wanted to appear in a weak and exposed position.

So far as negotiations themselves were concerned, attempts were often made to disarm the opposition by displays of personal magnaminity, or by attempts to develop the stance of the friendly but honest broker. Lord Citrine, an ex-general secretary of the TUC, reminiscing on his earlier days as a full-time officer of the Electricians said:

. . . I set about cultivating the acquaintance of the employers' officials, and of being as frank with them as my duty to my members permitted. I tried to play straight with them and I found they did the same by me. We knew that ours was a continuing relationship, and that if one snatched a temporary advantage by sharp practice the other would be sure to get his own back at some time or other. We fought each other in negotiations, but we never broke faith.[20]

Citrine, like many other union leaders, set great store by a 'decent', 'love-thy-neighbour' approach: 'We all felt (Charles Booth, a Liverpool shipowner) was a decent chap, and that counts for a great deal in industrial negotiations. I remember with pleasure that when on the occasion of his retirement a dinner was held in his honour . . . I was chosen as spokesman on behalf of the trade unions who were represented.'[21] Alf Allen, USDAW general secretary, had a similar view:

Negotiations can be carried on in a friendly or hostile way. I have always found that I have been able to get more for our members against a friendly, understanding background. But nevertheless a hard bargaining relationship and in the end an effective compromise – most settlements are compromises. If I set a hostility towards someone before I go and negotiate with them, I doubt that I am serving the best interests of my people. There are some employers with whom you cannot have a reasonable, above the board, friendly but hard bargaining attitude. They know no other than a provocative and hostile

environment and atmosphere. If it *has* to be there the
trade union official will live up to it. He will do his
stint in those circumstances. Whether he would get, at the
end of the day, as much out of that employer as he
would get out of another where the relationship is friendly
in the work-a-day sense, is open to question. I would
always back the latter rather than the former.[22]

The key phrase was Citrine's 'we knew that ours was
a continuing relationship' – where was the point in
hostility if each took the continued presence of the
other for granted? Union leaders and businessmen
did not relate to each other in a political sense where
the one saw himself as the representative of labour,
and the other as the representative of capital. The
very reverse – private views notwithstanding, they
looked upon each other as professionals who respected
each other as people who had a job to do. As Alf
Allen put it: 'The employer is defending what he has
and I'm after some of it. I do that and I hope he
thinks none the less of me because of it. He has to do
his job, and I have to do mine.'[23] This professional
attitude was exactly what was required – though some
chose to slip in the odd political innuendo:

We have, whether we like it or not, to negotiate with
state employed administrators and we shake their hands
and sit down across the table. Sometimes we have polite
exchanges and sometimes impolite exchanges. But I think
the general attitude of most trade union leaders I know
of is one of suspicion. I don't think it is necessary to have
a good personal relationship with the people with whom
one is negotiating. . . . We have always got to pursue the
immediate interests of our members, but we have got to
make it clear at the same time that what we want is a
complete change of system.[24]

Union leaders had to pursue the immediate interests
of their members, and to do that they *had* to establish
reasonable working relationships with employers. If
personal bitterness, hostility, and acrimony continually

punctuated their meetings, then efficient negotiations would have been almost impossible. That, presumably, would only have suited trade union leaders had they been operating in a near revolutionary situation with the working class politically prepared in outlook and organisation. With the working class prepared in neither of those respects, even the union leader who would have had it otherwise had no choice but to become a professional, a master of what George Woodcock called the 'shabby compromise'.*

A manager of discontents

Sir Sidney Greene of the Railwaymen told the 1965-68 Royal Commission '. . . in a democratic organisation it is not much good my signing an agreement if I am doubtful about my members accepting it.'[25] Some twenty years earlier C. Wright Mills told the readers of his book on American trade union leaders: '. . . even as the labor leader rebels, he holds back rebellion, exploiting it in order to maintain a continuous organisation; the labor leader is a manager of discontent.'[26] On the one hand then a response to pressure from below, on the other a containment and utilisation of that pressure. These were not contradictory views – together they approximately summed up the relationship between the union leader and the rank and file.

At this point it is necessary to emphatically stress again the risks of identifying the actions of the union leader with his own personal gratifications. Such grati-

*Just how careful union leaders were with respect to their dealings with employers was brought resoundingly home to me when I compared what they actually said to me in tape-recorded interviews with what they were prepared to let me quote them as saying. Unsatisfactory though it is, I must ask readers to accept my assurance that there was often a considerable gap between what I was told in confidence and what I have been allowed to say in public. I might add that fears of the possibility of libel suits did not account for the discrepancy.

fications were obviously available, for as Joel Seidman said: 'By becoming a working class leader . . . the union official in an important sense may have risen out of the working class. Here are rewards, both psychological and material, that are worth holding on to. Defeat for re-election means, not release from the burdens of office, but reverting to a much less desirable way of life.'[27] And their availability was certainly a factor in the leader's dealings with the rank and file: his own self-interest was bound up with the survival of the union as a viable organisation. However, the form that the union took and the way that it adapted to its political and economic environment was not merely an extension of the leader's personality. The leader was caught up in a whole set of social processes that preceded his arrival and over which he, as an individual, had little influence. He may have been a key figure in some of those processes but he was more their creature than their creator. The fact that his own interest was bound up in the future of the union was secondary to the preceding fact that the union had evolved out of the *collective* actions of people – actions which were answers to historical situations responsive only to the power of collectivities. The union leader was continuously involved in establishing and re-establishing his credibility to his members. To achieve that more or less successfully he had to engage in 'debate' with his members so as to bridge the gap between what he considered as achievable and desirable and what his members thought achievable and desirable.

Previous chapters should have made it abundantly clear that the rank and file was always in ragged order. Consisting of a wide range of sectional interests distributed over a large geographical area, the rank and file was a large fragmented mass united only by its common union membership. The rank and file, never confronting the leadership as a coherent, organised, more or less homogeneous mass, was never in a position to challenge the leader's claim to represent the majority. Challenges therefore came in isolated, spontaneous outbursts. These, because they were isolated, could be contained: the leadership possessed the organisational weapons of containment, the necessary political skills, and most of all a position that guaranteed continuity. He could survive a challenge because he remained in his office long after the conferences were over or the men back at work.

In situations of full employment the commonest threat to leaders was the unofficial strike – which was the one they could do least about, and cope with the best. The unofficial strike took place outside the union machine by definition – 'unofficial', in fact, meant 'unconstitutional'. The challenge, that is, was not directed at the leadership in the sense that it was an attempt to unseat him or embarrass him in his role as political boss of the union. The threat was rather more vague in that it was implicitly directed at him in his role as a negotiator with employers. Even so, it still left the leader in a delicate position. In the earlier decades of trade unionism it tended to undermine the employer's willingness to enter into agreements; in the later decades employers were more sympathetic to the problems of union leadership and understood its fragile control over membership – a measure of that sympathetic understanding was the employer's willingness to call in the leader to help solve an unofficial strike. What made the leader's position delicate was not so much the effect it had on his relationship with the employer as on the strike's potential for undermining his credibility as a negotiator and hence for spreading disaffection to other members. Leaders therefore tended to co-opt the strike by tacitly ignoring its unconstitutional nature, and doing a deal behind the scenes. If that did not work, or where other considerations rendered it inexpedient, recourse could be made to the mass media who would obligingly repeat allegations that the strikers were being led by the nose by 'subversive elements'. A useful tactic in that it exonerated the mass of his members from any 'blame' by pinning it on a handful.

Relatively easy to cope with as most unofficial strikes were, the union leaders still found them extremely distasteful. Some, like Will Paynter, disliked them for principled political reasons:

I have some misgivings about this move towards the stewards. Frankly, it seems to me to divide, to fractionalise. It creates too many bargaining centres inside the trade union movement. It is divisive, not unifying. In the short term, for the strong, it gets results. But in the long term, from the standpoint of consolidating and creating a consciousness of what has to be done in this society I think it militates against it.[28]

Others found unofficial strikes distasteful for pragmatic political reasons: unofficial strikes and their shop steward leaders, particularly in the post-war period, severely hampered union leaders in their attempts to help Labour governments operate incomes policies. But most of all, unofficial strikes were disliked because they were a denial of the leadership's right to decide how and when collective action should be exerted. The ultimate justification of leadership was that those vested with it were, by virtue of their special knowledge and skills, best qualified to judge at what points shows of strength were necessary. From the earliest days of modern trade unionism (see chapter 2) union leaders had accordingly insisted that the right to call strikes was firmly the property of the union. Always viewing strikes as potentially destructive of the organisation at worst, and disruptive of attempts to produce an orderly machine with a predictable pattern of events at best, many leaders of unofficial strikes could depend upon round condemnation, or in rare cases expulsion.

Union leaders were agreed without exception that they were democratic leaders. One of them could have been speaking for all leaders at all times when he said:

I was elected on a ballot vote and it is my duty to represent the members interests as they express it to me. I may have differences with the members in which case they have to be hammered out through the union's democratic procedures.[29]

He went on to say however that:

There are some trade union leaders who do tend to see themselves as shepherds of a flock and adopt a cynical attitude toward the rank and file. I think the best way of guarding against this, despite all the disadvantages, is periodic elections. Of course the union leader does tend to develop specialist skills. And it is possible for him to manipulate the membership – rules for example can be interpreted in ways favourable to the leadership or dominant clique. It may happen unconsciously.[30]

Trade union leaders were undoubtedly in a very strong position to impose their views on their unions. If, like the shop stewards, they had always to cast an eye over their shoulders to see if the troops were following, unlike the shop stewards they had the union machinery as an instrument of protection. To be sure, leaders had to contend with their executive committees which nominally were the final repositories of union authority, and executive members by comparison with the rank and file were usually well-informed men and women. But by comparison with senior full-time officials they were innocents. As V. L. Allen said of Arthur Deakin, former general secretary of the Transport Workers:

(His) intimate contact with the affairs of the union, with the trade union movement at home and abroad, and with political events generally, gave him a depth of knowledge and an understanding of problems that the executive members could hardly have hoped to possess. The skills that had developed in committee and conference work, in negotiating and representing the union, combined with the specialist services of different departments of the Union that he had at his disposal, gave him an undoubted position of authority.[31]

And of Ernest Bevin, Deakin's predecessor: 'Though sometimes the Executive rebuffed Bevin, in the main and on important Union issues his superior ability and knowledge enabled him to persuade them to accept his proposals as their own.'[32]

In principle at least there was nothing Machiavellian about this, nothing notably devious or underhand – the widely and popularly accepted role of the representative leader actually imposed on him the *duty* of acquiring specialist knowledge and abilities. It also imposed on him the obligation to ensure that his electors were not deprived of politically relevant knowledge – while yet leaving it to him to define what was relevant. This meant of course that the extent to which union politics was relatively 'open' or 'closed' was partly dependent upon the personality and political convictions of the leader. (Generally speaking a left-wing leader favoured more open policies than a leader of the right. Herbert Smith, president of the Miners Federation, speaking at the 1921 Labour Party conference on the Communist Party's application for affiliation, said that while he disbelieved in Communism he saw no reason to be frightened of it. Disruption was necessary in every trade union for otherwise there would be no check on its leadership.[33] Such classical liberal views were not to be heard from the right-wing.)

That the definition of relevancy remained the gift of leadership was often the basis of rank and file attack. Allen reported that:

(Bevin) was pressed by a number of branches before the 1923 delegate conference of the union to distribute

Executive minutes to branches; their claim was based on democratic rights but he successfully opposed it. To distribute the Executive minutes he said, would be equivalent to broadcasting what action the Union was going to take, and on what scale. He wanted the Executive to have a free hand. Employers' organisations did not publish their minutes. In addition he thought it was unwise to show the divisions within an Executive over taking a particular course of action.[34]

In 1936 Bevin returned to the same theme: '. . . the lay members must be conscious that there are certain things they cannot do, and they must leave the Officers to carry out the tasks in which they are employed to specialise, the lay member supplementing this work and thereby making a very happy combination.'[35] There was sound reasoning in those arguments. Dealings with employers inevitably contained an element of bluff, and the effectiveness of bluff depended on withholding information that would allow it to be called if it were known. It was important, too, that divisions within the union should be concealed because if known they were open to exploitation. Nevertheless the withholding of information served to strengthen the hand of leadership because it deprived the rank and file of the ability to engage in criticism at the appropriate time. To the extent that it was ever possible for the rank and file to deliver informed criticism, it had to be after the event – at which point it could be dismissed as being 'past history', an 'unnecessary opening of old wounds', or whatever other well-tried cliché seemed suitable.

If, despite leadership opposition, people continued to insist on their 'right' to be informed they might have been told, as was the 1962 congress of the TUC by George Woodcock: 'The General Council do not as a rule welcome motions on the Congress agenda. Our general attitude to motions is that if they tell us to do what we already intend to do they are redundant, and if they try to tell us what we do not intend to do they are offensive.'[36] Such breathtakingly aggressive pronouncements may only have been possible at the TUC where motions were only accepted if sponsored by unions. Certainly it is difficult to imagine a union leader at a conference of his own delegate members being so audacious even if predisposed. The more typical response from a challenged leadership was a call for loyalty of the form: 'Trust the Executive – you elected us, and you must trust us to act in your best interests. Some matters are too delicate to be discussed in public because public discussion may prejudice the outcome.' This sort of appeal implied a choice between 'open' or 'closed' diplomacy and expressed a preference for the closed variety where people could speak in confidence with one another and make deals without publicly being seen to do so. The open alternative, by contrast and implication, was much less effective because it exposed people to oppositional pressures that could prove personally embarrassing.

Appeals to be allowed to work in confidence were almost invariably allowed: partly because it was the traditional and accepted way of doing things; partly because of the sentiment that maybe it really was safer to let certain things remain unsaid; partly because a challenge implied a lack of personal integrity in the leader; and partly because the leadership's speaking skills were often such as to make a monkey out of the critic or rebel. In most respects and from nearly every angle the rank and file dissident had little going for him. His relative lack of political skills was often his most telling disadvantage – to challenge the leadership was tantamount to an invitation to a personal confrontation, and it was a rare member who had the courage to offer himself for public humiliation. Trade union leaders were adept at the put-down, as Blaxland noted when talking of Jimmy Thomas:

'. . . the men were always worsted, tackling as they were a past master at the art of throwing ridicule on hecklers. One of his aids was stealthily to obtain from the branch chairman the names and identity of interrupters. They found it very disconcerting to receive a rebuke directed at them by surname or a scathing witticism with christian name appended.'[37]

It has already been pointed out that progress toward becoming a leader entailed the acquisition of political capital. Barry Hindess described this process well when he said that it involved:

. . . making speeches, pertinent comments, relevant points of order. It requires that one marshals one's thoughts, is able to think quickly and preferably on one's feet, that one chooses words carefully, learns to summarise complex situations in a few sentences . . . All this is only a beginning. Those who progress beyond the elementary stage must develop a personal style, learn to acquire appropriate allies and enemies, to score debating points, to raise relevant questions.[38]

The rank and file activists who were prepared to challenge the leadership and had some of the necessary skills to put up a good showing had often served an apprenticeship in the Communist Party or in one of the other left-wing sects. That they had done so cancelled out their speaking and debating abilities. Where they were not already known to the leadership, their distinctive vocabulary immediately gave them away. Once identified as 'politicals' they could be tagged as such and discredited. Sheila Cunnison quoted two workers – one Conservative and one Labour – commenting on their union's AGM: 'We had a lot of fun at the last union meeting. Any time anyone got up and objected to one of the proposals that the executive committee made, the general secretary got up and banged the table and said he didn't want to hear from Communist agitators.'[39] In dealing with the 'politicals' the leadership could be assured of having the bulk of the members on its side: with the latter's consciousness firmly rooted in the workplace, they shared their leader's predelictions for rigidly compartmentalising the world into the mutually exclusive spheres of politics and economics. As Deakin said on one occasion: 'We cannot afford to allow the Communists' attempted infiltration into, and domination of the trade unions to succeed. It is important that members should record their votes and take their full part in making sure that their representatives are prepared primarily to do an *industrial job of work* (emphasis added).'[40]

The branch was the only part of the union machine open as of right to every member. That the right was not exercised and the reasons for it were discussed in the previous chapters. The absence of large-scale participation at branch level naturally meant that it was controlled by a very small number of activists who lacked any mass basis. This, as Joseph Goldstein pointed out, served to undermine the authority of the activist and placed control in the hands of the full-time official. The official had the confidence and the security of the permanence of office, and knew that the branch officers acted on behalf of a small active group which could seldom effectively rally the majority of the membership to action. Thus the final decision as to what policy would best serve the interests of the membership often rested with the full-time officer rather than with the branch activists.[41]

Goldstein then proceeded to give an example of his analysis by quoting a case – to which he was a witness – where an official openly violated branch policy by concluding an agreement with an employer which was self-evidently against the members' interests, ridiculed the branch officers, and subsequently refused to explain his conduct.[42] It appeared there was nothing unusual about that:

The usurpation of policy-making authority . . . is reflected on all higher levels of the T & GWU's organisation [*This was in the early fifties* – author's note]. At area level, for example, one of the most responsible officials in the union frankly admits that so long as he feels he is acting in the best interests of the union, he does not hesitate to break its rules . . . this permanent officials' method is to 'present your executive (the elected representatives) with a *fait accompli ;* if necessary look to the rules to explain your action.' This attitude of disregard for the rank and file member as an individual to be consulted on matters of policy . . . is precisely summarised by a remark made during this interview: 'We know what is best and do it.'[43]

As if to underline the irony, Deakin, then general secretary, told the 1947 Biennial Delegate Conference: 'Above all . . . you are the people in this BDC who determine the policy of this organisation. Our job is to apply it.'[44]

'What they don't know they can't shout about' was a crude and ancient adage – but every potential autocrat knew that it was a neat summary of political realism. The general truth of that has already been shown above: to appeal for confidence was at the same time to ask the membership to be content in its ignorance. However, ignorance could be maintained in more positive ways than that. As early as the 1890s the Webbs felt able to comment on the use of the union journal as an instrument of control (see chapter 2). Most union rule books, then as now, made it clear that it was the responsibility of the general secretary. By the 1960s many unions of any size retained full-time editors who, though enjoying an area of discretion, knew that the general secretary would want in every issue a prominent place for his views and would expect to be consulted over any item critical of him and union policy. If the journals were not widely read, they were closely scrutinised by the people who mattered – the rank and file activists. Although the journal was not their only source of knowledge, its importance was still considerable for the printed word was more potent than gossip.

Possession of the journal clearly meant that union leaders were in a strong position to determine their members' general state of knowledge and to define what issues were relevant. Possession also meant that it could be used to build up what could only be called a 'cult of leadership'. The GMWU *Journal* sometimes pushed leader-worship to the frontier of hilarity.

Lord Cooper tells me that he and Lady Cooper have a lively and amusing travelling companion. He is Maxie, a six-year-old budgerigar who often accompanies them on union business. According to the general secretary, the little bird recognizes landmarks and aptly comments on them. Indeed, Lord Cooper believes that Maxie knows the turning from the M1 and M6. He is a gay and voluble talker. Tape recordings have been made of his chatter for the amusement of friends.[45]

The general tenor of most union journals was well-summarised by Goldstein's comment on Deakin's use of the Transport Workers *Record:* 'Though the *Record* devoted considerable space to (the Unofficial Dock Strike of 1948), all of it was taken by Arthur Deakin . . . in defence of the Union's attitude and actions. The membership was provided with the facts only as the Union official saw them, or at least as he wished the membership to see them.'[46]

Education was also a means of maintaining ignorance for, apart from a few areas in the Miners' union, political education was never an activity that the unions took seriously. This did not mean that educational services were not provided. Indeed most unions provided money or scholarships to Ruskin College and other adult educational establishments having links with the labour movement, and subsidised members who wanted to take correspondence courses through the National Council of Labour Colleges and the TUC. Education, however, was one of the frills available to the curious and the ambitious. Alone amongst the unions, only the South Wales Miners made any attempt to make it a central part of union activity.

There were broadly two reasons for this. The one was rooted in the pragmatic nature of trade unionism. George Woodcock, when asked to account for the failure of the unions to do much in the way of education, replied:

They haven't done anything have they? Trade unionism is a straightforward routine business despite all the glamour that is attached to individuals; it's as routine as peeling potatoes. I don't know anybody in whom it has induced a mood of reflection. At least not inside the trade union movement. The lads themselves don't seem to reflect very much. They have a stock issue – and they just pull a stock solution off the shelf . . . There is this essential conservatism. There is a distrust of what they would call the theorist and the academic – and they would block them both together. They are fearful that he will cause them unnecessary work.[47]

The other reason stemmed from this accurate assessment. Linked as the leaders were to managing the *status quo,* they did not, as Woodcock suggested, want to do anything that would cause them 'unnecessary work'. Will Paynter in a separate interview suggested what that could mean:

They don't do much in politicising their members. In most of the areas of the Miners union the leaders would be reluctant to take the risk because they would be afraid that they might create opponents to themselves. They would be afraid of creating a political consciousness amongst the active element of their membership who might eventually challenge them and their positions.[48]

The maintenance of ignorance amongst members was not therefore simply derived from their desire for self-protection, for that desire itself was derivative of the practice of trade unionism.

The fact that union leaderships had many methods at their disposal for controlling their members – and the methods in principle were no different from those used by other leaders in other contexts – did not mean that their members were straight-jacketed. As was shown in chapter four, the most arresting characteristic of trade unionism after 1945 was the ability of more and more groups of workers to pursue their own claims regardless of the wishes of their nominal leaders. It was shown in the same chapter that the membership had nothing like that strength in the inter-war years: in other words there was an inverse relationship between the ability of the unions to control its members and the level of employment, such that the higher the one rose the lower the other fell. What *this* meant, to spell it out, was that insofar as members were well-organised and well-led at their place of work they were more or less immune from any constraints that the union leadership could have applied. Leadership constraints were only generally felt when unofficial action was ill-timed or inefficiently conducted, i.e. on occasions when it was necessary to fall back on the union machine for protection, or when governments intervened with legal or quasi-legal measures to upset the balance of power in the workplace. Those not altogether exceptional circumstances apart, union leaders were more restrained than restraining. Their situation as over-viewers of the national and international scene, their experience of governmental pressures to induce 'order' into industrial relations in the name of the 'national interest', produced in many if not most of them a desire to comply. Yet compliance was out of the question for, given the mode of consciousness of the rank and file, it would have involved a mass disciplining of the members and a consequent breakdown

of the unions as established and organised. Thus
George Woodcock's observation, born of first-hand
experience of the 1960s:

What you get at the top of a union is the inhibition from
the realisation that they can't carry their own people with
them. You can see them almost physically pulled up by
the reins at a certain point when intellectually they would
want to go further. By then they become conscious that
they may have to deal with this or that man, this or that
group in the union and you can see them start backing
away.[49]

So long as the rank and file concentrated most of
their political resources in the place of work they
were free from the coils of union politics; as soon as
they ventured into the intricate workings of the
union machine they were liable to become entangled
and bested. Notwithstanding what has been said of
the relative power of leadership versus rank and file
in the post-war years, most union activists at some
time in their careers did find it necessary to draw on
union resources. Where for many it was no doubt a
cordial and fruitful experience, for those who dared
a challenge there were only bitter memories.

8. Trade Unionism and Capitalism

Are we sitting at the sickbed of capitalism, not only
as doctors who want to cure the patient, but as
prospective heirs who cannot wait for the end and
would like to hasten it by administering poison? We
are condemned, I think, to be doctors who seriously
wish a cure, and yet we have to retain the feeling
that we are heirs who wish to receive the entire legacy
of the capitalist system today rather than tomorrow. This
double role, doctor and heir, is a damned difficult task.

*Fritz Tarnow, a German trade union leader, speaking
in 1931*[1]

'The lessons learned related more with how to cope
with capitalism, and less with how to overthrow it.'
That was the verdict on the period 1800-1850; a
verdict that could have equally applied to 1972.
Despite the hopes and the dreams, the dedication and
unremitting energy of successive generations of trade
unionists, the British political economy was still
governed by the principles of capitalism. Trade union
leaders of the 1960s claimed with pride to have some
stature in the community: in similar vein had William
Allan, secretary of the Engineers almost exactly one
hundred years previous, spoken of the unions' desire
to be 'respected and respectful'. Thus did the prominent men of organised labour speak across a
century to each other in a political language not much
eroded by time and great events.

The explanation of the historical development of trade

unionism lies not in the actions of individuals who
featured prominently in the events of importance.
Trade unionism was what it was, not through the arbit-
rary dictate of an individual in search of a definition,
but because of a *common* appreciation that labour
could only withstand capital if organised in collectivities. As Marx said in his discussion of trade unionism
amongst Lancashire cotton workers in the 1840s:

The first attempts of workers to *associate* among themselves always take place in the form of combinations.
Large-scale industry concentrates in one place a crowd
of people unknown to one another. Competition divides
their interests. But the maintenance of wages, this common
interest which they have against their boss, unites them
in a common thought of resistance – *combinations*. Thus
combination always has a double aim, that of stopping
competition among the workers, so that they can carry
on general competition with the capitalist.[2]

In the absence of a union, labour came face to face
with capital as a mass of isolated individuals. Each
worker, having only his labour-power to bargain with,
confronted his employer alone; as an individual in
a sea of others he was devoid of any bargaining
strength. Bargaining required that the respective
parties had the ability to employ sanctions, and the
only sanction at the command of labour was its
refusal at the offered price. But that sanction was
worthless and empty when he was but one amongst
hundreds or thousands. The spontaneous lesson from
that situation was clear: only through a combination
of workers did a threat of withdrawal of labour become real. Only through combinations did labour as
a whole begin to meet the power of capital.

The solitary worker, once organised in a union, had
placed a buffer between himself and his employer –
though the effectiveness of that buffer depended upon
a great deal more than its mere existence. Much
depended upon the general level of employment, the

scarcity of the skills of the workers in question, the legal status of the unions (restrictions on the use of the strike, on the use of funds, on the actions of officials etc.), the efficiency and responsiveness of the union organisation with respect to rank and file demands. Furthermore, not all workers found it easy to organise themselves into unions – which is to say that the spontaneous response could only be activated in certain conditions. The American experience from the 1880s to the 1930s showed that ruling class hostility, as manifested through the repressive use of the law, the police, and the military could be extremely effective in breaking some unions and severely retarding the growth of others. Trades typified by seasonal variations and the use of casual labour drawn from a large pool of unemployed made it relatively easy for an employer to resist trade unions – as seamen and dockers found in the 1890s and 1900s. Where a working force was small the objective relationship between employer and employed could be obscured and overlaid by close social relationships, and the exposed position of potential activists left them open to swift victimisation. In other cases 'labour-only' sub-contractors stood between the worker and the capitalist. In yet others, especially in white-collar occupations and in rural areas, traditional attitudes of deference stood in the way of solidarity and unification. Overall, and at the back of these various modifying factors, stood the more general consideration of the level of unemployment and the degree of expectation of suffering unemployment: nothing inhibited trade union activity quite as much as mass unemployment.

Where trade unionism was established it was about wages and wage payment systems, about bonus and overtime rates, about who should do what jobs and with what manner of assistance, about redundancy and hiring and firing, about limitations on the exercise of managerial authority, about working conditions – in

short, about everything that immediately affected the
worker in his mine, factory, warehouse, ship, office, or
wherever. At its most elementary, trade unionism drew
its inspiration from the desire of separate groups of
workers to insist upon 'rights' attached to the job. It
could exist quite independently of any organisation as
H. A. Turner said: '. . . people of the same occupation, who are regularly brought together in the same
workplace or town, may acknowledge regular leaders,
develop customs of work-regulation and systematic
"trade practices", and produce a disciplined observance
of the latter, without embedding these procedures in
any formal records . . .'[3] Thus trade unionism properly
so called was, as Marx pointed out, a step beyond the
taken-for-granted customs and practices of job control, an attempt to by-pass (not eliminate) the divisive
consequences of work-group practices and to empha-
sise common interests. More generally, as even Allan
Flanders acknowledged,[4] trade unionism was about
power: about the power of organised labour to confront the power of organised capital and to insist on a
regularisation of the relationships between them. Trade
unionism was a standing and continuing assertion of a
fundamental cleavage of interest, yet simultaneously,
because of its insistence on the regulation of that conflict, it could not be the vehicle of its abolition. Hence
Perry Anderson's comment: 'As institutions, trade
unions do not *challenge* the existence of a society
based on a division of classes, they merely *express* it
. . . They can bargain within the society, but not
transform it.'[5]

The trade unions could not transform society because their very nature – as signified by their spontaneous formation and the character of their aims –
required them to work within it, to take it for granted.
Thus trade unionism regarded the present as remedi-
able; and to look upon the present in that way ensured
that the unions remained anchored to it. The present

did not impinge upon the unions homogeneously, with an undifferentiated face. The variations within the political economy of competitive pressures, technologies, skills etc., meant that the unions were, at any particular moment, faced with a bewildering variety of circumstances. The unions accordingly reflected the complexities of the face that capitalism, taken as a whole, presented to its workers.

What the unions saw was not capitalism as a *system* but capitalism as a range of separate and unique elements, each of which threw up its own distinctive set of 'problems'. It thus followed that the unions adjusted to capitalism in a piecemeal, *ad hoc* way rather than as a *movement*. The inability to act as a movement, coupled with its tenacious grasp of the doctrine of 'we'll cross that bridge when we come to it', implicitly guaranteed the continuance of sectionalism.

The term 'movement' as used by trade unionists was merely a loose expression, a formal linguistic convention for talking of unions in the plural. The term hinted at, and was redolent of, the dead decades of 'new unionism' when the progressive men and women looked upon the unions as being in the vanguard of socialist advance. Its continued usage thereafter was a sentimental nod in the direction of the aspirations of the past – and a not totally submerged belief amongst some that the unions remained, in some vague and unspecified way, an indication of a different future. 'Movement' implied a disciplined unity aimed at the fulfilment of a coherent and comprehensive strategy. If there were odd moments, such as 1926, when the unions achieved a temporary unity, that very unity was undermined by the absence of a political strategy. Precisely the same factors accounted for the failure of the unions in 1971 and 1972 to cope with the passing through parliament of the Industrial Relations Act.

Sectionalism was regarded as one of the cardinal sins by every conscientious trade unionist – and amply indulged in by all of them: inevitably produced by the nature of their practice; inevitably reproduced by the inability of that practice to be other than it was. Sectionalism could only have been held in check if the unions had been capable of generating a programme of a sufficiently broad sweep as to make the differences between workers seem petty and trivial. Such a programme would, of necessity, have needed to be a *political* programme: trade union practice stood in the way of that, too. Thus did union squabble with union over areas of jurisdiction and job demarcation; thus did work group squabble with work group over pay differentials and over anything else that set them apart. All trade unionists knew that it was ludicrous, weakening, and divisive. And all were helpless in its face, resigned to the perennial patchwork of mediation that gave only temporary solutions to enduring questions.

Sectionalism, in the absence of any politically unifying force at work in the working class, gave rise to a deformed mode of political consciousness thoroughly deceptive in its implications. The working class was possessed of a collective consciousness, but it was rooted in the workplace because it was only there that it came up against capitalism as an immediately experienced reality. The social relations of production in particular workplaces generated an 'us' and 'them' consciousness which the daily encounters with work discipline and authority served only to reinforce. The timidly reform-oriented Labour Party, which did precisely nothing to help the working class understand the politics of capitalism, yet further enhanced the tendency for consciousness to 'end' at the factory gates.

Where the job was concerned there was, by the 1970s, an extraordinarily well-developed determination to protect what had come to be regarded as 'property'. But this deep antagonism of the workplace did not extend outside it, it was in no firm way generalised beyond the article of faith that 'all bosses are the same'. The only significant political consequence was that the suspicion of bosses spread out to encompass all those in positions of authority. Thus, despite the growing participation of the working class in the world of more-than-minimum-consumption, there remained strong sentiments of separateness and resentment: resentment that the working class was usually on the receiving end of whatever 'pushing around' was going on. These feelings, however, did not congeal into a socialist consciousness. Indeed where they were expressed in such community organisations as tenants' associations and claimants' unions, there was a strong tendency for these groupings to emulate the structures and ideology of trade unionism.

Trade union leaders were not as a rule much more politically sophisticated than their members – though tactically they were incomparably more proficient. Immersed as they were in the world of the big-time professional fixers, they had but little choice to learn the rules. But learning the rules and rituals of the fix was not the same as learning the governing principles of the historical process: in fact the more embroiled the union leader became in the wheelings and dealings of producing and selling compromises, the more convinced he was likely to become that these, rather than the clash of great interests, determined the course of history. Certainly it was easy to understand the union leader's round contempt for 'academic theorists' if they were of the left-wing sort.*

The union leader did not have a simple choice

*Lord Citrine, commenting on a discussion at the London School of Economics held by the Socialist League in 1933, said: 'It was an altogether interesting evening and in response to an invitation to meet the group again I wound up by saying I thought we had come to discuss practical politics. What I had found, however, was that we were discussing ultimate Socialist objectives of a theoretical character. I did not propose to waste my time further in doing so.'[6]

between becoming either a fixer or a man of the people. The logic of his situation demanded that he became the former no matter how distasteful he may have found it. That same logic also demanded that he played the part of the latter as well. Every trade union leader was two men; privately a man of the quiet and secretive world of power, and publicly a tribune of the people. This did not necessarily mean that he was a subtle practitioner of duplicity, for a public perform-ance in the role of the tribune could be used as a weighty backing for what he was negotiating privately. A show of strength from the grass-roots was often a decisive bargaining counter, for it could be essential to demonstrate that threats were not idle. This process of private and public dealings set the leader apart from his members. It made an oligarch of even the most scrupulous Communist who was of a type well-fitted to be appreciative of the political danger of his situation.

Oligarchy was doubly present in the logic of trade unionism. The attainment of objectives required the leader to enter into durable relationships with poli-ticians, employers, and state officials both nationally and locally. And the effectiveness with which those aims could be pursued depended on the efficiency, the coherence, and the discipline of the union organisa-tion. These two factors were each different aspects of the same reality.

The necessity of negotiations had the effect of creat-ing a small cadre of activists – some lodged in the union machine, others operative largely in the work-place. Wherever located they took on the role of the representative and as such were, to a greater or lesser extent, isolated from the rank and file. The function of the representative had strong élitist tenden-cies built in to it. It assigned to the person elected or appointed the task of acquiring specialist skills and knowledge; it imposed the duty of moving in circles that had codes and patterns of interaction foreign to the experience of the ordinary constituents, of moving in circles whose inhabitants had interests running directly counter to those of the representative's followers. The representative was marked out as a man apart, removed from the direct scrutiny of those in whose name he acted, he was nevertheless expected to remain loyal to them.

In that role he was afforded little protection. The acceptance of the politico-economic status quo, the acceptance of the enduring nature of capitalist institutions and the political apparatus that supported it, all combined to make the representative a supplicant – albeit a sometimes very powerful one. The lack of a developed political consciousness amongst his constituents underlined his potential weakness. The people who owned and controlled the means of production and dissemination of knowledge were from the same 'thought-world' as those with whom he negotiated. Thus, through their possession of the means of mass communication they could appeal over the heads of the leaders in terms subversive to his position. It was not only right-wing leaders who had the uncomfortable experience of being disowned by their members. Thus the leader's basic weakness, founded in his acceptance of the logic of the economics of capitalism, was compounded by the political suggestibility of his members.

The people with whom the trade union leader had to deal were trained in the ways of abstractions and generalities, briefed by men of professional expertise, reared in an ethos which assured them of their right to rule and confident of the biddability of others, possessed of the subtle charm and courtesy that could be so beguiling to those brought up in a political culture admiring of aristocratic 'coolness'. The union leader needed strong armour to find all that resistable. Yet if relatively few could withstand the culturally transmitted 'allure' of the mighty, it mattered not greatly that others could not. Either way deals had to be done, compromises had to be arrived at – and not infrequently by the techniques of secret diplomacy.

The union leader's situation in the union machine also served to insulate him from the mass of the membership as his prime preoccupation came to be with union administration. And administration meant adjusting and balancing the competing sectional claims on the union's resources. The unions could not afford to risk strike action in chase of every claim, nor could they afford to approve of every dispute that the members ventured into on their own account. Funds were finite, and most annual balance sheets delicately poised. Thus it fell to the leadership to survey the overall situation, to assess where resources should be allocated. Decisions were not, however, 'rational' in the sense that different claims were judged purely on their individual merits. On the contrary, decisions were determined by the balance of internal union politics, by judgements as to the future consequences on the memberships' jobs through following a certain line.

Not all sections of the membership were equally well-organised, either on the ground or within the union. Those that were well-organised in the workplace and in their penetration of the lay apparatus of the union were disproportionately powerful: thus constituting blocs especially needy of attention and not lightly to be crossed. Still, even these could be flouted with impunity in the name of organisational survival. As Hugh Scanlon told a conference of the Engineers in 1971, by way of explaining his intervention in the Ford strike of that year: 'There comes a time, particularly after a strike has been on nine weeks and when there seems not even a remote possibility of any meeting of the sides within the foreseeable future, when there are responsibilities on the president of this union that exceed the responsibilities of anyone else.'[7] There came a time, that is, when even a trade union leader committed to militant policies found it necessary to tell a section of his membership: 'I know what's good for you better than you know yourselves.' The trade union leader was in some position to say that with truth and conviction, for different sections of the rank and file did not generally know much about the affairs of the others and, moreover, were not much interested.

Naturally the union leader's own position was bound up with the continuance of the organisation. But it would be altogether too facile to believe that as a consequence his only reason for preservation of the union was self-interest and self-aggrandizement. To believe that would be to attribute to him *total* dominance. Clearly leaders *did* play an important part in holding their organisations together, and the extent to which those with strong personalities could stamp their own idiosyncratic views on union policies *did* influence the course of union development. There was, to put it briefly, an area of tolerance in which the union leader could go his own way and trample over objectors – an area which the conception of the leader-representative tacitly ceded to him. That area, though, was set in a wider complex of internal political groupings and shifting alliances that permanently featured in the leader's calculations and definitions of the possible.

The significant thing about the factors that made for the insulation of leadership and gave it its area of autonomy was that none of them were ultimately rooted in the organisation as an independent entity. Michels told but a part of the story when he said: 'who says organisation, says oligarchy.'[8] Organisations may have had relative autonomy but they did not exist in historical vacuums, sealed off from other aspects of the social structure. The form that organisation took, and the sorts of roles it provided and defined were basically determined by the mode of adaptation to the society in which it operated. Where the unions were concerned, that mode of adaptation was one of parallelism. V. L. Allen put it this way:

Developments in the trade union movement were always, inevitably, responses to changes in the environment of the unions. When markets for commodities, including labour, were small and localised, so were trade unions. As industrial units grew and became more complex in their organisation so the tasks of unions became more complicated . . . The changes in the democratic structure of unions . . . were all responses to alterations in market structures which enabled firms to expand. The movement from complete lay administration to the employment of full-time officials was made necessary.[9]

Every stage in the development of capitalism, not excluding the more contemporary one of wide State intervention in overall economic management, created an enormously complicated matrix of institutions. And at every stage the trade union official was implicated, thus endowing him with more and more specialised knowledge and distancing him from the rank and file. The fact to seize upon, however, was not the distancing, but the logic of the process that created it. As long as trade unionism was about remedying the present, so long was it inevitable that the union leader was abstracted from his roots, forced into the patterns and practices of 'secret diplomacy', the 'shabby compromises' that so aroused the anger of the rank and file from time to time. If some union leaders proved less than resilient and fell victim to the reflected grandeur of the powerful, then that certainly proved that they hadn't the character for the job. But it proved most of all that the possibility of corruption was inherent in trade unionism unsupported by a vigorous socialist movement. The oligarchic tendency was determined by the nature of trade unionism; corruption was but a possible side effect. Thus where moral condemnations were sometimes justified, they were quite out of place and counter-productive if not underpinned with an understanding of how it was that transgressions could be produced.

'This double role, doctor and heir, is a damned difficult task.'

Blinkered politics: as it was in the beginning

Trade unionism in its contemporary form of a centralised bureaucracy and an established set of relations between its leading personnel and employers and politicians, waited upon two developments: first, the creation of a disciplined 'factory' proletariat, and second, the appreciation of the ruling class that trade unionism was not synonymous with insurrectionism or revolutionism. Before either of those two factors were noticeably present, forms of trade unionism fluctuated between foreshadowing the future and echoing the past.

The trade union 'instinct', the notion of combining for the settlement of a common grievance, certainly preceded trade unionism as it is now understood. The rick-burning followers of Captain Swing and the machine-breakers of General Ned Ludd were practising, it has been suggested, 'collective bargaining by riot'; a revealing and enlightening description. It corrects the historical record by pointing out that the destruction of property was not 'senseless acts of violence', but spontaneous responses to solid grievances that were resistant to resolution by other means. At a time when the labouring classes were not recognised as having a legitimate political existence, resort to violent direct action against *property* was an objectively legitimate tactic. These tactics echoed the past in that by the beginning of the nineteenth century there was a well-established tradition of rioting as a means of regulating the price of bread, the main component of the workers' diet.[10] They foreshadowed the future in two respects. First was the spontaneous combination accompanied by direct action, and second was the exertion of that action at the immediate source of complaint – the price of bread, the threshing machine, the steam-powered loom. Rioting, that is to say, was primarily economic rather than political in motivation, although underlying the destruction of property there was, in the words of Rudé, '. . . a "levelling" instinct or the belief in a rough sort of social justice, which prompt(ed) the poor to settle accounts with the rich . . .'[11]; instincts which were always present in the more organised strikes of subsequent decades. Nascent trade unionism was present in other forms, too: the informal practices of work groups in regulating their output, the thinly disguised activities of friendly societies to the same end.

In sum, wherever men were gathered together, or wherever grievances were commonly held and deeply felt enough to override differences of individual circumstances, there was the ever-present tendency to combination and direct action. This tendency was eventually canalised into the organised trade union as the progress of capitalism required a stable work force working to fixed routines, and as the overall stability of capitalism required that this new disciplined force be accepted into political citizenship. At every stage in its development trade unionism as a formalised set of institutions drew on the spontaneous 'urge' to combine – which was never so apparent as in that great period of union growth, the 1890s and 1900s. In the 1890s the new unions grew out of strikes. If in some cases, such as the London dockers, a small nucleus existed around one small and relatively privileged group of workers, that nucleus became transformed into a larger and more generalised organisation as the strike moved from group to group. Thus the strike itself *created* the union by welding men together in an atmosphere conducive to the recruiting efforts of the organiser. In the 1900s the unions capitalised on strikes as new sources of membership. Although strikes were typically embarked upon by men who knew little or nothing of trade unionism, once 'out on the stones' with the first flush of enthusiasm somewhat lessened by a cooler appreciation of their audacity, they were ripe for the experienced counsel of the professional organiser. Thus did unions as permanent organisations at once capitalise on spontaneity and seek to harness it: to discipline workers in their own interests as capitalists sought to discipline them in theirs. The unions, however, never succeeded in extinguishing the will to direct action. In fact, if anything they broadcast its efficiency by extending to backward areas the news of its success. This was especially true of the 1950s and 1960s when larger numbers of workers than ever before demonstrated their belief in the practices of their ancestors. The wildcat strike, far from being a new phenomenon, was the rock on which the unions were built.

With the development of unions as institutions, a new word entered the vocabulary – sectionalism – a word designed to express the failure of the unions to control and direct the source of their inspiration. The failure was endemic and ineradicable. The lack of a suitable politics meant that the plurality of the unions never gelled into a movement, and the inability to form a movement meant that groups of workers organised in different unions fell into conflict with each other. The presence of differences in the job situations of workers organised in one union made it impossible for that union to produce a common programme. Sectionalism literally wrecked the several ambitious attempts at all-embracing unions in the 1830s: the National Association of United Trades for the Protection of Labour collapsed within eighteen months of its foundation, the Operative Builders Union within three years, the Grand National Consolidated Trade Union within a year. Sectionalism defeated the Triple Alliance in the 1920s almost a century later, and fifty years after that the attempts of the Union of Post Office Workers in 1971 and 1972 to get a united strategy among the unions in the public sector of employment did not even get a serious hearing. Always and everywhere small groups of workers and powerful national unions refused to sink their identities in a common cause. Sectionalism was at the root of many a conflict between trade union leaders and was the characteristic basis of rank and file rebellions, even accounting for the intrusion of other factors. The Shop Stewards Movement in the engineering industry in World War I drew its strength from the tradesman's fear of dilution of his craft, and even the thoroughly political Minority Movement of the 1920s sometimes found it hard to resist capitalising on sectional discontents. And finally the great wave of unofficial action of one sort or another from the 1950s onward was sectional by definition, being utterly devoid of any political intent. Despite amendments and reamendments of union constitutions, the only thing that proved capable of checking sectional action was mass unemployment. The activities of the Communist Party notwithstanding, union leaders had a fairly quiet time in the 1920s and 30s.

So long as industry catered largely for local markets or was concentrated in small areas and not much differentiated, sectionalism was not a major problem for the unions: they too were localised, and their lay officers conversant with local conditions. But as soon as unions started to operate on a national scale sectionalism became a major problem – and necessarily so, for while the small local union could closely mirror local conditions it was quite impossible for the national union to do so. That the union had moved to London or one of the great provincial cities did not alter the fact that workers lived in specific places and worked for specific employers. From thenceforward there were continual struggles as the men in the localities resisted the subordination of their powers to that of the centre, or attempted to closely circumscribe what central control they were ready to concede. In some unions the head office was moved around from town

to town so that local men could take it in turn to act
as the executive committee – and keep a close eye on
the secretary. In others the national executive was
drawn only from the area in which the national office
was situated – acting on the principle that only local
men had the time and the opportunity to keep a check
on leadership. In other unions the national secretary
had his powers limited to that of acting merely as a
means of keeping the various branches informed of
their different activities. These and other devices –
such as the referendum – were characteristic of the
second half of the nineteenth century, but had nearly
everywhere fallen into disuse by the early 1920s. As
the unions grew in size to embrace a widening diversity
of particular interests, sectional jealousies themselves
ensured that more powers would accrue to the centre.
The local executive did in many cases act as a considerable constraint on general secretaries or their
equivalents, but at the same time it came under fire
from men in other localities who complained – usually
with cause – that their own interests were not being
properly attended to. Eventually, then, the local
executives were replaced by bodies composed of men
from all areas. The new national executives, if much
more representative of the spread of membership,
greatly enhanced the power of their leaders. Meeting
much less frequently – monthly or quarterly as against
the weekly meeting of the local executive – the leader's
activities were much less visible, while on the other
hand the explicit divisions within the union allowed
him to play the role of peacemaker.

The pattern of evolution of leadership authority outlined above applied mainly to the unions of the labour
aristocracy. The story was somewhat different where
the new unions of the semi- and unskilled workers were
concerned. By the period of maximum union growth
in 1890–1920 the aristocratic unions were established –
the new members moved into an already well-defined

structure of organisation. The new unions, by contrast, grew from scratch to mass organisations almost overnight. In those circumstances there was no opportunity for a period of 'experimentation' with different forms of government. While basic constitutional forms were borrowed from the old unions (the London Dockers in 1889 based their rules on the ASE), the commitment to a mass membership regardless of occupation dictated the immediate recruitment of full-time officials. From the outset the new unions had a professional bureaucracy of dimensions unknown (and unwanted) in the craft unions. These officials, because of their key role in organisation drives and their possession of skills barely present in the semi-literate workers they organised, immediately assumed positions of considerable authority: the setting-up of branches and the teaching of basic administrative skills was the province of the organiser. And once established in the role of mentor he was not easily displaced. Thus was the oligarchical tendency embedded in the fabric of the large general unions from the very beginning, and indeed continued to remain much more pronounced in them than the unions which remained nominally 'craft' in the decades that followed. Turner had cause for classifying the large general unions as 'popular bossdoms'.

In the 1960s the search for constitutional answers on the part of union leaders to the perennial question of sectionalism was more or less ended. Only in a few odd unions like the Engineers and the Railwaymen did executive committees exercise a strong restraining influence. If that was at times personally frustrating for their respective leaders, they were really in no better case than other less trammelled leaders. With effective full employment, constitutional checks were mostly irrelevant to the activities of the rank and file in the workplace. Thus did attempts to check sectionalism take a new form. Sectionalism, it was decided, was a consequence of 'wrong attitudes', 'mis-understandings', 'failures of communication'. So union journals were made more attractive, shop stewards sent on training courses and called to conferences, and more 'experts' employed in the union head offices. At the time of writing none of this had any visible pay-off, for rank and file militancy was on the increase rather than the reverse. It was obviously naïve to think that sectionalism was just a state of mind, an aberration of people wedded to false precepts. Sectionalism, to repeat yet again, was the elementary consequence of a trade unionism that followed the cycles and contours of a capitalist economy.

There was no heroic age of trade unionism when the men who stood at the head of the 'movement' had superhuman qualities of courage and integrity. Trade union leaders, being professional compromisers, did not believe in leading epic lives for the sake of glorifying biographers of future generations. Neither did they believe, at least as a general rule, in using their positions to feather their own nests: those that did tended to set up in the business late in their careers when they swapped trade unionism for politics. Alexander Macdonald, the Miners leader in the 1870s, seems to have been one of the very few who made a modest fortune out of his incumbency; John Burns and Jimmy Thomas made theirs only when well-launched on their careers as Members of Parliament. There was, from the late nineteenth century onward, a steady procession of union leaders leaving the move-ment for State employment, particularly between 1945 and 1951 with the creation of the large nationalised industries. It was rare, however, for a man established as a general secretary or executive president to leave while still in office. He either took a job when he was at or near retirement, or much earlier in his career before he was within striking distance of the general secretaryship. The jobs were not usually handed out for services rendered – and were not usually accepted for acquisitive reasons. They were offered because the union leader had experience that could be of use to the State. And they were accepted because most union leaders were thoroughly imbued with the liberal ethic of 'public service'. Thus did the offering and the accepting reveal the political conceptions of trade unionism as held by the ruling classes and the leaders of organised labour.

The co-option of the union leaders was not a crude and messy business, a process in which ambitious and avaricious union leaders sold themselves to Brechtian caricatures of capitalists (although there were, incredibly, situations that did not much depart from that characterisation at the local level of union officialdom). On the contrary, it was a much more gentlemanly business, even in the days of William Allan and Robert Applegarth when union leaders generally were looked upon as upstart clods. And it could be a gentlemanly business because the union leaders were not revolutionaries but patient reformers. Once this was understood by politicians – and it seems to have been done so from as early as the 1850s by many of those that counted – little stood in the way (except class prejudice) of their political acceptability and subsequent offers of State posts.

The acceptance of trade union leaders was not, however, to be confused with a complete and unequivocal acceptance of trade unionism. Trade union leaders could be amenable and personally related to. Trade union*ism* was a different sort of animal for it mobilised and at least partly disciplined the working class on its own behalf. There was at *all* times a fear, sometimes submerged, sometimes near the surface, but always present: a fear that the working class might be mobilised as a revolutionary force.

From their very earliest days the trade unions were closely watched by some branch or other of the police.

The most infamous spy in the history of the labour movement was Oliver, so superbly described in Frank Peel's book, *The Rising of the Luddites*:

Oliver was a paid spy in the employ of the Government – only one of ˙a great number – but the most wicked, unscrupulous, and infamous of the whole vile troop. He had had many splendid jobs during the year 1817, and had grown fat and scant of breath. The times indeed were rife for the informer and the detective.

In later years spies and informers got cleverer and harder to detect, but they were still around right enough as some right-wing trade union leaders very well knew. Organisations were infiltrated, informers recruited, mail intercepted, houses watched, men followed, telephones tapped.

In 1918 the Shop Stewards Movement discovered that one of its most prominent members had turned police informer. In 1925 the National Unemployed Workers Committee Movement found that one of its most active London branches was led by a man in the pay of the police. In 1926 Lord Citrine noted Jimmy Thomas as saying: 'The government are well-informed. By God, you don't know! When I was in the government the railway sectional strike was on . . . Well, do you know that I had on my desk every morning full details, photographs of letters that had passed, speeches made at private meetings . . .'[12] Will Paynter said that in the thirties 'I know that my phone was tapped when I was a trade union official and active Communist in South Wales. And as active organisers of the Communist Party we used to get our post opened and investigated.'[13] And more recently, as Harold Wilson's memoirs made plain, comprehensive reports were reaching the government of what was going on inside the National Union of Seamen during their 1966 strike.[14]

In the 1960s most large strikes were observed and reported upon by the Special Branch, and some

managements used the Special Branch as a private
detective agency for spying on their own employees.
There was not much doubt either that certain trade
union leaders got tipped-off as to the activities of their
members and fellow officials.* The very nature of this
subject does not lend itself readily to proof or regular
exposure: secret police naturally tend to be secretive.
There are certainly some newspaper reporters who
have a detailed knowledge of how the Special Branch
and MI6 operates. They never reveal it of course
because of their reliance on their contacts for tips.
Detailed information is kept in Home Office files —
which Office is notably reluctant to reveal to historians
such information even when fifty years old.

The fear of what the working class might do has
been evident in a number of other ways: the right-
wing press's love-affair with the agitator theory of
industrial relations and the near hysterical insistence
of some managements in the same belief. (A full year
after the Pilkington strike some of that Company's
directors continued to believe that they had been the
victims of a left-wing plot — despite their receipt of a
Special Branch report assuring them to the contrary.)
Even less politically naïve employers and managers
had a hatred of strikes that went beyond resentment
at loss of profits. Hatred implied fear — and it was
justified in some measure. Strikes were not just with-
drawals of labour, refusals to work at the offered price
and conditions — they were also *temporary* rebellions
against managerial authority and thus an implied nega-
tion of management itself. Strikes carried with them
that 'levelling instinct' that Rudé talked of in his discussion of the motivation of rick-burners and machine-

---

*A friend of the author, now a respectable Labour MP, once
had an opportunity to look through his personal file in the head
office of his union. He was amazed to discover in it a police
report on his activities and contacts during the course of an
official strike. He also had conclusive proof that in the same
strike his phone had been tapped.

breakers, though it was almost unknown for it to break surface. *That* eventuality would have made strikes overtly political – and we have seen that the factory consciousness prevalent in the working class made it easy for struggles to be taken up and defused by unions which were the embodiment of that consciousness.

As a broad general rule the ruling class in different periods sought to exploit the divisions within the working class. When there were no divisions of any consequence, then life was that little bit easier as in the years 1850 to 1890: a period of considerable prosperity until the late eighties; the socialists and ex-Chartists confined to their little debating clubs and societies; the labour aristocracy largely imbued with the petit bourgeois morality of thrift and self-help; members of the wealthy bourgeoisie prepared to assist in the short-lived wave of general unionism in the early seventies. In that climate the most visible and organised part of the working class did not seem in the least threatening – and altogether worthy of encouragement. Thus were the unions helped on their way with liberalising legislation that removed impediments to their progress. Thus was the 'respectable' working class rewarded with electoral reform.

By the years immediately before the First World War the scene had changed traumatically from the point of view of the ruling class. The unions had cast aside their Liberal connection, strikes multiplied, socialist agitators got enthusiastic audiences and made an impact on union policies. Yet the ruling class did not panic. Its more intelligent members had the political nous to see that all was not as it superficially seemed. Ramsay MacDonald had formed a secret electoral pact with the Liberals in time for the 1906 election – and the trade union leaders who made up the bulk of the subsequent thirty Labour MPs rapidly proved themselves 'sound' and 'moderate' men. The willing collaboration of trade union leaders with government and employers during the War, proved conclusively to the ruling class that the men who led the unions were not to be confused with the Manns, Gallaghers, and Pollitts who agitated at the grass-roots. Policies were thenceforward adopted – by large employers as well as governments – of making sufficient concessions to the right-wing men of labour as to help them in their attempts to beat off the left. That policy was pursued right through to the 1970s with invariable success.

The recruitment of union leaders to State posts and the bestowal of peerages and the like were not in themselves important. Symbolically, however, those gestures were of immense significance, They showed that culturally the labour establishment had been incorporated into the 'thought-world' of the ruling class, and politically that the labour establishment was a highly effective instrument of dominance.

The 'new model unions' of the 1850s and 1860s were quite clear about politics – they wanted none of it. Mindful of the disasters of Chartism and of the petit bourgeois status of the labour aristocrat, they were insistent that the unions were not to be instruments of political change. The lobbying of parliament and the recruitment of political allies was legitimate; extra-parliamentary agitation was not. Thus was born the unions' highly peculiar definition of politics, a definition, incidentally, that has traditionally been associated with conservativism: people who were prepared to accept the *status quo* and work within it for piecemeal reform were not political; people who wanted to overturn the established order were, in the words of Harold Wilson, 'politically motivated' – a very neat demagogic device for imputing neutrality to one's own actions and bias to those of others. The men of the mid-nineteenth century would have understood Wilson perfectly.

Despite the distortion of the English language in a

manner that anticipated George Orwell's 'newspeak' by a hundred years, the separation of the world into mutually exclusive spheres of politics and pressure group activity made a limited sort of sense. Pragmatically, it gave the unions an aura of respectability which freed them from State repression at a time when repression was a very vivid memory. And logically it had a certain philistine appeal. If politics was about recasting the social order, and trade unionism was about doing deals with employers, then it followed that trade unionism was non-political. That logic, and the perverse definition that it rested upon, persisted with an unshakeable tenacity. It was employed with increasing frequency and growing shrillness after the tentative socialist revival of the late 1960s and early 70s.

With the trade union's creation of the Labour Party in 1900 the unions were especially well-equipped to impose their definition of politics on their left-wing dissidents – they could be told that their proposals were the province of the 'political wing' of the movement, thereby revealing fully what they had always understood as being 'political'. Parliamentary politics was not the same as agitational politics. If the limitations of the language required that the same term be used in conjunction with forms of activity greatly at variance with one another, everyone understood the nuances; parliamentarism was 'good', agitation was 'bad'. The creation of the Labour Party reinforced this distinction.

The Labour Party was never a socialist party despite its claims to the contrary. That fact was guaranteed from the outset by its ideological and financial enslavement to the trade unions. The unions did not establish the Labour Party because of a commitment to a socialist society. They established it because the Liberal Party was no longer capable of coping with the growing demands made upon it by a more aggressive working class. The demands were reformist, but too radically reformist for a ruling-class party in which business elements dominated. Furthermore, the coalescence of the landed and industrial factions of the ruling class forbade the continuation of two ruling-class parties at a time when the working class was being welded together by the advance of monopoly capital. These were considerations not lost upon the more far-sighted leaders of the Conservative Party – nor for that matter upon the heads of some of the larger companies who had started to desert the Liberals for the Tories in the 1890s.* Different Liberal governments between 1906 and 1914 made determined populist appeals in attempts to contain the Labour Party and retain their slice of the working-class vote. They failed – as did further attempts after the War. Middle-class Liberals defected to the Tories, working-class Liberals to Labour: by 1935 the Liberals were politically dead.

The Labour Party, thanks to its trade union roots, was held doubly captive. The practice of trade unionism as an industrial activity led, as we have seen, to its orientation to the present. A present that was shorn of any time dimension, a present that had no past and no future. This compression of time simultaneously cut off any attempts to look at society as a system caught up in a process of historical change and development, and ensured that attention would be exclusively focused on defects, on 'social problems' – social problems, that is, that were to be considered in themselves rather than as structural products of an historical process. The trade unions, to use a crude analogy, acted like a gauche motor mechanic who thought he could tinker around with the carburettor without understanding its relationship to the overall workings of the engine. Or to put it more simply: the

*Other considerations also entered into the desertion. The monopolists, for solid economic reasons, preferred the restrictionist policies of the Tories to the free trade policies of the Liberals.

everyday practice of trade unionism in no wise suggested that there was any need of a social and political theory. What the trade unions saw were isolated problems – and what they sought were pragmatic solutions. Therefore, by their 'ownership' of the Labour Party, they were able to impose on the party their own stunted view of the world. What they wanted out of the Labour Party was in principle no different than what they had previously sought from the Liberals. This was why, for the entire decade of the nineties, the TUC's Parliamentary Committee resisted all attempts from those to the left of them to form their own party. Why form their own party when they could, for the most part, get what they wanted anyway? Once the party was established, with the men of the 'new unions' proving themselves basically as conservative as the men of the old, the liberal future of Labour was assured. So, too, was the absence of a socialist consciousness within the working class.

The Labour Party carried from its birth the conception of politics as a pressure group activity – so that when it formed governments it attemped merely to carry out what it had previously pressed for, namely limited, *ad hoc* reforms. The fact that many of them were of immediate benefit to the working class should not, however, be allowed to obscure the further fact that the *means of their attainment* held back a socialist advance. The pressure-group conception of politics implicitly meant a *de*-activation of the working class. It meant a recognition of the established institutions of power, especially parliament, and thus a clear and sharp break between the party's activists and its mass following. Effective pressure group politics depended upon the acceptability of its leading echelons, an acceptability that could not have been forthcoming if that leadership was engaged in mass agitation. The practice of parliamentarism as an *overriding principle* therefore excluded agitation, i.e. the political mobilisation of the working class. The detailed practice of parliamentarism

– the acceptance of its stylised courtesies, its archaic rituals, its bestowal of 'confidential' information, the sham conflicts of a debating society – served as a subsidiary reinforcement of the division between the activist and the mass. Parliamentary socialism could not on its own, unsupported by an awakened and politically conscious working class, be a serious business; not when it enabled close personal friendships across party lines, such as those between Aneurin Bevan and Lord Beaverbrook who were stereotyped symbols of the Labour left and the Tory right in the 1950s.

The Labour Party became a more or less perfect expression of the sort of politics embodied in trade unionism. Creating no socialist consciousness amongst the working class, it ensured that the class remained locked up in the factory consciousness that developed out of collective action in the workplace. With the dominant institutions of the labour 'movement' as a whole bereft of any clear and coherent understanding of the historical processes of capitalism, it produced *ad hoc* 'solutions' to *ad hoc* problems and left the working class wide open to such reactionary mystifications as nationalism, racism, and 'benevolent' capitalism. That was the case in the 1900s. And it remained the case in the 1960s. Thus did trade unionism deny its non-political claims and work, directly and indirectly, as a powerful integrative and stabilising force.

That the trade unions proved an integrative force did *not* mean that they had been totally absorbed and incorporated into the State – despite appearances to the contrary and the implications of the stand-points of some right-wing trade union leaders. Paradoxically, there were times when in limited respects rank and file sectionalism proved a progressive force. At no time was this more evident than in the 1960s. In that decade – which extended into the 1970s – British capitalism was entering into a phase of deepening crisis which by 1972 had forced a Tory government committed to an unleashing of market forces to resort to an 'incomes policy' that it had hitherto despised. That crisis was due in no small part to the 'wage militancy' of the working class.[15] The Labour and Conservative governments both tried, with varying degrees of ardour, to get the TUC to collaborate in operating 'incomes policies'. Or put another way, they tried to use the unions as instruments of State policy. The union leaders, with widely varying amounts of enthusiasm, agreed. Their agreement was insubstantial and eventually revealed as utterly hollow – they could not control the rank and file which insisted on going its own way and taking a plastic market for all it would bear. The rank and file, in short, undermined at one stroke their leaders' willingness to play ball demonstrating thus the fragility of their dominance. Trade union leaders could be as obliging as they liked in the committee rooms of Whitehall and the Cabinet room at No. 10 Downing Street – but they still had to keep half an ear cocked for the sound of the men dropping their tools. The insistence of the rank and file on job control, which in other respects concealed latent reactionary tendencies, in this respect at least effectively stopped the unions from becoming part of the apparatus of a corporate State.

And so the story may end as it was almost in the beginning:

In a general way (the British workman's) political thoughts and aspirations, though they scarcely recognise them as being strictly political, turn exclusively upon improving the position of labour in relation to capital. And this they seek to accomplish by direct action – as, for instance, by strikes and the strengthening of trades unions – and not by the establishment of entirely new social systems.

That comment could have been written in 1972. In fact it was written in 1871 by Thomas Wright, a Liverpool man.

A Personal Postscript

Several friends who read this book while it was still only a manuscript with an uncertain future told me that I ought not to have finished the story at the point I did. While they broadly agreed with what I had done in the way of analysis, they thought that left as it was it seemed too negative. What needed to be done, they said, was a 'What is to be done?' I replied that I was too conscious of my limitations to aspire to be another Lenin, and that anyway what they were really asking for was another book. All this in a comradely spirit you understand.

What worried them was that the book as it stood might be understood as an attack on the unions and as a counsel of political despair; that it could be read as though there were *nothing* to be done. They appreciated that that was not my position. Indeed knew very well that implicit in my negative assessment of the politics of trade unionism was a very positive call for the urgent renewal of a socialist politics firmly grounded in a socialist party. They knew, too, that I had no intention of embracing a form of lunacy that would advocate the dismemberment of the trade unions. After all, I had chosen the title with some care.

To make the call, however implicitly, for a socialist politics is, in a way, to beg the question. What does it mean to make that plea?

A socialist politics requires both a theory and a strategy. A survey of the left-wing press reveals an abundance of strategies. It does not reveal, as yet anyway, any theoretical work with a finely-honed cutting edge. But to call for a socialist politics is to call for exactly that. Thus at one level what needs to be done is some intellectual work, some solid development of Marxist theory that will enable us to comprehend the reality of contemporary capitalism.

Notwithstanding the extraordinary virulence of sectarianism on the left in recent years – on a scale that bears comparison with the first few decades of the century – there are grounds for optimism. A bit nebulous perhaps, but grounds just the same. In the last ten years or so Marxism has at last started to make a serious impact on British intellectual life. (Our indebtedness to the various people associated with *The New Left Review* is profound.) The works of Marx, Engels and Lenin are once again being read for the first time on any scale since the twenties and thirties. And, furthermore, being read in the way those authors intended. Marxism is starting to emerge as a way of thinking, as a way of reflecting upon the world. This is something which is largely new. In earlier decades the Marxist writers tended to be regarded either as scriptural authorities, or as instant bases for *ad hoc* analyses. Although that tendency still persists, it is quite evidently waning. After the political deadliness of the 1950s and early 60s, so reminiscent of the same period in the previous century, there is room for hope once more. There is a world to win.

Tony Lane
Liverpool
June 1974

On Borrowing or Buying Books

It's a bit difficult to know where to start. There has been a lot written on how the union makes us strong, on the politics and trade unionism of the British working class. The quality varies considerably. Some of the better known and widely read books are frankly best left to gather dust. On the other hand are books not so well known and not so readily available which are really rather good.

Very broadly I have used three standards for the selection that follows: availability, readability, and the employment of a theoretical line that I find not too objectionable. Some of the books I have recommended do not score equally on all three counts. Indeed some of them I'm pretty indifferent about: they are included because there's nothing much else available on the particular subject. Other works, because of my criteria, do not appear at all. For example I have completely omitted all of those pieces of article length that appear in the various academic journals. Not because I have anything against them. On the contrary, some of the very best work on aspects of the labour movement appear in their pages. The major problem with the journals is that they are only easily accessible to those who live in large cities whose central libraries stock them, or to those who can get at university or polytechnic libraries. To help those who are fortunate in any of those respects I have included a short list of journals at the end.

To help readers get what they want out of librarians and bookshops I have included in brackets the name of the publisher and the year of publication. Where a cheap paperback edition is available I have also included price. For those who are keen to have their own collection of books I have indicated what you might get for the fairly modest outlay of a tenner.

Librarians in local libraries are usually helpful people: if they don't have the book you want just ask them to order you a copy. It helps to ensure that they provide a good service for other readers – and it costs you nothing. Buying books can be a bit of a problem if your tastes are broader than pseudo-erotic novels, thrillers and science fiction. If you live in a university town then the university bookshop *might* be useful. It's certainly worth having a look at. A growing number of cities are seeing the rebirth of left-wing bookshops, and they are certain to have good selections of books on the labour movement. Otherwise you could do a lot worse than write to: *Collet's Bookshop, 64–66, Charing Cross Road, London, WC2H 0BD*. They have an excellent postal service.

There are two books which are *absolutely basic* and should be read before anything else: Karl Marx and Frederick Engels, *Selected Works* (Lawrence and Wishart, 1970, £1.50), and V. I. Lenin, *What Is To Be Done?* (Panther paperback, 1970, 30p). Marx, Engels and Lenin, contrary to popular belief, are not always difficult to read. Neither are they turgid and humourless figures – which is more than can be said for most of their detractors. Marx had a very lively wit and a sharp eye for absurdity; both Engels and Lenin had a great gift for explaining complicated ideas in everyday language. The selected works of Marx and Engels contains a number of items indispensable to clear thinking: above all the 1848 *Manifesto of the Communist Party*, an inarguably brilliant summary of Marx's theory. Lenin's book, although first written in 1902 and especially for a Russian audience, remains the standard analysis of trade unionism. Care should be taken in trying to directly transpose his theory to contemporary Britain (or anywhere else). The general principles, however, remain valid. This, like all of Lenin's work, is a masterpiece of clarity and forcefulness. Two other books are useful. T. B. Bottomore and M. Rubel, *Karl Marx* (Pelican, 1972, 30p), and R. Hyman, *Marxism and the Sociology of Trade Unionism* (Pluto Press, 1971, 30p). The first of these contains a well-chosen selection from the main body of Marx's and Engels' works. The second, despite its intimidating title and occasional lapses into academicism, is a short (fifty-three pages) but generally reliable survey of Marxist theory of the trade unions.

Of general histories of the British labour movement there is the monumental *The Common People, 1746–1946* by G. D. H. Cole and Raymond Postgate. Written with a light touch, and yet packed with detail, it's about the best overall work. (Published by Methuen, 1963. The paper edition is about £1.) Much shorter and spanning a briefer period is A. L. Morton and George Tate, *The British Labour Movement 1770–1920* (Lawrence and Wishart, hardback edition for 75p). Written with feeling, it is one of the few books that capture the sense of drama of great labour struggles. E. J. Hobsbawm's *Labouring Men* (Weidenfeld and Nicholson, 1968) is a collection of superb essays on the labour movement in the nineteenth century ranging from 'The Machine Breakers', an analysis of Ludd, to a piece on the influence of 'Labour Traditions'. Most of the other of Hobsbawm's works are also well worth reading (see your library catalogue). As far as E. P. Thompson's *The Making of the English Working Class* is concerned I can do no better than quote the blurb on the cover of the Penguin edition (1972, £1.25): '. . . probably the greatest and most imaginative post-war work of English social history. This account of artisan and working-class society in its formative years, 1780 to 1832, adds an important dimension to our understanding of the nineteenth century, for Edward Thompson sees the ordinary people of England not as statistical fodder, nor as merely passive victims of political repression . . . He shows that the working class took part in its own making.' Thompson is an exuberant romantic at times – and why not? Surely that's a luxury we can occasionally afford? Still, correctives are in order. A. E. Musson's *British Trade Unions 1800–1875* (Macmillan, 1972) provides an antidote to Thompson as well as other historians on the left. Despite his resort to such prejudiced phrases as 'mob violence' and 'primitive barbarism', and his talk of doctrinaire writers as if he himself was devoid of any political opinion, it is nevertheless a very solid book with the merit of having only sixty-seven pages. It is also a reminder that it is quite possible for writers on the labour-right to be as balanced in their judgements as those on the left.

On the Chartists the best available is Asa Briggs' collection of articles by various authors, *Chartist Studies* (Macmillan, 1960). There is also R. G. Gammage's *History of the Chartist Movement*, reprinted by Merlin Press, 1969. Gammage, a doctor, had himself been a leading Chartist. His account has deficiencies (akin to those of Musson mentioned above), but dryness is not one of them. The Swing revolt has been admirably captured in E. J. Hobsbawm and George Rudé, *Captain Swing* (Lawrence and Wishart, 1969, and Penguin, 1973, £1.50), while the best work on Ludd is Frank Peel, *The Risings of the Luddites*, an old work recently reprinted (1970) by Frank Cass.

Royden Harrison's *Before the Socialists* (Routledge & Kegan Paul, 1965) covers in dashing style the years of the top-hatted trade unionist. As they say in the ads: 'this is one you can't afford to do without'. Also on the years around mid-century is E. P. Thompson's and Eileen Yeo's collection of Mayhew's reports on life and labour in London, *The Unknown Mayhew* (Merlin Press, 1971, and Penguin, 1973, £1). Some of the best material on the 'new unionism' in the late nineteenth century is in Hobsawm's *Labouring Men*, and Asa Briggs' and John Saville's collection *Essays in Labour History, Vol. I* (Macmillan, 1960). For detail presented in the most incredibly drab way see Hugh Clegg and others, *A History of British Trade Unions Since 1889, Vol. I* (Oxford University Press, 1964). Some of the judgements in this latter book should be viewed with deep suspicion: they range from the simple to the simple-minded.

There is surprisingly little on the growth of the shop stewards' movement during and after the First World War. There is a very good essay by James Hinton in Asa Briggs' and John Saville's *Essays in Labour History, Vol. II* (Macmillan, 1971). The essay is being transformed into a book, *Union Militancy and the First World War*, yet to be published. G. D. H. Cole's *Workshop Organisation*, first published in 1923 and recently reprinted by Hutchinson (1973), has a supremely boring title: a pity since it is a really excellent account of the growth of shop stewards in the engineering industry in the First World War. Writing on roughly the same period is Walter Kendall with his *The Revolutionary Movement in Britain, 1900–1921* (Weidenfeld and Nicolson, 1969). In spite of a scatty conclusion that the Communist Party could not have established itself in Britain but for help from Moscow, it's an exciting book to read and the only source worth bothering with for those who want (or need) to understand where the revolutionary left was at fifty-odd years ago. L. J. Macfarlane's *The British Communist Party* (MacGibbon and Kee, 1966) is a reasonably fair and adequate account of the CP until 1929: if it doesn't exactly take you by the ears it must be counted essential reading. It should be supplemented by the CP's own multi-volume official history which is as yet incomplete. Volumes so far published are by James Klugman (Lawrence and Wishart). As far as the Labour Party is concerned there is only one good book: *Parliamentary Socialism* by Ralph Miliband (second edition, Merlin Press, 1972). Henry Pelling's *The Origins of the Labour Party, 1800–1890* (Oxford University Press, 1971) does not set the pulse racing but has to be read until such times as Tom Nairn completes his long-rumoured book. In the meantime there is a pay-off to be had from a search for the now out of print *Towards Socialism*, edited by Perry Anderson and Robin Blackburn for Fontana Books (1965): it contains Tom Nairn's exotic yet telling article on the Labour Party. It first appeared in *New Left Review*, Numbers 27 and 28, 1964.

One of the most revealing works on the Labour Party is in fact a history of the Conservative Party: Maurice Cowling's *Impact of Labour* (Cambridge University Press, 1971). Cowling is not an historian's historian. Perhaps it is partly because he believes in telling a story with gusto and relish. Cowling is a High Tory, but don't let that put you off. It's a marvellous book to read. At once subtle and provocative, it's a splendid account of the intrigue in the Conservative Party in the early 1920s that led to the ascendency of Stanley Baldwin. You need to know how the ruling class operates and this book will help you on the way. So, too, will Nigel Harris's *Competition and the Corporate Society* (Methuen, 1972). Dealing mainly with the Tories since 1945, it has a very helpful chapter on the 1930s. Robert Blake's *The Conservative Party from Peel to Churchill* (Fontana, 1972, 60p) covers the period from 1830 to 1955. *The Economist's* reviewer said Blake 'knows how to tell a good story'. I agree. The best book on Conservatism is Benjamin Disraeli's novel, *Sybil*. Written about 130 years ago, and currently out of print (I think), it goes to the very heart of Toryism. It's bound to be in your library. The Liberal Party also needs to be understood. If nothing else it will broaden your perspective on the Labour Party. Try John Vincent's *The Formation of the British Liberal Party 1857–1868* (Pelican, 1972, 50p). It's beautifully written. Try also Trevor Wilson's *The Downfall of the Liberal Party, 1914–1935* (Fontana, 1968, 60p). According to the blurb, A. J. P. Taylor commented: 'a good political mystery, and Mr Wilson has told it in fine dramatic style'.

Labour historians have yet to do much work on the 1920s and 30s. Fortunately there are some really good books written by the activists themselves. At the top of the list must go Wal Hannington's *Unemployed Struggles* (Lawrence and Wishart, 1936): it's as exciting as any Raymond Chandler thriller. Great stuff, it is. Harry Pollitt's *Serving My Time* (Lawrence and Wishart, 1940) is very good on the 1920s and earlier. Will Paynter's *My Generation* (Allen and Unwin, 1972, £1.50): it says on the cover 'portrays the roving twilight life of a pithead revolutionary', and so it does.

The General Strike has been poorly served. The best book has been out of print for ages and is very hard to get hold of. It's W. H. Crook's *The General Strike* (University of North Carolina Press, 1931). Julian Symons, best known as a crime-writer, made a creditable attempt with *The General Strike* (Cresset Press, 1957). The most recent is Christopher Farman's *The General Strike May 1926* (Rupert Hart-Davis, 1972). It looks destined for future publication as a Paladin paperback. Its deficiencies are the same as those of the other books: it concentrates far too much on the comings and goings of trade union leaders and politicians, and is far too sparse on what was going on in the localities. It's the best going at the moment even if Farman is unable to restrain himself from making the usual clichéd and mindless gibes at the CP. Somebody should reprint Raymond Postgate's *A Workers*

History of the Great Strike (Plebs League, 1927). A. Mason's *The General Strike in the North East* (Hull University Press, 1970) is very thorough. D. E. Baines' and R. Bean's 'The General Strike on Merseyside, 1926' appearing in J. R. Harris, ed., *Liverpool and Merseyside* (Frank Cass, 1969), is interesting though rather thin.

Books on the more recent period are few and far between. Huw Beynon's *Working for Ford* (Penguin, 1973, 90p) is a cracker. It portrays with terrific vividness and sympathy shop floor struggles. It's a 'can't put it down' sort of book. Tony Cliff's *The Employers' Offensive* (Pluto Press, 1970) was a best-seller amongst shop stewards. Deservedly. The book I wrote with Kenneth Roberts, *Strike at Pilkington's* (Fontana, 1971, 50p), contains serious flaws but is still the best account of a post-1945 strike. A good one to have around is Robin Blackburn's and Alexander Cockburn's *The Incompatibles: Trade Union Militancy and the Consensus* (Penguin, 1967, 30p). Amongst other items it includes Michael Frayn's hilarious piece, 'A Perfect Strike', which starts: 'Public opinion, so far as I can tell, unquestioningly concedes the right of men in a free society to withdraw their labour. It just draws the lines at strikes.' Barry Hindess's *The Decline of Working Class Politics* (Paladin, 1971, 60p) is a very good story about the decline of the Labour Party in Liverpool. Finally, though this book is hardly recent, is that great working-class novel: Robert Tressel's *The Ragged Trousered Philanthropists* (Panther, 1972, 60p). To have not read it is unforgivable.

Journals

The International Review of Social History
Labor History
Past and Present
Economic History Review
Bulletin of the Society for the Study of Labour History

Best Buys for a Tenner

K. Marx and F. Engels, *Selected Works*, Lawrence and Wishart, £1.50

V. I. Lenin, *What Is To Be Done?*, Panther, 30p

R. Hyman, *Marxism and the Sociology of Trade Unionism*, Pluto Press, 30p

R. Tressel, *The Ragged Trousered Philanthropists*, Panther, 60p

E. P. Thompson, *The Making of the English Working Class*, Penguin, £1.25

A. L. Morton and George Tate, *The British Labour Movement 1770–1920*, Lawrence and Wishart, 75p

E. J. Hobsbawm, *Labouring Men*, Weidenfeld and Nicolson Goldback, £2

H. Beynon, *Working for Ford*, Penguin, 90p

W. Paynter, *My Generation*, Allen and Unwin, £1.70

B. Hindess, *The Decline of Working Class Politics*, Paladin, 60p

G. Orwell, *The Clergyman's Daughter*, Penguin, 35p

G. Orwell, *The Road to Wigan Pier*, Penguin, 30p

References

Introduction

1. I am grateful to my colleague Norman Wilson for this personal reminiscence.
2. Quoted in Christopher Farman, *The General Strike May 1926*, London, 1972, p.29.
3. ibid. p.50.
4. ibid. pp.122–3.
5. Julian Symons, *The General Strike,* London, 1957, p.57.
6. Farman, op. cit. p.116.
7. ibid. p.154.
8. ibid. p.225.
9. ibid. p.233.
10. ibid. p.243.

Chapter 1 .

1. Quoted in E. J. Hobsbawm & George Rudé, *Captain Swing*, London, 1969, p.208.
2. Quoted in F. Engels, *The Condition of the Working-Class in England in 1844*, London, 1952, p.229.
3. Quoted in A. Aspinall, *The Early English Trade Unions,* London, 1949, p.324.
4. E. P. Thompson, *The Making of the English Working Class*, London (Pelican ed.), 1968, p.604.
5. G. Rudé, 'English Rural and Urban Disturbances on the Eve of the First Reform Bill, 1830–31,' *Past & Present,* Nos. 36-8, 1967, p.91.
6. See for detailed accounts G. Rudé, *Paris and London in the 18th Century, Studies in Popular Protest, London*, 1970.

7. Quoted in W. Houghton, *The Victorian Frame of Mind*, London, 1957, p.39.
8. H. Perkin, *The Origins of Modern English Society*, London, 1969, p.188.
9. Quoted in E. P. Thompson, op cit. p.295.
10. S. & B. Webb, *The History of Trade Unionism*, London, 1920, p.292.
11. ibid. p.73.
12. P. A. Brown, *The French Revolution in English History*, London, 1965, p.167.
13. E. J. Hobsbawm, *Industry and Empire*, London, 1968, p.4.
14. J. F. C. Harrison, *The Early Victorians*, London, 1971, p.161.
15. V. A. C. Gatrell, 'Introduction', in Robert Owen, *Report to the County of Lanark*, London (Pelican ed.), 1970, p.43.
16. R. Williams, *Culture and Society 1780–1950*, London (Pelican ed.), 1961, p.43.
17. E. P. Thompson, op. cit. p.859.
18. ibid, p.869.
19. ibid, p.861.
20. P. Hollis, *The Pauper Press*, London, 1970, p.217.
21. P. Quennell (ed.), Henry Mayhew, *Mayhew's London*, London, 1969, p.553.
22. For details see F. C. Mather, *Public Order in the Age of the Chartists*, Manchester, 1959.
23. F. C. Mather, 'The Government and the Chartists,' in A. Briggs (e.), *Chartist Studies*, London, 1960.
24. See the Home Office documents reproduced in A. Aspinall, op. cit.
25. J. Dugan, *The Great Mutiny*, London (Mayflower ed.), 1970, p.94.
26. I. J. Prothero, 'London Chartism and the Trades', *Econ. Hist. Rev.*, Vol. XXIV, 1971, p.203.
27. E. P. Thompson, op. cit. p.531.

28. S. Pollard, *A History of Labour in Sheffield*, Liverpool, 1959, p.50.
29. S. & B. Webb, *Industrial Democracy*, Vol. I, London, 1897, p.9.
30. S. Pollard, op. cit. p.67.
31. W. H. Warburton, *The History of Trade Union Organisation in North Staffordshire Potteries*, London, 1931, p.41.
32. Quoted in G. D. H. Cole, *Attempts at General Union*, London, 1953, p.5.
33. For the best overall account see ibid.
34. A. E. Musson, *British Trade Unions 1800-1875*, London, 1972, p.37.
35. G. D. H. Cole, *A Short History of the British Working Class Movement*, London, 1948, p.85.
36. Quoted in G. D. H. Cole, *Attempts at General Union*, op. cit. p.144.
37. J. Child, *Industrial Relations in the British Printing Industry*, London, 1967, p.78.
38. S. & B. Webb, *Industrial Democracy*, Vol. I, op. cit. pp.91-2.

Chapter 2

1. Quoted from 'The Journeyman Engineer', in R. Harrison (ed.), *The English Defence of the Commune*, London, 1971, p.134.
2. G. Best, *Mid-Victorian Britain 1851-1875*, London, 1971, p.230.
3. J. T. Wood (ed.), *Popular Movements c. 1830-1850*, London, 1970, p.5.
4. H. Perkin, *The Origins of Modern English Society 1780-1880*, London, 1968, p.271.
5. Quoted in G. D. H. Cole & R. Postgate, *The Common People*, London (Methuen ed.), 1961, p.389.
6. Quoted in W. Houghton, *The Victorian Frame of Mind*, London, 1957, p.47.
7. G. D. H. Cole & R. Postgate, op. cit. p.368.

8. See John Taylor, *From Self-Help to Glamour: The Working Man's Club, 1860-1972,* History Workshop Pamphlets No. 7, Oxford, 1972, pp.3-5 for a most illuminating list of patrons.

9. Quoted in W. Houghton, op. cit. p.58.

10. E. Phelps Brown, *The Growth of British Industrial Relation,* London, 1960, pp.117-18.

11. S. G. Checkland, *The Rise of Industrial Society in England 1815-1885,* London, 1964, pp.363-4.

12. See F. M. Leventhal, *Respectable Radical,* London, 1971.

13. Quoted in W. H. C. Armytage, *A. J. Mundella: The Liberal Background to the Labour Movement,* London, 1951, and 1957.

14. M. Dobb, *Studies in the Development of Capitalism,* London, 1963 (revised ed.), p.226.

15. R. Harrison, *Before the Socialists,* London and Toronto, 1965, p.26.

16. Quoted, ibid. p.28.

17. E. J. Hobsbawm, *Labouring Men,* London, 1964, p.228.

18. G. Stedman Jones, *Outcast London,* Oxford, 1971, p.343.

19. E. Genovese, *The World the Slaveholders Made,* London, 1970, p.4.

20. Quoted in H. A. Turner, *Trade Union Growth, Structure, and Policy,* London, 1962, p.181.

21. Quoted in R. Harrison, *Before the Socialists,* pp.19-20.

22. See Stan Shipley, *Club Life and Socialism in Mid-Victorian London,* History Workshop Pamphlets No. 5, Oxford, 1972.

23. R. Harrison, op. cit. pp.232-3.

24. R. Postgate, *The Builders History,* London (n.d.), p.185.

25. S. & B. Webb, *Industrial Democracy,* Vol. I, London, 1897, p.8.

26. ibid. p.27.

27. R. Challinor, *Alexander Macdonald and the Miners,* CPGB, 'Our History Pamphlets', No. 48, 1967/8.
28. See ibid. pp.30-2.
29. J. B. Jefferys, *The Story of the Engineers,* London, 1945, p.57.
30. V. L. Allen, *The Sociology of Industrial Relations,* London, 1971, p.68.
31. J. H. Porter, 'Wage Bargaining Under Conciliation Agreements, 1860-1914', *Econ. Hist. Rev.,* Vol. XXIII, p.461.
32. E. Halevy, *Imperialism and the Rise of Labour,* London, 1951, p.211.
33. Quoted in Cole & Postgate, op. cit. p.385.
34. For a full account of this intriguing story see R. Harrison, op. cit.
35. Cole & Postgate, op. cit. p.406.
36. ibid. p.367.

Chapter 3

1. Quoted in H. J. Fyrth & H. Collins, *The Foundry Workers,* Manchester, 1959, p.83.
2. J. Saville, 'Trade Unions and Free Labour: The Background to the Taff Vale Decision', in A. Briggs & J. Saville (eds.), *Essays in Labour History,* Vol. I, London, 1960, p.317.
3. Quoted in P. Bagwell, 'The Triple Industrial Alliance, 1913-1922', in A. Briggs & J. Saville (eds.), *Essays in Labour History 1886-1923,* Vol. II, London, 1971, p.106.
4. Quoted in B. W. Tuchman, *The Proud Tower,* New York (Bantam ed.), 1967, p.58.
5. M. Cowling, *The Impact of Labour,* Cambridge, 1971, p.423.
6. See for example E. P. Thompson, 'Homage to Tom Maguire', in Briggs & Saville, Vol. I, op. cit. Also *Tom Mann's Memoirs,* London, 1967.

7. S. & B. Webb, *The History of Trade Unionism,* London, 1920, p.386.

8. P. S. Foner, *History of the Labour Movement in the United States,* Vol. III, New York, 1964, p.368.

9. G. D. H. Cole, *A Short History of the British Working Class Movement,* 1789-1947, London, 1948, p.325.

10. ibid. pp.321-2.

11. M. Cowling, op. cit. p.40.

12. E. J. Hobsbawm, *Labouring Men,* London, 1964, pp.324-5.

13. Quoted in H. Clegg et. al., *A History of British Trade Unions Since 1889, Vol. I 1889-1910,* Oxford, 1964, p.90.

14. See R. Bean, 'Working Conditions, Labour Agitation and Origins of Unionism on the Liverpool Tramways, *Transport History,* Vol. V, No. 2, 1972.

15. Quoted in J. Lovell, *Stevedores and Dockers,* London, 1969, p.123.

16. P. Bagwell, *The Railwaymen,* London, 1963, p.303.

17. J. Saville, op. cit. p.319.

18. R. Hyman, *The Workers' Union,* London, 1971, p.113.

19. ibid. p.115.

20. H. Clegg, *General Union in a Changing Society,* London, 1964, p.20.

21. ibid. p.20.

22. J. Lovell, op. cit. p.116.

23. H. Clegg, op. cit. p.52.

24. S. & B. Webb, *Industrial Democracy,* London, 1897, Vol. II, p.825.

25. H. Clegg et. al., op. cit. p.432.

26. See J. Hinton, 'The Clyde Workers' Committee and the Dilution Struggle', in A. Briggs & J. Saville (eds.), Vol. II, op. cit.

27. B. Pribicevic, *The Shop Stewards Movement 1910-1922*, Oxford, 1959, p.102-3.

28. V. L. Allen, *Trade Unions and the Government*, London, p.167.

29. P. Bagwell, 'The Triple Industrial Alliance 1913-1922', in Briggs & Saville, Vol. II, op. cit. p.127.

30. P. Thompson, *Socialists, Liberals, and Labour*, London, 1967, p.293.

31. M. Cowling, op. cit. p.424.

32. Quoted in S. R. Graubard, *British Labour and the Russian Revolution*, Cambridge, Mass., 1956, p.41.

33. M. Cowling, op. cit. p.425.

34. A. Fox, *A History of the National Union of Boot and Shoe Operatives 1874-1957*, Oxford, 1958, pp.329-30.

35. See A. Fox, op. cit. p.451.

36. Quoted in A. Bullock, *The Life and Times of Ernest Bevin*, Vol. I, London, 1960, p.70.

Chapter 4

1. Phillip Higgs, 'The Convenor', in R. Fraser (ed.), *Work*, Vol. II, London, 1969, p.110.

2. Quoted in *Attitudes in British Management*, P.E.P., London (Pelican ed.), 1966, p.89.

3. Quoted in V. L. Allen, *Trade Union Leadership*, London, 1957, p.32.

4. Quoted in H. Fyrth & H. Collins, *The Foundry Workers*, Manchester, 1959, p.225.

5. J. Lovell & B. C. Roberts, *A Short History of the TUC*, London, 1968, p.162.

6. R. Skidelsky, *Politicians & the Slump*, London (Pelican ed.), 1970, p.433.

7. *Minutes of Evidence No. 17*, p.622.

8. See D. Sutherland, *The Landowners*, London, 1968.

9. Quoted in N. Harris, *Competition & the Corporate Society*, London, 1972, pp.136-7.

10. *The Times,* 6 March 1962.
11. *The Guardian,* 23 February 1972.
12. Quoted in P. Thompson, *Socialists, Liberals, and Labour,* London, 1967, p.290.
13. See W. Kendall, *The Revolutionary Movement in Britain, 1900-1921,* London, 1969.
14. A. Flanders & H. Clegg, *The System of Industrial Relations in Great Britain,* Oxford, 1963, p.277.
15. ibid. pp.278-9.
16. H. Clegg, *General Union in a Changing Society,* London, 1964, pp.147-8.
17. ibid. p.148.
18. S. Graubard, *British Labour & the Russian Revolution,* Cambridge, Mass., 1956, p.291.
19. Quoted in *The Times,* 21 September 1961.
20. Quoted in *The Times,* 13 December 1961.
21. *The Times,* 6 July 1963.
22. A. Bullock, *The Life and Times of Ernest Bevin,* Vol. I, London, 1960, p.394.
23. H. Pelling, *A History of British Trade Unionism,* London, 1963, p.188.
24. J. P. Nettl, 'Consensus or Elite Domination: The Case of Business', *Political Studies,* Vol. XIII, 1965, pp.22-41.
25. ibid. p.36.
26. In an interview with the author, April 1972.
27. W. K. Hancock & M. M. Gowing, *The British War Economy, History of the Second World War,* London, 1944, p.56, quoted in Flanders & Clegg, op. cit. p.307.
28. H. A. Turner, *Collective Bargaining & the Eclipse of Incomes Policy,* Manchester, 1970, p.8.
29. H. Clegg & R. Adams, *The Employers' Challenge,* Oxford, 1957, p.20.
30. Brian Pearce, *Some Past Rank & File Movements* (privately published pamphlet, n.d.), p.16.

31. *Report of the Royal Commission on Trade Unions and Employers Associations 1965-1968,* London, 1968, p.29, para.110.
32. For breakaway unions generally, see S. Lerner, *Breakaway Unions & the Small Trade Union,* London, 1961. For the Pilkington strike see T. Lane & K. Roberts, *Strike at Pilkingtons,* London, 1971.
33. For an example of this situation see K. Weller & E. Stanton, *What Happened at Fords,* Solidarity Pamphlet No. 26, London, (n.d.).

Chapter 5

1. Quoted in Huw Beynon, *Working for Ford,* London, 1973, p.112-13.
2. G. Clack, *Industrial Relations in a British Car Factory,* Cambridge, 1967, p.20.
3. Huw Beynon, op. cit. p.99.
4. Will Paynter, *My Generation,* London, 1972, p.110.
5. G. Clack, op. cit. p.36.
6. See Huw Beynon, op. cit., & H. A. Turner et. al., *Labour Relations in the British Motor Industry,* London, 1967, chap.4.
7. C. L. Goodrich, *The Frontier of Control,* London, 1920.

Chapter 6

1. Quoted in J. B. Jefferys, *The Story of the Engineers,* London, 1945, p.261.
2. H. A. Turner, *Trade Union Growth, Structure and Policy,* London, 1962, p.85.
3. W. E. J. McCarthy & S. R. Parker, 'Shop Stewards & Workshop Relations', Report No. 10 of *The Royal Commission on Trade Unions and Employers Associations,* London, 1968, p.17.

4. A. Fox, *A Sociology of Work in Industry,* London, 1971, pp.120-1.
5. Carl Dreyfuss, 'Prestige Grading: A Mechanism of Control', in R. K. Merton et. al. (eds.), *Reader in Bureaucracy,* New York, 1952, p.259.
6. H. A. Turner et. al., *Labour Relations in the Motor Industry,* London, 1967, p.223.
7. ibid. p.222.
8. op. cit. p.31.
9. ibid. p.33.
10. Huw Beynon, *Working for Ford,* London, 1973, p.158.
11. H. Clegg et. al., *Trade Union Officers,* Oxford, 1961, p.178.
12. op. cit. p.14.
13. *Minutes of Evidence No. 30,* p.1236.
14. G. Clack, *Industrial Relations in a British Car Factory,* Cambridge, 1967, p.64.
15. In an interview with the author, June 1970.
16. op. cit. p.105.
17. ibid. p.183.
18. ibid. pp.183-4.
19. In an interview with the author, April 1972.
20. op. cit. p.32.
21. op. cit. p.211.
22. Report of *The Royal Commission on Trade Unions etc., 1965-68,* London, 1968, paras.701-2, p.188.
23. A. Marsh, *Managers and Shop Stewards,* London, 1963, p.20.
24. A. Fox, *A History of the National Union of Boot and Shoe Operatives,* Oxford, 1958, p.412.
25. op. cit. p.206.
26. ibid. p.221.
27. *Minutes of Evidence No. 57,* p.2451.
28. S. W. Lerner & J. Bescoby, 'Shop Steward Combine Committees in the British Engineering Industry', *Brit. Jnl. Industrial Relations,* Vol. IV, 1966, p.159.

29. op. cit. p.214.
30. ibid. p.222.

Chapter 7

1. Quoted in K. Weller & E. Stanton, *What Happened at Fords,* Solidarity Pamphlet No. 26, London (n.d.), p.6.
2. Quoted in V. L, Allen, *Power in Trade Unions,* London, 1954, p.195.
3. Quoted in Huw Beynon, *Working for Ford,* London, 1973, p.300.
4. For a full and fascinating list see, *The Financial Times,* 12 November 1969.
5. *The Sunday Times,* 16 February 1969.
6. *The Manchester Guardian,* 11 June 1959.
7. N. Chamberlain, 'The Corporation and the Trade Union', in E. S. Mason (ed.), *The Corporation in Modern Society,* Cambridge, Mass., 1959, p.125.
8. Quoted in *Industry Week,* 5 September 1969, p.15.
9. In an interview with the author, April 1972.
10. *Minutes of Evidence No.53,* p.2287.
11. *Minutes of Evidence No. 42,* p.1780.
12. Quoted in *The Times,* 4 March 1970, p.28.
13. In an interview with the author, April 1972.
14. In an interview with the author, April 1972.
15. In an interview with the author, April 1972.
16. Quoted in S. Graubard, *British Labour and The Russian Revolution,* Cambridge, Mass., 1956, p.179.
17. *Labouring Men,* London (Weidenfeld Goldback ed.), 1968, p.339.
18. V. L. Allen, *Trade Union Leadership,* London, 1957, p.28.
19. *Minutes of Evidence No. 30,* p.1232.
20. Lord Citrine, *Men & Work,* London, 1964, p.51.
21. ibid. p.53.
22. In an interview with the author, June 1972.

23. ibid.
24. The leader who said this in an interview with the author preferred to remain anonymous.
25. *Minutes of Evidence No. 17*, p.622.
26. C. Wright Mills, *The New Men of Power*, New York, 1948.
27. *The Worker Views His Union*, Chicago, 1958, p.168.
28. In an interview with the author, April, 1972.
29. The leader who said this in an interview with the author preferred to remain anonymous.
30. ibid.
31. V. L. Allen, *Trade Union Leadership*, op. cit. p.251.
32. ibid. p.86.
33. See Graubard, op. cit. p.147.
34. V. L. Allen, *Trade Union Leadership*, op. cit. p.84.
35. ibid. p.84.
36. *TUC Report*, 1962, p.298.
37. G. Blaxland, *J. H. Thomas: A Life for Unity*, London, 1964, p.160.
38. Barry Hindess, ' "Participation" and the Failure of Party Politics', *Proceedings of The British Association for The Advancement of Science*, 1970.
39. *Wages & Work Allocation, London,* 1966, pp.97-8.
40. Quoted in J. Goldstein, *The Government of British Trade Unions*, London, 1952, p.61.
41. ibid. pp.219-20.
42. ibid. pp.220-3.
43. ibid. p.224.
44. ibid. p.227.
45. GMWU *Journal,* Vol. XXXIV, No. 2, 1971.
46. op. cit. p.92.
47. In an interview with the author, April 1972.
48. In an interview with the author, April 1972.
49. In an interview with the author, April 1972.

Chapter 8

1. Quoted in A. Sturmthal, *The Tragedy of European Labour 1918-1939,* London, 1944, p.71.
2. K. Marx, *The Poverty of Philosophy,* New York, 1963, p.172.
3. H. A. Turner, *Trade Union Growth, Structure and Policy,* London, 1962, p.52.
4. 'The Nature of Collective Bargaining', in A. Flanders (ed.), *Collective Bargaining,* London, 1969, p.19.
5. 'The Limits and Possibilities of Trade Union Action', in R. Blackburn & A. Cockburn (eds.), *The Incompatibles: Trade Union Militancy and the Consensus,* London, 1967, pp.264-5.
6. Lord Citrine, *Men and Work,* London, 1964, p.300.
7. Quoted in J. Mathews, *Ford Strike,* London, 1972, p.151.
8. R. Michels, *Political Parties,* New York (Collier ed.), 1962.
9. *The Sociology of Industrial Relations,* London, 1971, p.122.
10. See G. Rudé, *Paris and London in the Eighteenth Century,* London, 1970.
11. ibid. p.31.
12. Citrine, op. cit. p.157.
13. In an interview with the author, April 1972.
14. H. Wilson, *The Labour Government: 1964-70,* London, 1971, pp.233-41.
15. See A. Glyn & B. Sutcliffe, *British Capitalism, Workers and the Profits Squeeze,* London, 1972.

Index